Texas

Pattern Jury Charges

Oil • Gas

TEXAS
PATTERN JURY CHARGES

Oil • Gas

Prepared by the

COMMITTEE

on

PATTERN JURY CHARGES

of the

STATE BAR OF TEXAS

Austin   2020

The State Bar of Texas, through its Texas Bar Books Department, publishes practice books prepared and edited by knowledgeable authors to give practicing lawyers as much assistance as possible. The competence of the authors ensures outstanding professional products, but, of course, neither the State Bar of Texas, the editors, nor the authors make either express or implied warranties in regard to their use. Each lawyer must depend on his or her own knowledge of the law and expertise in the use or modification of these materials.

IRS CIRCULAR 230 NOTICE: To ensure compliance with requirements imposed by the IRS, we inform you that (1) this written material was not intended or written by the author(s) to be used for the purpose of avoiding federal penalties that may be imposed on a taxpayer; (2) this written material cannot be used by a taxpayer for the purpose of avoiding penalties that may be imposed on the taxpayer; (3) this written material cannot be used in promoting, marketing, or recommending to another party any tax-related transaction or matter; and (4) a taxpayer should seek advice based on the taxpayer's particular circumstances from an independent tax advisor.

The use of the masculine gender throughout this publication is purely for literary convenience and should, of course, be understood to include the feminine gender as well.

International Standard Book Number: 978-1-938873-91-1

Printed in the United States of America

FSC
www.fsc.org
MIX
Paper from
responsible sources
FSC® C020980

To the memory of Dick Watt, 1947–2020, and Michael E. McElroy, 1952–2020,
both true legal legends whose immeasurable contributions to
Texas jurisprudence will be with us forever.

COMMITTEE ON PATTERN JURY CHARGES—OVERSIGHT

2018–2021

HON. JANE BLAND, *Chair*

HON. DAN HINDE, *Chair*

HON. ANA ESTEVEZ, *Vice-Chair*

HON. JOHN P. DEVINE, *Supreme Court Liaison*

J. ARNOLD AGUILAR

BROCK C. AKERS

ALEXANDRA W. ALBRIGHT

SCOTT ARMSTRONG

KIRSTEN M. CASTAÑEDA

JAMES DEAN

HON. DIANE DEVASTO

MICHAEL W. EADY

HON. AIDA SALINAS FLORES

STEWART W. GAGNON

JOHN BLAISE GSANGER

MARY T. HENDERSON

JAY JACKSON

DAVID C. KENT

SUSAN R. KLEIN

JEFFREY S. LEVINGER

H. E. MENDEZ

BRIAN MILLER

HON. EMILY MISKEL

JOYCE MOORE

HON. LANA MYERS

LADAWN H. NANDRASY

SARAH PATEL PACHECO

DAN POZZA

HON. ROBERT SCHAFFER

MICHAEL L. SLACK

HON. CATHERINE STONE

HON. TIMOTHY SULAK

HON. ANDREW A. WRIGHT

COMMITTEE ON PATTERN JURY CHARGES

Oil • Gas

2013–2018

Chair

RICARDO E. MORALES, 2013–2018

Vice-Chairs

ELIZABETH N. MILLER, 2013–2014

LAURA H. BURNEY, 2014–2018

Members

HON. PATRICIA O'CONNELL ALVAREZ

RICHARD F. BROWN

ALLEN D. CUMMINGS

CHARLES W. GORDON, IV

CRAIG A. HAYNES

ISAIAH ROBY JACKSON

EZRA A. JOHNSON

MICHAEL D. JONES

LISA VAUGHN LUMLEY

MICHAEL E. MCELROY

KAREN S. PRECELLA

C. E. RHODES, JR.

SUSAN RAFFERTY RICHARDSON

BENJAMIN ROBERTSON

MARK C. RODRIGUEZ

PAUL F. SIMPSON

SCOTT P. STOLLEY

JAMES "MARTY" TRUSS

DICK WATT

PAT LONG-WEAVER

COMMITTEE ON PATTERN JURY CHARGES

Civil

1990–1991

J. HADLEY EDGAR, *Chair*

HON. WILLIAM L. HUGHES, JR., *Vice-Chair*

BLAKE BAILEY

R. DOAK BISHOP

GEORGE E. CHANDLER

STEPHEN C. DILLARD

ROBERT L. GIBBINS, JR.

DOUGLASS D. HEARNE

KAREN M. KACIR

STEPHEN R. LEWIS

WAYNE H. PRESCOTT

THOMAS T. ROGERS

CONTENTS

CONTENTS

PREFACE

The year 2020 has been challenging for all of us. Despite these unprecedented times, I am proud of our hard-working Committee's dedication to see this year's edition through to completion. Sadly, and for the first time in several years, our Committee would have to complete its charge without two of its most crucial stalwarts: Richard "Dick" Watt (1947–2020) and Michael E. McElroy (1952–2020). Dick and Mike dedicated years of service to the oil and gas pattern jury charges project, both as members of this Committee and when the project was directed by the Council of the Oil, Gas & Energy Resources Law Section (OGERL). Dick and Mike, legends of the oil and gas bar in their own right, were made of the mold that would fight like hell in court against you and then show up the next day at a Committee meeting with a warm handshake, ready to dedicate the day to meticulously scrutinizing each phrase, comma, and cite in the oil and gas volume. Whatever the endeavor and whether for their clients or for the benefit of the bench and bar, Mike and Dick worked tirelessly to get it right. Those who had the privilege of working with them (or against them) in the courthouse are better lawyers because of their example. Their expertise, advocacy, generosity, and unique personalities are irreplaceable and will be missed. This 2020 volume is dedicated to both Dick and Mike.

For decades, oil and gas litigators had to rely on their own research to write a jury charge. The charge often had to be crafted from scratch or built upon previous charges from earlier cases and took days to assemble. We hope this volume has changed all of that for practitioners, and we believe that the 2020 edition improves on the good work done by so many over the last twenty years, including Dick and Mike. This project was started in 2000 by OGERL. Susan Richardson brought the original idea to the Council, and she served as the first chair of that first committee, followed by Elizabeth "Becky" Miller, who served with Susan as cochair. Dick Watt and Jesse Pierce also served as cochairs of the Section's committee, which included Arnold "Arne" Johnson, Patton Lochridge (1949–2017), Allen Cummings, Jeff Hart, Rick Strange, and others. Charles B. Harris and Judge Bob Parks from Monahans both contributed ideas and suggestions to those early versions. These lawyers and judges helped shape the current version you see today.

In 2013, the State Bar of Texas moved toward its own stand-alone oil and gas pattern jury charges project. Many of the members that worked for years on OGERL's committee were brought on along with new members to help with the State Bar project. I commend the State Bar for having the wisdom to bring many of those that have worked for so many years on this project to complete the 2016 volume, the 2018 volume, and now this 2020 volume. I continue to be awed by the hours spent by so many and thank all of those that volunteered their time over the last twenty years for the benefit of other practitioners.

This Committee has met on a monthly basis for the last three years, often meeting with Committees from other volumes to work toward consistency between volumes. I am so thankful for their service to this cause. A special note of thanks to the Oversight Committee and its leadership, including Justice Tracy Kee Christopher, Justice Jane Bland, and Judge Dan Hinde for their important comments. On behalf of the entire Committee, I want to give special recognition to Elma Garcia, our project legal editor, for her patience and grace in keeping our colorful group on course.

—Ricardo E. Morales, *Chair*

CHANGES IN THE 2020 EDITION

The 2020 edition of *Texas Pattern Jury Charges—Oil & Gas* includes the following changes from the 2018 edition:

1. Adverse Possession—Clarified language on acknowledgment of title (301.2–301.6)

2. Improper Use of Real Property—

   a. Revised title and instruction on use of the surface estate (302.2)

   b. Added discussion on negligent use of the surface estate (302.2)

   c. Revised question and commentary on accommodation doctrine (302.3)

   d. Added question and instruction on statutory waste (302.8)

   e. Added question and instruction on reasonably prudent operator defense to statutory waste claim (302.9)

3. Executive Rights—

   a. Expanded the discussions on the executive's duty and actionable self-dealing to include *Texas Outfitters Limited, LLC v. Nicholson*, 572 S.W.3d 647 (Tex. 2019) (304.1)

   b. Revised question and added discussion on *Texas Outfitters Limited, LLC*, 572 S.W.3d 647 (304.2)

4. Oil and Gas Industry Agreements—

   a. Updated citations on broad-form discussion to reflect revised Tex. R. Civ. P. 277 throughout

   b. Revised discussion on formation of agreement to include recent case law (305.4)

   c. Expanded discussion on court's duty to interpret unambiguous contract and deleted comment on construction of contract as an issue for the court

   d. Clarified discussion on when to use and deleted discussion on whether construction of a contract is an issue for the court (305.9)

   e. Revised comment on trade custom to add recent case law (305.10)

   f. Clarified discussion on when to use and deleted discussion on construction of contract being an issue for the court (305.19)

5. Defenses—

   a. Updated citations on broad-form discussion to reflect revised Tex. R. Civ. P. 277 throughout

   b. Revised discussion on plaintiff's material breach to reflect elements as listed in *Mustang Pipeline Co. v. Driver Pipeline Co.*, 134 S.W.3d 195 (Tex. 2004), and deleted discussion on compliance with a bilateral contract (312.2)

   c. Updated instruction on anticipatory repudiation (312.3)

   d. Expanded discussion on source of definition (312.4)

   e. Revised discussion on description of land (312.14)

6. Damages—

   a. Revised title of question (313.3)

   b. Revised title and updated discussion on damages recoverable (313.5)

   c. Added question on intrinsic value of trees damages (313.8)

   d. Revised question to be consistent with liability question (313.16)

   e. Revised question, instruction, and comments on attorney's fees to reflect *Rohrmoos Venture v. UTSW DVA Healthcare, LLP*, 578 S.W.3d 469 (Tex. 2019), and other recent case law (313.33)

7. Preservation of Charge Error—Revised discussion on objections required to preserve error (314.2)

INTRODUCTION

1. PURPOSE OF PUBLICATION

The purpose of this volume, like those of the others in this series, is to assist the bench and bar in preparing the court's charge in jury cases. It provides definitions, instructions, and questions needed to submit jury charges in the following cases:

- adverse possession
- improper use of real property
- issues between the lessor and lessee
- executive rights; and
- contracts between working interest owners.

It also contains questions and comments pertaining to defenses to the above actions and sections on damages and preservation of charge error.

The pattern charges are suggestions and guides to be used by a trial court if they are applicable and proper in a specific case. The Committee hopes that this volume will prove as worthy as have the earlier *Texas Pattern Jury Charges* volumes.

2. SCOPE OF PATTERN CHARGES

The infinite combinations of possible facts in oil and gas cases make it impracticable for the Committee to offer questions suitable for every occasion. The Committee has tried to prepare charges to serve as guides for the usual litigation encountered in these types of cases. However, a charge should conform to the pleadings and evidence of a case, and occasions will arise for the use of questions and instructions not specifically addressed here.

3. USE OF ACCEPTED PRECEDENTS

Like its predecessors, this Committee has avoided recommending changes in the law and has based this material on what it perceives the present law to be. It has attempted to foresee theories and objections that might be made in a variety of circumstances but not to express favor or disfavor for particular positions. In unsettled areas, the Committee generally has not taken a position on the exact form of a charge. However, it has provided guidelines in some areas in which there is no definitive authority. Of course, trial judges and attorneys should recognize that these recommendations may be affected by future appellate decisions and statutory changes.

4. PRINCIPLES OF STYLE

a. *Preference for broad-form questions.* Tex. R. Civ. P. 277 provides that "the court shall, whenever feasible, submit the cause upon broad-form questions." Accordingly, the basic questions are designed to be accompanied by one or more instructions.

See Tex. R. Civ. P. 277–78. For further discussion, see PJC 314.2 regarding broad-form issues and the *Casteel* doctrine.

b. *Simplicity.*   The Committee has sought to be as brief as possible and to use language that is simple and easy to understand.

c. *Definitions and instructions.*   The supreme court has disapproved the practice of embellishing standard definitions and instructions, *Lemos v. Montez*, 680 S.W.2d 798 (Tex. 1984), or of adding unnecessary instructions, *First International Bank v. Roper Corp.*, 686 S.W.2d 602 (Tex. 1985). The Committee has endeavored to adhere to standard definitions and instructions stated in general terms rather than terms of the particular parties and facts of the case. If an instruction in general terms would be unduly complicated and confusing, however, reference to specific parties and facts is suggested.

d. *Placement of definitions and instructions in the charges.*   Definitions and instructions that apply to a number of questions should be given immediately after the general instructions required by Tex. R. Civ. P. 226a. *See Woods v. Crane Carrier Co.*, 693 S.W.2d 377 (Tex. 1985). However, if a definition or instruction applies to only one question or cluster of questions (e.g., damages questions), it should be placed with that question or cluster. Specific guidance for placement of definitions and instructions can be found in the individual PJCs and comments.

e. *Burden of proof.*   As authorized by Tex. R. Civ. P. 277, it is recommended that the burden of proof be placed by instruction rather than by inclusion in each question. When the burden is placed by instruction, it is not necessary that each question begin: "Do you find from a preponderance of the evidence that . . ." The admonitory instructions contain the following instruction, applicable to all questions:

> Answer "yes" or "no" to all questions unless you are told otherwise. A "yes" answer must be based on a preponderance of the evidence [unless you are told otherwise]. Whenever a question requires an answer other than "yes" or "no," your answer must be based on a preponderance of the evidence [unless you are told otherwise].

> The term "preponderance of the evidence" means the greater weight of credible evidence presented in this case. If you do not find that a preponderance of the evidence supports a "yes" answer, then answer "no." A preponderance of the evidence is not measured by the number of witnesses or by the number of documents admitted in evidence. For a fact to be proved by a preponderance of the evidence, you must find that the fact is more likely true than not true.

f. *Hypothetical examples.*   The names of hypothetical parties and facts have been italicized to indicate that the names and facts of the particular case should be substituted. In general, the name *Paul Payne* has been used for the plaintiff and *Don Davis* for the defendant. *Larry Lessee* refers to the lessee, and *Suzie Surface Owner* refers to the surface owner. Additionally, in PJC 312.17, *Polly Payor* indicates the payor, and *Perry Payee* is used to indicate the payee.

5. COMMENTS AND CITATIONS OF AUTHORITY

The comments to each PJC provide a ready reference to the law that serves as a foundation for the charge. The primary authority cited is Texas case law. In some instances, secondary authority—for example, Smith & Weaver, 1 *Texas Law of Oil and Gas*—is also cited. The Committee wishes to emphasize that secondary authority is cited solely as additional guidance to the reader and not as legal authority for the proposition stated. Some comments also include variations of the recommended forms and additional questions or instructions for special circumstances.

6. USING THE PATTERN CHARGES

Matters on which the evidence is undisputed should not be submitted by either instruction or question. Conversely, questions, instructions, and definitions not included in this book may sometimes become necessary. Finally, preparation of a proper charge requires careful legal analysis and sound judgment.

7. INSTALLING THE DIGITAL DOWNLOAD

The complimentary downloadable version of *Texas Pattern Jury Charges—Oil & Gas* (2020 edition) contains the entire text of the printed book. To install the digital download—

1. go to **https://manage.texasbarpractice.com**;
2. if prompted to log in, do so; and
3. in the "Downloadables" column, click the download button for this book's title.

Use of the digital download is subject to the terms of the license and limited warranty included in the documentation at the end of this book and on the digital download web pages. By accessing the digital download, you waive all refund privileges for this publication.

8. FUTURE REVISIONS

The contents of questions, instructions, and definitions in the court's charge depend on the underlying substantive law relevant to the case. This volume as updated reflects all amendments to Texas statutes enacted through 2019. The Committee expects to publish updates as needed to reflect changes and new developments in the law.

PJC 300.1   Instructions to Jury Panel before Voir Dire Examination

[Brackets indicate optional, alternative, or instructive text.]

MEMBERS OF THE JURY PANEL:

Thank you for being here. We are here to select a jury. Twelve [six] of you will be chosen for the jury. Even if you are not chosen for the jury, you are performing a valuable service that is your right and duty as a citizen of a free country.

Before we begin: Turn off all phones and other electronic devices. While you are in the courtroom, do not communicate with anyone through any electronic device. [For example, do not communicate by phone, text message, email message, chat room, blog, or social networking websites such as Facebook, Twitter, or Myspace.] [I will give you a number where others may contact you in case of an emergency.] Do not record or photograph any part of these court proceedings, because it is prohibited by law.

If you are chosen for the jury, your role as jurors will be to decide the disputed facts in this case. My role will be to ensure that this case is tried in accordance with the rules of law.

Here is some background about this case. This is a civil case. It is a lawsuit that is not a criminal case. The parties are as follows: The plaintiff is _____, and the defendant is _____. Representing the plaintiff is _____, and representing the defendant is _____. They will ask you some questions during jury selection. But before their questions begin, I must give you some instructions for jury selection.

Every juror must obey these instructions. You may be called into court to testify about any violations of these instructions. If you do not follow these instructions, you will be guilty of juror misconduct, and I might have to order a new trial and start this process over again. This would waste your time and the parties' money, and would require the taxpayers of this county to pay for another trial.

These are the instructions.

  1. To avoid looking like you are friendly with one side of the case, do not mingle or talk with the lawyers, witnesses, parties, or anyone else involved in the case. You may exchange casual greetings like "hello" and "good morning." Other than that, do not talk with them at all. They have to

follow these instructions too, so you should not be offended when they follow the instructions.

2.   Do not accept any favors from the lawyers, witnesses, parties, or anyone else involved in the case, and do not do any favors for them. This includes favors such as giving rides and food.

3.   Do not discuss this case with anyone, even your spouse or a friend, either in person or by any other means [including by phone, text message, email message, chat room, blog, or social networking websites such as Facebook, Twitter, or Myspace]. Do not allow anyone to discuss the case with you or in your hearing. If anyone tries to discuss the case with you or in your hearing, tell me immediately. We do not want you to be influenced by something other than the evidence admitted in court.

4.   The parties, through their attorneys, have the right to ask you questions about your background, experiences, and attitudes. They are not trying to meddle in your affairs. They are just being thorough and trying to choose fair jurors who do not have any bias or prejudice in this particular case.

5.   Remember that you took an oath that you will tell the truth, so be truthful when the lawyers ask you questions, and always give complete answers. If you do not answer a question that applies to you, that violates your oath. Sometimes a lawyer will ask a question of the whole panel instead of just one person. If the question applies to you, raise your hand and keep it raised until you are called on.

Do you understand these instructions? If you do not, please tell me now.

The lawyers will now begin to ask their questions.

COMMENT

When to use.   The foregoing oral instructions are prescribed in Tex. R. Civ. P. 226a. The instructions, "with such modifications as the circumstances of the particular case may require," are to be given to the jury panel "after they have been sworn in as provided in Rule 226 and before the voir dire examination."

Rewording regarding investigation by jurors.   In an appropriate case, the sentence "Do not post information about the case on the Internet before these court proceedings end and you are released from jury duty" may be added in the second paragraph of this instruction, and the instructions admonishing against independent investigation by the jurors contained in item 6 of PJC 300.2 may be included in the instruction.

PJC 300.2   Instructions to Jury after Jury Selection

[Brackets indicate optional or instructive text.]

[Oral Instructions]

MEMBERS OF THE JURY:

You have been chosen to serve on this jury. Because of the oath you have taken and your selection for the jury, you become officials of this court and active participants in our justice system.

[Hand out the written instructions.]

You have each received a set of written instructions. I am going to read them with you now. Some of them you have heard before and some are new.

1.   Turn off all phones and other electronic devices. While you are in the courtroom and while you are deliberating, do not communicate with anyone through any electronic device. [For example, do not communicate by phone, text message, email message, chat room, blog, or social networking websites such as Facebook, Twitter, or Myspace.] [I will give you a number where others may contact you in case of an emergency.] Do not post information about the case on the Internet before these court proceedings end and you are released from jury duty. Do not record or photograph any part of these court proceedings, because it is prohibited by law.

2.   To avoid looking like you are friendly with one side of the case, do not mingle or talk with the lawyers, witnesses, parties, or anyone else involved in the case. You may exchange casual greetings like "hello" and "good morning." Other than that, do not talk with them at all. They have to follow these instructions too, so you should not be offended when they follow the instructions.

3.   Do not accept any favors from the lawyers, witnesses, parties, or anyone else involved in the case, and do not do any favors for them. This includes favors such as giving rides and food.

4.   Do not discuss this case with anyone, even your spouse or a friend, either in person or by any other means [including by phone, text message, email message, chat room, blog, or social networking websites such as Facebook, Twitter, or Myspace]. Do not allow anyone to discuss the case with you or in your hearing. If anyone tries to discuss the case with you or in your

hearing, tell me immediately. We do not want you to be influenced by something other than the evidence admitted in court.

5.   Do not discuss this case with anyone during the trial, not even with the other jurors, until the end of the trial. You should not discuss the case with your fellow jurors until the end of the trial so that you do not form opinions about the case before you have heard everything.

After you have heard all the evidence, received all of my instructions, and heard all of the lawyers' arguments, you will then go to the jury room to discuss the case with the other jurors and reach a verdict.

6.   Do not investigate this case on your own. For example, do not:

    a.   try to get information about the case, lawyers, witnesses, or issues from outside this courtroom;

    b.   go to places mentioned in the case to inspect the places;

    c.   inspect items mentioned in this case unless they are presented as evidence in court;

    d.   look anything up in a law book, dictionary, or public record to try to learn more about the case;

    e.   look anything up on the Internet to try to learn more about the case; or

    f.   let anyone else do any of these things for you.

This rule is very important because we want a trial based only on evidence admitted in open court. Your conclusions about this case must be based only on what you see and hear in this courtroom because the law does not permit you to base your conclusions on information that has not been presented to you in open court. All the information must be presented in open court so the parties and their lawyers can test it and object to it. Information from other sources, like the Internet, will not go through this important process in the courtroom. In addition, information from other sources could be completely unreliable. As a result, if you investigate this case on your own, you could compromise the fairness to all parties in this case and jeopardize the results of this trial.

7.   Do not tell other jurors about your own experiences or other people's experiences. For example, you may have special knowledge of something in the case, such as business, technical, or professional information. You may even have expert knowledge or opinions, or you may know what

happened in this case or another similar case. Do not tell the other jurors about it. Telling other jurors about it is wrong because it means the jury will be considering things that were not admitted in court.

8.   Do not consider attorneys' fees unless I tell you to. Do not guess about attorneys' fees.

9.   Do not consider or guess whether any party is covered by insurance unless I tell you to.

10.   During the trial, if taking notes will help focus your attention on the evidence, you may take notes using the materials the court has provided. Do not use any personal electronic devices to take notes. If taking notes will distract your attention from the evidence, you should not take notes. Your notes are for your own personal use. They are not evidence. Do not show or read your notes to anyone, including other jurors.

You must leave your notes in the jury room or with the bailiff. The bailiff is instructed not to read your notes and to give your notes to me promptly after collecting them from you. I will make sure your notes are kept in a safe, secure location and not disclosed to anyone.

[You may take your notes back into the jury room and consult them during deliberations. But keep in mind that your notes are not evidence. When you deliberate, each of you should rely on your independent recollection of the evidence and not be influenced by the fact that another juror has or has not taken notes. After you complete your deliberations, the bailiff will collect your notes.]

When you are released from jury duty, the bailiff will promptly destroy your notes so that nobody can read what you wrote.

11.   I will decide matters of law in this case. It is your duty to listen to and consider the evidence and to determine fact issues that I may submit to you at the end of the trial. After you have heard all the evidence, I will give you instructions to follow as you make your decision. The instructions also will have questions for you to answer. You will not be asked and you should not consider which side will win. Instead, you will need to answer the specific questions I give you.

Every juror must obey my instructions. If you do not follow these instructions, you will be guilty of juror misconduct, and I may have to order a new trial and start this process over again. This would waste your time and the parties' money, and would require the taxpayers of this county to pay for another trial.

Do you understand these instructions? If you do not, please tell me now.

Please keep these instructions and review them as we go through this case. If anyone does not follow these instructions, tell me.

COMMENT

When to use.   The foregoing instructions are prescribed in Tex. R. Civ. P. 226a. The instructions, "with such modifications as the circumstances of the particular case may require," are to be given to the jury "immediately after the jurors are selected for the case."

If no tort claim is involved.   Item 9 should be deleted from the foregoing instructions unless a tort claim is involved in the case.

PJC 300.3   **Charge of the Court**

PJC 300.3A   **Charge of the Court—Twelve-Member Jury**

[Brackets indicate optional or instructive text.]

MEMBERS OF THE JURY:

After the closing arguments, you will go to the jury room to decide the case, answer the questions that are attached, and reach a verdict. You may discuss the case with other jurors only when you are all together in the jury room.

Remember my previous instructions: Do not discuss the case with anyone else, either in person or by any other means. Do not do any independent investigation about the case or conduct any research. Do not look up any words in dictionaries or on the Internet. Do not post information about the case on the Internet. Do not share any special knowledge or experiences with the other jurors. Do not use your phone or any other electronic device during your deliberations for any reason. [I will give you a number where others may contact you in case of an emergency.]

[Any notes you have taken are for your own personal use. You may take your notes back into the jury room and consult them during deliberations, but do not show or read your notes to your fellow jurors during your deliberations. Your notes are not evidence. Each of you should rely on your independent recollection of the evidence and not be influenced by the fact that another juror has or has not taken notes.]

[You must leave your notes with the bailiff when you are not deliberating. The bailiff will give your notes to me promptly after collecting them from you. I will make sure your notes are kept in a safe, secure location and not disclosed to anyone. After you complete your deliberations, the bailiff will collect your notes. When you are released from jury duty, the bailiff will promptly destroy your notes so that nobody can read what you wrote.]

Here are the instructions for answering the questions.

     1.   Do not let bias, prejudice, or sympathy play any part in your decision.

     2.   Base your answers only on the evidence admitted in court and on the law that is in these instructions and questions. Do not consider or discuss any evidence that was not admitted in the courtroom.

3.   You are to make up your own minds about the facts. You are the sole judges of the credibility of the witnesses and the weight to give their testimony. But on matters of law, you must follow all of my instructions.

4.   If my instructions use a word in a way that is different from its ordinary meaning, use the meaning I give you, which will be a proper legal definition.

5.   All the questions and answers are important. No one should say that any question or answer is not important.

6.   Answer "yes" or "no" to all questions unless you are told otherwise. A "yes" answer must be based on a preponderance of the evidence [unless you are told otherwise]. Whenever a question requires an answer other than "yes" or "no," your answer must be based on a preponderance of the evidence [unless you are told otherwise].

The term "preponderance of the evidence" means the greater weight of credible evidence presented in this case. If you do not find that a preponderance of the evidence supports a "yes" answer, then answer "no." A preponderance of the evidence is not measured by the number of witnesses or by the number of documents admitted in evidence. For a fact to be proved by a preponderance of the evidence, you must find that the fact is more likely true than not true.

7.   Do not decide who you think should win before you answer the questions and then just answer the questions to match your decision. Answer each question carefully without considering who will win. Do not discuss or consider the effect your answers will have.

8.   Do not answer questions by drawing straws or by any method of chance.

9.   Some questions might ask you for a dollar amount. Do not agree in advance to decide on a dollar amount by adding up each juror's amount and then figuring the average.

10. Do not trade your answers. For example, do not say, "I will answer this question your way if you answer another question my way."

11. [Unless otherwise instructed] The answers to the questions must be based on the decision of at least ten of the twelve jurors. The same ten jurors must agree on every answer. Do not agree to be bound by a vote of anything less than ten jurors, even if it would be a majority.

As I have said before, if you do not follow these instructions, you will be guilty of juror misconduct, and I might have to order a new trial and start this process over again. This would waste your time and the parties' money, and would require the taxpayers of this county to pay for another trial. If a juror breaks any of these rules, tell that person to stop and report it to me immediately.

[Definitions, questions, and special instructions given to the jury will be transcribed here.]

Presiding Juror:

1.   When you go into the jury room to answer the questions, the first thing you will need to do is choose a presiding juror.

2.   The presiding juror has these duties:

    a.   have the complete charge read aloud if it will be helpful to your deliberations;

    b.   preside over your deliberations, meaning manage the discussions, and see that you follow these instructions;

    c.   give written questions or comments to the bailiff who will give them to the judge;

    d.   write down the answers you agree on;

    e.   get the signatures for the verdict certificate; and

    f.   notify the bailiff that you have reached a verdict.

Do you understand the duties of the presiding juror? If you do not, please tell me now.

Instructions for Signing the Verdict Certificate:

1.   [Unless otherwise instructed] You may answer the questions on a vote of ten jurors. The same ten jurors must agree on every answer in the charge. This means you may not have one group of ten jurors agree on one answer and a different group of ten jurors agree on another answer.

2.   If ten jurors agree on every answer, those ten jurors sign the verdict.

If eleven jurors agree on every answer, those eleven jurors sign the verdict.

If all twelve of you agree on every answer, you are unanimous and only the presiding juror signs the verdict.

3.   All jurors should deliberate on every question. You may end up with all twelve of you agreeing on some answers, while only ten or eleven of you agree on other answers. But when you sign the verdict, only those ten who agree on every answer will sign the verdict.

4.   *[Added if the charge requires some unanimity.]* There are some special instructions before Questions _____ explaining how to answer those questions. Please follow the instructions. If all twelve of you answer those questions, you will need to complete a second verdict certificate for those questions.

Do you understand these instructions? If you do not, please tell me now.

_____
JUDGE PRESIDING

Verdict Certificate

Check one:

_____ Our verdict is unanimous. All twelve of us have agreed to each and every answer. The presiding juror has signed the certificate for all twelve of us.

_____   _____
Signature of Presiding Juror   Printed Name of Presiding Juror

_____ Our verdict is not unanimous. Eleven of us have agreed to each and every answer and have signed the certificate below.

_____ Our verdict is not unanimous. Ten of us have agreed to each and every answer and have signed the certificate below.

          Signature   Name Printed

1. _____   _____

2. _____   _____

3. _____   _____

4. _____   _____

5. _____   _____

6. _____   _____

7. _____   _____

8. _____   _____

9. _____   _____

10. _____   _____

11. _____   _____

If you have answered Question No. _____ [*the exemplary damages amount*], then you must sign this certificate also.

Additional Certificate

[Used when some questions require unanimous answers.]

I certify that the jury was unanimous in answering the following questions. All twelve of us agreed to each of the answers. The presiding juror has signed the certificate for all twelve of us.

[Judge to list questions that require a unanimous answer, including the predicate liability question.]

_____   _____
Signature of Presiding Juror   Printed Name of Presiding Juror

PJC 300.3B   Charge of the Court—Six-Member Jury

[Brackets indicate optional or instructive text.]

MEMBERS OF THE JURY:

After the closing arguments, you will go to the jury room to decide the case, answer the questions that are attached, and reach a verdict. You may discuss the case with other jurors only when you are all together in the jury room.

Remember my previous instructions: Do not discuss the case with anyone else, either in person or by any other means. Do not do any independent investigation about the case or conduct any research. Do not look up any words in dictionaries or on the Internet. Do not post information about the case on the Internet. Do not share any special knowledge or experiences with the other jurors. Do not use your phone or any other electronic device during your deliberations for any reason. [I will give you a number where others may contact you in case of an emergency.]

[Any notes you have taken are for your own personal use. You may take your notes back into the jury room and consult them during deliberations, but do not show or read your notes to your fellow jurors during your deliberations. Your notes are not evidence. Each of you should rely on your independent recollection of the evidence and not be influenced by the fact that another juror has or has not taken notes.]

[You must leave your notes with the bailiff when you are not deliberating. The bailiff will give your notes to me promptly after collecting them from you. I will make sure your notes are kept in a safe, secure location and not disclosed to anyone. After you complete your deliberations, the bailiff will collect your notes. When you are released from jury duty, the bailiff will promptly destroy your notes so that nobody can read what you wrote.]

Here are the instructions for answering the questions.

    1.   Do not let bias, prejudice, or sympathy play any part in your decision.

    2.   Base your answers only on the evidence admitted in court and on the law that is in these instructions and questions. Do not consider or discuss any evidence that was not admitted in the courtroom.

    3.   You are to make up your own minds about the facts. You are the sole judges of the credibility of the witnesses and the weight to give their testimony. But on matters of law, you must follow all of my instructions.

    4.   If my instructions use a word in a way that is different from its ordinary meaning, use the meaning I give you, which will be a proper legal definition.

    5.   All the questions and answers are important. No one should say that any question or answer is not important.

    6.   Answer "yes" or "no" to all questions unless you are told otherwise. A "yes" answer must be based on a preponderance of the evidence [unless

you are told otherwise]. Whenever a question requires an answer other than "yes" or "no," your answer must be based on a preponderance of the evidence [unless you are told otherwise].

The term "preponderance of the evidence" means the greater weight of credible evidence presented in this case. If you do not find that a preponderance of the evidence supports a "yes" answer, then answer "no." A preponderance of the evidence is not measured by the number of witnesses or by the number of documents admitted in evidence. For a fact to be proved by a preponderance of the evidence, you must find that the fact is more likely true than not true.

7.   Do not decide who you think should win before you answer the questions and then just answer the questions to match your decision. Answer each question carefully without considering who will win. Do not discuss or consider the effect your answers will have.

8.   Do not answer questions by drawing straws or by any method of chance.

9.   Some questions might ask you for a dollar amount. Do not agree in advance to decide on a dollar amount by adding up each juror's amount and then figuring the average.

10.   Do not trade your answers. For example, do not say, "I will answer this question your way if you answer another question my way."

11.   [Unless otherwise instructed] The answers to the questions must be based on the decision of at least five of the six jurors. The same five jurors must agree on every answer. Do not agree to be bound by a vote of anything less than five jurors, even if it would be a majority.

As I have said before, if you do not follow these instructions, you will be guilty of juror misconduct, and I might have to order a new trial and start this process over again. This would waste your time and the parties' money, and would require the taxpayers of this county to pay for another trial. If a juror breaks any of these rules, tell that person to stop and report it to me immediately.

[Definitions, questions, and special instructions given to the jury will be transcribed here.]

Presiding Juror:

1.   When you go into the jury room to answer the questions, the first thing you will need to do is choose a presiding juror.

2.   The presiding juror has these duties:

a.   have the complete charge read aloud if it will be helpful to your deliberations;

b.   preside over your deliberations, meaning manage the discussions, and see that you follow these instructions;

c.   give written questions or comments to the bailiff who will give them to the judge;

d.   write down the answers you agree on;

e.   get the signatures for the verdict certificate; and

f.   notify the bailiff that you have reached a verdict.

Do you understand the duties of the presiding juror? If you do not, please tell me now.

Instructions for Signing the Verdict Certificate:

1.   [Unless otherwise instructed] You may answer the questions on a vote of five jurors. The same five jurors must agree on every answer in the charge. This means you may not have one group of five jurors agree on one answer and a different group of five jurors agree on another answer.

2.   If five jurors agree on every answer, those five jurors sign the verdict.

If all six of you agree on every answer, you are unanimous and only the presiding juror signs the verdict.

3.   All jurors should deliberate on every question. You may end up with all six of you agreeing on some answers, while only five of you agree on other answers. But when you sign the verdict, only those five who agree on every answer will sign the verdict.

4.   *[Added if the charge requires some unanimity.]* There are some special instructions before Questions _____ explaining how to answer those questions. Please follow the instructions. If all six of you answer those questions, you will need to complete a second verdict certificate for those questions.

Do you understand these instructions? If you do not, please tell me now.

_____

JUDGE PRESIDING

Verdict Certificate

Check one:

_____ Our verdict is unanimous. All six of us have agreed to each and every answer. The presiding juror has signed the certificate for all six of us.

_____   _____
Signature of Presiding Juror   Printed Name of Presiding Juror

_____ Our verdict is not unanimous. Five of us have agreed to each and every answer and have signed the certificate below.

              Signature   Name Printed

1. _____   _____

2. _____   _____

3. _____   _____

4. _____   _____

5. _____   _____

If you have answered Question No. _____ [*the exemplary damages amount*], then you must sign this certificate also.

Additional Certificate

[Used when some questions require unanimous answers.]

I certify that the jury was unanimous in answering the following questions. All six of us agreed to each of the answers. The presiding juror has signed the certificate for all six of us.

[Judge to list questions that require a unanimous answer,
including the predicate liability question.]

_____   _____
Signature of Presiding Juror   Printed Name of Presiding Juror

COMMENT

When to use.   The above charge of the court includes the written instructions pre-scribed in Tex. R. Civ. P. 226a. Before closing arguments begin, the court must provide each member of the jury a copy of the charge, including the written instructions, "with such modifications as the circumstances of the particular case may require."

Modification of additional certificate.   The additional certificate set forth in Tex. R. Civ. P. 226a lists the questions that require unanimous answers for an award of exemplary damages and requires the presiding juror to sign the certificate only if the jury answered unanimously to all of the listed questions. This format may require modification in cases involving multiple claims and/or multiple parties. In such cases, the jury's answers might be unanimous as to some but not all of the listed questions, and therefore the presiding juror will be unable to sign the certificate even though an award of exemplary damages might be appropriate based on the questions to which the jury answered unanimously. The Committee suggests that the additional certificate be modified in such multiclaim, multiparty cases. One possible approach is as follows:

Additional Certificate

I certify that the jury was unanimous in answering the following questions or parts of questions marked "yes" below. All [twelve/six] of us agreed to each of the answers marked "yes." The presiding juror has signed the certificate for all [twelve/six] of us.

Answer "yes" or "no" for each of the following:

Question No. 1   _____

Question No. 2

    Defendant 1   _____

    Defendant 2   _____

    Defendant 3   _____

Question No. 3

    Defendant 1   _____

Defendant 2 _____

Defendant 3 _____

_____

Signature of Presiding Juror

_____

Printed Name of Presiding Juror

PJC 300.4   **Additional Instruction for Bifurcated Trial**

[Brackets indicate optional, alternative, or instructive text.]

MEMBERS OF THE JURY:

In discharging your responsibility on this jury, you will observe all the instructions that have been previously given you.

_____

JUDGE PRESIDING

Certificate

I certify that the jury was unanimous in answering the following questions. All twelve [six] of us agreed to each of the answers. The presiding juror has signed the certificate for all twelve [six] of us.

[Judge to list questions that require a unanimous answer,
including the predicate liability question.]

_____   _____
Signature of Presiding Juror   Printed Name of Presiding Juror

COMMENT

When to use. PJC 300.4 should be used as an instruction for the second phase of a bifurcated trial pursuant to Tex. Civ. Prac. & Rem. Code § 41.009. *See also Transportation Insurance Co. v. Moriel*, 879 S.W.2d 10, 29–30 (Tex. 1994). If questions that do not require unanimity are submitted in the second phase of a trial, use the verdict certificate in PJC 300.3.

Source of instruction. The foregoing instructions are prescribed in Tex. R. Civ. P. 226a.

Actions filed before September 1, 2003. For actions filed before September 1, 2003, add the following instruction derived from *Hyman Farm Service, Inc. v. Earth Oil & Gas Co.*, 920 S.W.2d 452 (Tex. App.—Amarillo 1996, no writ), along with signature lines for jurors to use if the verdict is not unanimous:

I shall now give you additional instructions that you should carefully and strictly follow during your deliberations.

All jurors have the right and the responsibility to deliberate on [*this*] [*these*] question[*s*], but at least ten [five] of those who agreed to the verdict in the first phase of this trial must agree to this answer and sign this verdict accordingly. If your first verdict was unanimous, this second verdict may be rendered by the vote of at least ten [five] of you.

Modification of additional certificate.   The additional certificate set forth in Tex. R. Civ. P. 226a lists the questions that require unanimous answers for an award of exemplary damages and requires the presiding juror to sign the certificate only if the jury answered unanimously to all of the listed questions. This format may require modification in cases involving multiple claims and/or multiple parties. In such cases, the jury's answers might be unanimous as to some but not all of the listed questions, and therefore the presiding juror will be unable to sign the certificate even though an award of exemplary damages might be appropriate based on the questions to which the jury answered unanimously. The Committee suggests that the additional certificate be modified in such multiclaim, multiparty cases. One possible approach is as follows:

Additional Certificate

I certify that the jury was unanimous in answering the following questions or parts of questions marked "yes" below. All [twelve/six] of us agreed to each of the answers marked "yes." The presiding juror has signed the certificate for all [twelve/six] of us.

Answer "yes" or "no" for each of the following:

Question No. 1   _____

Question No. 2

Defendant 1   _____

Defendant 2   _____

Defendant 3   _____

Question No. 3

Defendant 1   _____

Defendant 2   _____

Defendant 3   _____

_____
Signature of Presiding Juror

_____

Printed Name of Presiding Juror

PJC 300.5   Instructions to Jury after Verdict

Thank you for your verdict.

I have told you that the only time you may discuss the case is with the other jurors in the jury room. I now release you from jury duty. Now you may discuss the case with anyone. But you may also choose not to discuss the case; that is your right.

After you are released from jury duty, the lawyers and others may ask you questions to see if the jury followed the instructions, and they may ask you to give a sworn statement. You are free to discuss the case with them and to give a sworn statement. But you may choose not to discuss the case and not to give a sworn statement; that is your right.

COMMENT

When to use.   The foregoing instructions are prescribed in Tex. R. Civ. P. 226a. The instructions are to be given orally to the jury "after the verdict has been accepted by the court and before the jurors are released from jury duty."

PJC 300.6   **Instruction to Jury If Permitted to Separate**

You are again instructed that it is your duty not to communicate with, or permit yourselves to be addressed by, any other person about any subject relating to the case.

COMMENT

When to use. The foregoing instruction is required by Tex. R. Civ. P. 284 "[i]f jurors are permitted to separate before they are released from jury duty, either during the trial or after the case is submitted to them."

PJC 300.7   Instruction If Jury Disagrees about Testimony

[Brackets indicate instructive text.]

MEMBERS OF THE JURY:

You have made the following request in writing:

[Insert copy of request.]

Your request is governed by the following rule:

> "If the jury disagree as to the statement of any witness, they may, upon applying to the court, have read to them from the court reporter's notes that part of such witness' testimony on the point in dispute . . . ."

If you report that you disagree concerning the statement of a witness and specify the point on which you disagree, the court reporter will search his notes and read to you the testimony of the witness on the point.

_____
JUDGE PRESIDING

COMMENT

When to use.   This written instruction is based on Tex. R. Civ. P. 287 and is to be used if the jurors request that testimony from the court reporter's notes be read to them.

PJC 300.8 Circumstantial Evidence (Optional)

A fact may be established by direct evidence or by circumstantial evidence or both. A fact is established by direct evidence when proved by documentary evidence or by witnesses who saw the act done or heard the words spoken. A fact is established by circumstantial evidence when it may be fairly and reasonably inferred from other facts proved.

COMMENT

When to use. PJC 300.8 may be used when there is circumstantial evidence in the case. It would be placed in the charge of the court (PJC 300.3) after the instruction on preponderance of the evidence and immediately before the definitions, questions, and special instructions. For cases defining circumstantial evidence, see *Blount v. Bordens, Inc.*, 910 S.W.2d 931, 933 (Tex. 1995) (per curiam), and *Russell v. Russell*, 865 S.W.2d 929, 933 (Tex. 1993). It is not error to give or to refuse an instruction on circumstantial evidence. *Larson v. Ellison*, 217 S.W.2d 420 (Tex. 1949); *Johnson v. Zurich General Accident & Liability Insurance Co.*, 205 S.W.2d 353 (Tex. 1947); *Adams v. Valley Federal Credit Union*, 848 S.W.2d 182, 188 (Tex. App.—Corpus Christi–Edinburg 1992, writ denied).

PJC 300.9   Instructions to Deadlocked Jury

I have your note that you are deadlocked. In the interest of justice, if you could end this litigation by your verdict, you should do so.

I do not mean to say that any individual juror should yield his or her own conscience and positive conviction, but I do mean that when you are in the jury room, you should discuss this matter carefully, listen to each other, and try, if you can, to reach a conclusion on the questions. It is your duty as a juror to keep your mind open and free to every reasonable argument that may be presented by your fellow jurors so that this jury may arrive at a verdict that justly answers the consciences of the individuals making up this jury. You should not have any pride of opinion and should avoid hastily forming or expressing an opinion. At the same time, you should not surrender any conscientious views founded on the evidence unless convinced of your error by your fellow jurors.

If you fail to reach a verdict, this case may have to be tried before another jury. Then all of our time will have been wasted.

Accordingly, I return you to your deliberations.

COMMENT

Source. The foregoing instructions are modeled on the charge in *Stevens v. Travelers Insurance Co.*, 563 S.W.2d 223 (Tex. 1978), and on Tex. R. Civ. P. 226a.

For use in civil trials only. The above charge is recommended for use in civil cases. For a sample instruction for use in criminal cases, see the current edition of State Bar of Texas, *Texas Criminal Pattern Jury Charges—General, Evidentiary & Ancillary Instructions* CPJC 10.1 (Instruction—*Allen* Charge).

PJC 300.10   Privilege—Generally No Inference

[Brackets indicate instructive text.]

You are instructed that you must not infer anything by [*name of invoking party*]'s refusal to answer questions because of [*name of invoking party*]'s claim of [*privilege asserted*] privilege.

COMMENT

When to use.   This instruction should be used in situations other than a claim of Fifth Amendment privilege. See PJC 300.11. On request by any party against whom the jury might draw any inference from a claim of privilege, the court must instruct the jury that no inference may be drawn therefrom. Tex. R. Evid. 513(d).

PJC 300.11   Fifth Amendment Privilege—Adverse Inference May Be Considered

[Brackets indicate instructive text.]

[Name of invoking party] refused to answer certain questions on the grounds that it may tend to incriminate *him*. A person has a constitutional right to decline to answer on the grounds that it may tend to incriminate *him*. You may, but are not required to, infer by such refusal that the answers would have been adverse to *[name of invoking party]*'s interests.

COMMENT

When to use.   On request by any party after another party has invoked his Fifth Amendment privilege against self-incrimination in the present case, the above instruction may be given at the court's discretion, as controlling authorities neither require nor prohibit its inclusion in the written charge of the court. *See Baxter v. Palmigiano*, 425 U.S. 308, 318 (1976); *Wilz v. Flournoy*, 228 S.W.3d 674, 677 (Tex. 2007); *Texas Department of Public Safety Officers Ass'n v. Denton*, 897 S.W.2d 757, 763 (Tex. 1995).

Nonparty witness.   The Committee expresses no opinion as to the propriety of such an instruction when a nonparty witness asserts a privilege.

PJC 300.12   Parallel Theories on Damages

In answering questions about damages, answer each question separately. Do not increase or reduce the amount in one answer because of your answer to any other question about damages. Do not speculate about what any party's ultimate recovery may or may not be. Any recovery will be determined by the court when it applies the law to your answers at the time of judgment.

COMMENT

When to use.   If several theories of recovery are submitted in the charge and any theory has a different legal measure of damages to be applied to a factually similar claim for damages, the Committee recommends that a separate damages question for each theory be submitted and that the above additional instruction be included earlier in the charge.

PJC 300.13   Proximate Cause

"Proximate cause" means a cause that was a substantial factor in bringing about an event, and without which cause such event would not have occurred. In order to be a proximate cause, the act or omission complained of must be such that a person using the degree of care required of him would have foreseen that the event, or some similar event, might reasonably result therefrom. There may be more than one proximate cause of an event.

COMMENT

Source of instruction.   This definition of proximate cause is based on language from *Transcontinental Insurance Co. v. Crump*:

> [W]e first examine the causation standards for proximate cause and producing cause. "The two elements of proximate cause are cause in fact (or substantial factor) and foreseeability. . . . Cause in fact is established when the act or omission was a substantial factor in bringing about the injuries, and without it, the harm would not have occurred." *IHS Cedars Treatment Ctr. v. Mason*, 143 S.W.3d 794, 798–99 (Tex. 2004). "The approved definition of 'proximate cause' in negligence cases and the approved definition of 'producing cause' in compensation cases are in substance the same, except that there is added to the definition of proximate cause the element of foreseeableness." [*Texas Indemnity Insurance Co. v. Staggs*, 134 S.W.2d 1026, 1028–29 (Tex. 1940).] In other words, the producing cause inquiry is conceptually identical to that of cause in fact.

Transcontinental Insurance Co. v. Crump, 330 S.W.3d 211, 222–23 (Tex. 2010). *See also Ford Motor Co. v. Ledesma*, 242 S.W.3d 32, 46 (Tex. 2007).

The *Crump* and *Ledesma* opinions address the definitions of "producing cause" and "cause in fact." As of the publication date of this edition, there is no decision that expressly overrules the traditional definition of "proximate cause" below:

> "Proximate cause" means that cause which, in a natural and continuous sequence, produces an event, and without which cause such event would not have occurred. In order to be a proximate cause, the act or omission complained of must be such that a person using the degree of care required of him would have foreseen that the event, or some similar event, might reasonably result therefrom. There may be more than one proximate cause of an event.

Former PJC 2.4, 50.3, and 100.9. This definition was based on the definition approved by the court in *Rudes v. Gottschalk*, 324 S.W.2d 201, 207 (Tex. 1959), and has been cited in many cases.

When to use.   PJC 300.13 should be used in every case in which a finding of proximate cause is required. For discussion of the element of "foreseeability," see *Motsenbocker v. Wyatt*, 369 S.W.2d 319, 323 (Tex. 1963), and *Carey v. Pure Distributing Corp.*, 124 S.W.2d 847, 849 (Tex. 1939).

PJC 300.14   Instruction on Spoliation

[Brackets indicate optional, alternative, or instructive text.]

[Name of spoliating party] *[destroyed/failed to preserve/destroyed or failed to preserve]* *[describe evidence]*. You *[must/may]* consider that this evidence would have been unfavorable to *[name of spoliating party]* on the issue of *[describe issue(s) to which evidence would have been relevant]*.

COMMENT

When to use.   The above instruction is recommended for the adverse inference resulting from spoliation. In *Brookshire Bros., Ltd. v. Aldridge*, 438 S.W.3d 9 (Tex. 2014), the Texas Supreme Court clarified the standards governing spoliation and the parameters of a trial court's discretion to impose spoliation remedies based on the facts of the case. After the trial court has determined that a party has spoliated evidence, it has broad discretion to impose a remedy that is proportionate to the conduct, including, under appropriate circumstances, a spoliation instruction to the jury. *Brookshire Bros.*, 438 S.W.3d at 23–26. A spoliation instruction is a severe sanction the court may use to remedy an act of intentional spoliation that prejudices the nonspoliating party. *Brookshire Bros.*, 438 S.W.3d at 23. To find intentional spoliation, the spoliator must have "acted with the subjective purpose of concealing or destroying discoverable evidence." *Brookshire Bros.*, 438 S.W.3d at 24. To submit a spoliation instruction the trial court must find that "(1) the spoliating party acted with intent to conceal discoverable evidence, or (2) the spoliating party acted negligently and caused the nonspoliating party to be irreparably deprived of any meaningful ability to present a claim or defense." *Wackenhut Corp. v. Gutierrez*, 453 S.W.3d 917, 921 (Tex. 2015). Moreover, the court must find that a less severe remedy would be insufficient to reduce the prejudice caused by the spoliation. *Brookshire Bros.*, 438 S.W.3d at 25.

On rare occasions the negligent breach of the duty to reasonably preserve evidence may support the submission of a spoliation instruction. Where the spoliation "so prejudices the nonspoliating party that it is irreparably deprived of having any meaningful ability to present a claim or defense," the court has discretion to remedy the extreme prejudice by submitting a spoliation instruction. *Brookshire Bros.*, 438 S.W.3d at 26.

Caveat.   Because the imposition of a spoliation instruction is considered extremely severe, it should be used cautiously, as the wrongful submission of an instruction may result in a reversal of the case. *Brookshire Bros.*, 438 S.W.3d at 17 (citing *Wal-Mart Stores, Inc. v. Johnson*, 106 S.W.3d 718, 724 (Tex. 2003) ("[I]f a spoliation instruction should not have been given, the likelihood of harm from the erroneous instruction is substantial, particularly when the case is closely contested.")).

Required findings by the court. Whether a spoliation instruction is appropriate is a question of law for the court. *Brookshire Bros.*, 438 S.W.3d at 20 (citing *Trevino v. Ortega*, 969 S.W.2d 950, 954–55, 960 (Tex. 1998) (Baker, J., concurring)). Before considering whether to instruct the jury on spoliation as a remedy for the loss, alteration, or unavailability of certain evidence, a court must consider—

1. whether there was a duty to preserve the evidence at issue,

2. whether the alleged spoliator breached that duty, and

3. prejudice.

Brookshire Bros., 438 S.W.3d at 20.

In evaluating prejudice the court must analyze—

1. relevance of the spoliated evidence to key issues in the case;

2. the harmful effect of the evidence on the spoliating party's case (or conversely, whether the evidence would be helpful to the nonspoliating party's case); and

3. whether the spoliated evidence was cumulative.

Brookshire Bros., 438 S.W.3d at 20; *see also Petroleum Solutions, Inc. v. Head*, 454 S.W.3d 482 (Tex. 2014). Because the imposition of a spoliation instruction is such a severe sanction, courts must first determine whether a direct relationship exists between the conduct, the offender, and the sanction imposed, and the sanction must not be more severe than necessary. *Petroleum Solutions, Inc.*, 454 S.W.3d at 489 (citing *TransAmerican Natural Gas Corp. v. Powell*, 811 S.W.2d 913 (Tex. 1991)).

Use of "may" or "must." In *Brookshire Bros.*, the majority does not articulate the specific language that should be included in the instruction, particularly whether the jury "may" or "must" consider that the missing evidence would have been unfavorable to the spoliator. The dissent in *Brookshire Bros.* interpreted the majority as requiring the use of the term *must*. *Brookshire Bros.*, 438 S.W.3d at 34 (Guzman, J., dissenting). The overarching guideline, as with any sanction, remains proportionality. "Upon a finding of spoliation, the trial court has broad discretion to impose a remedy that, as with any discovery sanction, must be proportionate; that is, it must relate directly to the conduct giving rise to the sanction and may not be excessive." *Brookshire Bros.*, 438 S.W.3d at 14. Whether *may* or *must* is used should be based on the facts applied to the standards articulated above.

PJC 301.1   Adverse Possession (Comment)

The adverse possession statutes apply to recovery of possession of real property, including the minerals underlying the surface of the land. Tex. Civ. Prac. & Rem. Code §§ 16.021–.038; *see Rio Bravo Oil Co. v. Staley Oil Co.*, 158 S.W.2d 293, 295 (Tex. 1942). The adverse possession statutes are statutes of limitations intended to settle land titles. *Natural Gas Pipeline Co. of America v. Pool*, 124 S.W.3d 188, 198–99 (Tex. 2003); *Republic National Bank of Dallas v. Stetson*, 390 S.W.2d 257, 262 (Tex. 1965). Because title vests in the party who establishes the required limitations elements, adverse possession claims may be brought affirmatively or defensively, depending on the situation. Accordingly, the party asserting adverse possession may sometimes be the plaintiff, not the defendant.

The required adverse possession elements are provided by statute. For that reason, the pattern jury charges in this chapter track the statute. Generally, however, the party seeking to establish title by adverse possession must enter the land adversely, that is, without permission or consent of the record title owner; must occupy the land under a claim of right that is inconsistent with and hostile to the claim of another; and must maintain an actual and visible appropriation of the property continuously for the specified period of time. *See Tran v. Macha*, 213 S.W.3d 913, 914–15 (Tex. 2006); *Rhodes v. Cahill*, 802 S.W.2d 643, 645 (Tex. 1990); *Ellis v. Jansing*, 620 S.W.2d 569, 571 (Tex. 1981); *Calfee v. Duke*, 544 S.W.2d 640, 642 (Tex. 1976); *see also Pool*, 124 S.W.3d at 188, 193, 198. The time periods under the adverse possession statutes vary, depending on the nature of the claim and the indicia of title in the adverse possessor. *See* Tex. Civ. Prac. & Rem. Code §§ 16.021–.038; Tex. R. Civ. P. 783–809. The trespass-to-try-title statute is "*the* method [of] determining title to . . . real property." *Martin v. Amerman*, 133 S.W.3d 262, 267 (Tex. 2004) (quoting Tex. Prop. Code § 22.001(a)) (emphasis added); *see* Tex. Prop. Code § 22.001; Tex. R. Civ. P. 783–809; *see also* Tex. Civ. Prac. & Rem. Code § 37.004(c) (notwithstanding section 22.001, a declaratory relief action is allowed if the "sole issue concerning title to real property is the determination of the proper boundary line between adjoining properties").

Adverse possession of the surface estate results in adverse possession of the mineral estate unless the two estates have been severed. *Grissom v. Anderson*, 79 S.W.2d 619, 621 (Tex. 1935). Once severed from the surface estate, the mineral estate may be acquired only by adverse possession of the mineral estate but not by adverse possession of the surface estate. *Pool*, 124 S.W.3d at 192–93, 198; *Thedford v. Union Oil Co. of California*, 3 S.W.3d 609, 615 (Tex. App.—Dallas 1999, pet. denied); *Barfield v. Holland*, 844 S.W.2d 759, 767 (Tex. App.—Tyler 1992, writ denied); *Watkins v. Certain-Teed Products Corp.*, 231 S.W.2d 981, 985 (Tex. App.—Amarillo 1950, no writ). The severed mineral estate can be adversely possessed only by drilling and production operations for the statutory period of time. *Pool*, 124 S.W.3d at 193; *Sun Operating Ltd. Partnership v. Oatman*, 911 S.W.2d 749, 757 (Tex. App.—Amarillo 1995, writ denied); *Barfield*, 844 S.W.2d at 767; *Webb v. British American Oil Producing Co.*, 281 S.W.2d 726, 734 (Tex. App.—Eastland 1955, writ ref'd n.r.e.). The surface owner's possession of the severed surface estate is not adverse to the owner of the mineral estate. *Grissom*, 79 S.W.2d at 621.

Producing minerals after an oil and gas lease expires is similar to the permissive possession by a holdover tenant and therefore cannot be adverse until the title holder has notice that the permissive tenancy has been repudiated and become hostile to the interests of the title holder. *Pool*, 124 S.W.3d at 194. However, actual notice is not required; instead, "notice can be inferred, or there can be constructive notice." *Pool*, 124 S.W.3d at 194; *see also BP America Production Co. v. Marshall*, 342 S.W.3d 59, 72 (Tex. 2011); *Glover v. Union Pacific Railroad Co.*, 187 S.W.3d 201, 215 (Tex. App.—Texarkana 2006, pet. denied). For what may constitute notice, see *Pool* and *Marshall*.

If the lessee establishes the elements of adverse possession, the lessee acquires the same interest adversely possessed; that is, the oil and gas leasehold estate as defined by the original lease. *Pool*, 124 S.W.3d at 199; *see also Marshall*, 342 S.W.3d at 72. If the landowner prevails, title to the mineral estate remains in the landowner free of the leasehold.

The questions in this chapter should be appropriately modified, as discussed in the following pattern jury charges, to reflect whether the adverse possession claim involves an unsevered surface and mineral estate, a severed mineral estate, or a lease-hold estate.

**PJC 301.2   Question and Instructions on Adverse Possession—
               Three-Year Limitations Period**

QUESTION _____

Did [*Don Davis/Paul Payne*] hold the property in peaceable and adverse possession [*under color of title*] for at least three years before [*date cause of action was filed*]?

"Peaceable possession" means possession of real property that is continuous and is not interrupted by an adverse suit to recover the property.

"Adverse possession" means an actual and visible appropriation of real property, commenced and continued under a claim of right that is inconsistent with and hostile to the claim of another person.

"Claim of right" means an intention to claim the real property as one's own to the exclusion of all others.

A claim of right is hostile only if either (1) it provides notice, either actual or by implication, of a hostile claim of right to the true owner; or (2) the acts performed on the real property, and the use made of the real property, were of such a nature and character that would reasonably notify the true owner of the real property that a hostile claim is being asserted to the property.

[*"Color of title" means a consecutive chain of transfers to the person in possession that is not regular because of a muniment that is not properly recorded or is only in writing or because of a similar defect that does not lack intrinsic fairness or honesty. A "muniment" is documentary evidence of title.*]

Answer "Yes" or "No."

Answer: _____

COMMENT

When to use.   PJC 301.2 should be used to submit a claim of adverse possession for three years under title or color of title. If there is a fact dispute about whether the claim is under title or color of title, the question and instructions should be modified as described below. This claim may be raised either affirmatively or defensively. The burden of proof rests with the party raising the adverse possession claim or defense.

Source of question and instructions.   PJC 301.2 is derived from Tex. Civ. Prac. & Rem. Code §§ 16.021, 16.024; *see also BP America Production Co. v. Marshall*, 342 S.W.3d 59, 70–72 (Tex. 2011) (describing claim of right); *Tran v. Macha*, 213

S.W.3d 913, 914–15 (Tex. 2006) (discussing claim of right); *Calfee v. Duke*, 544 S.W.2d 640, 642 (Tex. 1976) (same); *Orsborn v. Deep Rock Oil Corp.*, 267 S.W.2d 781 (Tex. 1954) (discussing hostile claim of right); *Villarreal v. Guerra*, 446 S.W.3d 404, 410 (Tex. App.—San Antonio 2014, pet. denied) (defining the test for hostility); *Taub v. Houston Pipeline Co.*, 75 S.W.3d 606, 626 (Tex. App.—Texarkana 2002, pet. denied) (same); *McCuen v. Huey*, 255 S.W.3d 716, 732 (Tex. App.—Waco 2001, no pet.) (defining muniment).

Broad-form submission.   Submission of adverse possession elements in one question is proper. *Pinchback v. Hockless*, 158 S.W.2d 997, 1003 (Tex. 1942); *Davis v. Dowlen*, 136 S.W.2d 900, 905 (Tex. App.—Beaumont 1939, writ dism'd judgm't cor.). The entire time period over which adverse possession is claimed should be submitted in a single question. *Pinchback*, 158 S.W.2d at 1002.

Title.   "'Title' means a regular chain of transfers of real property from or under the sovereignty of the soil." Tex. Civ. Prac. & Rem. Code § 16.021. Construction of a deed is generally a question of law. *See, e.g., Terrill v. Tuckness*, 985 S.W.2d 97, 101–03 (Tex. App.—San Antonio 1998, no pet.) (trespass-to-try-title action discussing deed construction). Moreover, evidence may establish a regular chain of conveyances from the sovereign as a matter of law. *See, e.g., Longoria v. Lasater*, 292 S.W.3d 156, 165–69 (Tex. App.—San Antonio 2009, pet. denied) (deciding regular chain of title in trespass-to-try-title action by summary judgment); *Terrill*, 985 S.W.2d at 101–03 (nothing for jury to resolve in trespass-to-try-title suit when question of law as between two competing meanings of deed); *see also Moser v. Tucker*, 195 S.W. 259, 260 (Tex. App.—Amarillo 1917, no writ) ("The parties having contracted for an abstract showing a merchantable title, which we construe to mean a marketable title, as it appears upon the records only, the question under this record becomes one of law."). A jury, however, should resolve any issues of disputed fact with regard to title, which may require that additional questions precede the adverse possession question. *See, e.g., Terrill*, 985 S.W.2d at 101–03 (construction of ambiguous deed may present fact question); *Niles v. Houston Oil Co.*, 288 S.W. 614, 617 (Tex. App.—Beaumont 1926, writ dism'd w.o.j.) (alleged forgery of deed may present fact question); *Smith v. Cavitt*, 50 S.W. 167, 167 (Tex. App.—Dallas 1899, no writ) (same). Because title is generally a question of law, title is not included in the question and instead the jury is asked about the disputed facts on adverse, peaceable possession for the requisite period.

Color of title/muniments.   Color of title may be a fact question. *See, e.g., Meaders v. Moore*, 132 S.W.2d 256, 259 (Tex. 1939); *Capps v. Gibbs*, No. 10-12-00294-CV, 2013 WL 1701772, at *5 (Tex. App.—Waco Apr. 18, 2013) (holding reasonable fact finder could find evidence constituted color of title based on consecutive chain of transfers). If color of title is a disputed question, include the phrase *under color of title* in the question and its definition in the instructions. The definition tracks the statute. Tex. Civ. Prac. & Rem. Code § 16.021. For cases interpreting color of title, see *Capps*, 2013 WL 1701772, at *4–5, and *Oncale v. Veyna*, 798 S.W.2d 802, 804 (Tex. App.—

Houston [14th Dist.] 1990, no writ) (citing *Grigsby v. May*, 19 S.W. 343, 348 (Tex. 1892) (construing similarly worded predecessor statute)). "A quitclaim deed is not a conveyance or a muniment of title. By itself, it does not establish any title in those holding the deed, but merely passes the interest of the grantor in the property." *Rogers v. Ricane Enterprises*, 884 S.W.2d 763, 769 (Tex. 1994).

Color of title/other documents.   In addition to muniments of title, section 16.021 also defines color of title to include "a consecutive chain of transfers to the person in possession that . . . is based on a certificate of headright, land warrant, or land scrip." Tex. Civ. Prac. & Rem. Code § 16.021. If the case involves a certificate of headright, land warrant, or land scrip, modify the instruction on color of title and consider whether additional definitions should be included.

Color of title/similar defect.   In addition to muniments of title, section 16.021 also defines color of title to include "a consecutive chain of transfers to the person in possession that . . . is not regular because of a muniment that is not properly recorded or is only in writing or because of a similar defect that does not want of intrinsic fairness." Tex. Civ. Prac. & Rem. Code § 16.021(2)(a).   The term "intrinsic fairness" relates "to the means of proving the right of property in the land, [so as to make the defective] title equitably equal to a regular chain." *Grigsby*, 19 S.W. at 348 (construing similarly worded predecessor statute).   If the purported transfers of title cited by a party claiming property under color of title were "freely executed by the persons whose acts they appear to be," they are sufficient under Tex. Civ. Prac. & Rem. Code § 16.024 "if upon their faces they show such right to land as a court of equity would enforce as between the parties to the instruments . . . ." *Grigsby*, 19 S.W. at 349.   If the case involves an irregular chain of title not otherwise specified in Tex. Civ. Prac. & Rem. Code § 16.021(2)(b), modify the instruction on color of title and consider whether additional definitions should be included.

Under title/color of title.   If a case involves a claim of both title and color of title, modification of the question or an additional question may be required and further instruction from the trial court regarding legal title may be necessary. *See, e.g., Wilson v. Whetstone*, No. 03-08-00738-CV, 2010 WL 1633087, at *4 (Tex. App.—Austin Apr. 20, 2010, pet. denied) (instructing jury that defendants had record title to disputed area).

Possession of mineral estate.   Adverse possession of the surface estate results in adverse possession of the mineral estate unless the two estates have been severed. *Grissom v. Anderson*, 79 S.W.2d 619, 621 (Tex. 1935). Once severed from the surface estate, the mineral estate may be acquired only by adverse possession of the mineral estate and not by adverse possession of the surface estate. *Natural Gas Pipeline Co. of America v. Pool*, 124 S.W.3d 188, 192–93, 198 (Tex. 2003); *Thedford v. Union Oil Co. of California*, 3 S.W.3d 609, 615 (Tex. App.—Dallas 1999, pet. denied); *Barfield v. Holland*, 844 S.W.2d 759, 767 (Tex. App.—Tyler 1992, writ denied); *Watkins v. Certain-Teed Products Corp.*, 231 S.W.2d 981, 985 (Tex. App.—Amarillo 1950, no writ).

The severed mineral estate can be adversely possessed only by drilling and production operations for the statutory period of time. *Pool*, 124 S.W.3d at 193; *Sun Operating Ltd. Partnership v. Oatman*, 911 S.W.2d 749, 757 (Tex. App.—Amarillo 1995, writ denied); *Barfield*, 844 S.W.2d at 767; *Webb v. British American Oil Producing Co.*, 281 S.W.2d 726, 734 (Tex. App.—Eastland 1955, writ ref'd n.r.e.). The surface owner's possession of the severed surface estate is not adverse to the owner of the mineral estate. *Grissom*, 79 S.W.2d at 621. When the claim is made to a severed mineral estate, the definition of "adverse possession" may be modified as follows:

> "Adverse possession" means an actual and visible appropriation of real property by drilling and producing oil and gas, commenced and continued under a claim of right that is inconsistent with and hostile to the claim of another person.

Continuity of possession. Possession is "continuous" as long as (1) any temporary breaks in possession by the claimant are reasonable under the circumstances and (2) the claimant did not intend to abandon possession. *Grayson v. Dunn*, 581 S.W.2d 785, 788 (Tex. App.—Waco 1979) (citing *Dunn v. Taylor*, 113 S.W. 265, 267 (Tex. 1908)). Where there is a break in the continuity of possession, the claimant must show that possession was resumed within a reasonable time. *Hardy v. Bumpstead*, 41 S.W.2d 226 (Tex. Comm'n App. 1931). If continuity of possession is a disputed issue, an additional instruction may be included in the question.

Tacking. "To satisfy a limitations period, peaceable and adverse possession does not need to continue in the same person, but there must be privity of estate between each holder and his successor." Tex. Civ. Prac. & Rem. Code § 16.023; *Estrada v. Cheshire*, 470 S.W.3d 109, 124–26 (Tex. App.—Houston [1st Dist.] 2015, pet. denied); *Treviño v. Treviño*, 64 S.W.3d 166, 172 (Tex. App.—San Antonio 2001, no pet.); *First National Bank of Marshall v. Beavers*, 602 S.W.2d 327, 329 (Tex. App.— Texarkana 1980, no writ). If possessory periods are tacked, consider whether modification of the question (or additional questions) and an additional instruction are required.

Property identification and definition. In this question or the general instructions of the charge, the real property in question should be defined, including the specific surface or mineral estate at issue:

> "Property" means the [*insert definition, description, or identification*].

Accrual. "The structure of the adverse possession statute indicates that the 'cause of action' refers to the suit to recover real property held by another in peaceable and adverse possession." *Marshall*, 342 S.W.3d at 73. *See* Tex. Civ. Prac. & Rem. Code § 16.024. The cause of action accrues when the adverse possession begins. *Marshall*, 342 S.W.3d at 73; *see also Horton v. Crawford*, 10 Tex. 382, 390–91 (1853); *Waddy v. City of Houston*, 834 S.W.2d 97, 103 (Tex. App.—Houston [1st Dist.] 1992, writ denied); *Woolaver v. Texaco, Inc.*, 638 S.W.2d 153, 155 (Tex. App.—Fort Worth 1982, writ ref'd n.r.e.); *Crow v. Payne*, 242 S.W.2d 824, 825 (Tex. App.—Amarillo 1951, no writ). For a claim to have accrued, the jury must find that the adverse possession began more than three years before the cause of action was filed.

Multiple limitations questions. If multiple limitations questions will be submitted, consider whether the phrase "For this question" should precede any definition to clarify the requirements between statutes.

Repudiation of title requirement. Other than by the fifteen-year combined limitations period in Tex. Civ. Prac. & Rem. Code § 16.0265, a cotenant may not adversely possess against another cotenant in the absence of repudiation of the relationship or ouster. *See King Ranch, Inc. v. Chapman*, 118 S.W.3d 742, 756 (Tex. 2003); *Todd v. Bruner*, 365 S.W.2d 155, 160–61 (Tex. 1963); *see also Marshall*, 342 S.W.3d at 70–72; *Hardaway v. Nixon*, 544 S.W.3d 402, 409 (Tex. App.—San Antonio 2017, pet. denied). For additional discussion, see PJC 301.1. The same is true with a permissive holdover tenant. *See Pool*, 124 S.W.3d at 194 (" '[P]ossession cannot be considered adverse until the tenancy has been repudiated, and notice of such repudiation has been brought home to the titleholder.' But . . . actual notice of repudiation is not required. Rather, notice can be inferred, or there can be constructive notice.") (citing *Tex-Wis Co. v. Johnson*, 534 S.W.2d 895 (Tex. 1976)). "Whether there has been a repudiation of a nonpossessory cotenant's title is a question of fact [but] when the pertinent facts are undisputed, repudiation may be established as a matter of law." *King Ranch, Inc.*, 118 S.W.3d at 756; *see also Marshall*, 342 S.W.3d at 70–72. For additional discussion, see PJC 301.1.

When repudiation is disputed, an additional instruction may be required. *See, e.g., Dyer v. Cotton*, 333 S.W.3d 703, 711–13 (Tex. App.—Houston [1st Dist.] 2010, no pet.); *Bell v. Lyon*, 635 S.W.2d 586, 589–90 (Tex. App.—Houston [14th Dist.] 1982, writ ref'd n.r.e.). The court in *Dyer* affirmed submission of the following instruction in a suit between cotenants:

> [T]he possession by an owner of an interest in property will be presumed to be his right as a co-owner. The possession, to be adverse to the other owner, or owners, must be of such acts as to amount to an ouster of the other owner, or owners, and must be of such an unequivocal nature and so distinctly hostile to the others' rights that the intention to claim the property is clear and unmistakable.

Dyer, 333 S.W.3d at 711; *see also Todd*, 365 S.W.2d at 159–60. Although mere possession does not generally suffice, one exception may be when possession and assertion of a claim by one cotenant is so long-continued, at least in the absence of a claim by the nonpossessory cotenant, that it puts the nonpossessory cotenant on constructive notice of the repudiation. *Tex-Wis Co.*, 534 S.W.2d at 901 (jury may infer notice of repudiation from a cotenant's long-continued possession and absence of claim by the titleholder). *But see Hardaway*, 544 S.W.3d at 409–10 (cotenant's summary judgment burden on notice of repudiation not satisfied "based on an inference or presumption arising from long-continued possession and absence of a claim" without evidence of other unequivocal, hostile acts taken to disseize other cotenants).

Acknowledgment of title.   Acknowledgment of title in another may defeat an adverse possession claim if made before limitations title ripens but not after. But a possessor's acknowledgment of title in another after the limitation period may tend to show that the possession was not adverse. *Bruni v. Vidaurri*, 166 S.W.2d 81, 88 (Tex. 1942). Whether an adverse claimant's conduct or statement constitutes an acknowledgment of title in another is a question of fact. *Kinder Morgan North Texas Pipeline, L.P. v. Justiss*, 202 S.W.3d 427, 439 (Tex. App.—Texarkana 2006, no pet.); *Bell*, 635 S.W.2d at 590. If acknowledgment is a disputed fact issue, an additional question or instruction may be necessary.

Attorney's fees.   Tex. Civ. Prac. & Rem. Code § 16.034(a)(1) provides for the recovery of attorney's fees by a record title holder in a suit for possession of real property, if successful against another party claiming adverse possession of the property. If the court finds that the adverse possessor's claim was groundless and made in bad faith, the court *shall* award costs and reasonable attorney's fees. Tex. Civ. Prac. & Rem. Code § 16.034(a)(1). Without such a finding, the court *may* award costs and reasonable fees. Tex. Civ. Prac. & Rem. Code § 16.034(a)(2). The statute imposes demand requirements. Tex. Civ. Prac. & Rem. Code § 16.034(b)–(c). The amount of reasonable attorney's fees is generally a fact issue. *See Transcontinental Insurance Co. v. Crump*, 330 S.W.3d 211, 229–32 (Tex. 2010); *City of Garland v. Dallas Morning News*, 22 S.W.3d 351, 367 (Tex. 2000); *Bocquet v. Herring*, 972 S.W.2d 19, 21 (Tex. 1998); *RDG Partnership v. Long*, 350 S.W.3d 262, 277–78 (Tex. App.—San Antonio 2011, no pet.); *Cullins v. Foster*, 171 S.W.3d 521, 536 (Tex. App.—Houston [14th Dist.] 2005, pet. denied). For a question on and additional discussion of attorney's fees, see PJC 313.33.

**PJC 301.3   Question and Instructions on Adverse Possession—
                 Five-Year Limitations Period**

QUESTION _____

Did [*Don Davis/Paul Payne*] hold the property in peaceable and adverse possession for a period of at least five years before [*date cause of action was filed*]?

"Peaceable possession" means possession of real property that is continuous and is not interrupted by an adverse suit to recover the property.

"Adverse possession" means an actual and visible appropriation of real property, commenced and continued under a claim of right that is inconsistent with and hostile to the claim of another person.

"Claim of right" means an intention to claim the real property as one's own to the exclusion of all others.

A claim of right is hostile only if either (1) it provides notice, either actual or by implication, of a hostile claim of right to the true owner; or (2) the acts performed on the real property, and the use made of the real property, were of such a nature and character that would reasonably notify the true owner of the real property that a hostile claim is being asserted to the property.

[*For this question,*] To establish peaceable and adverse possession, a claimant must also have—

    1.   cultivated, used, or enjoyed the property;

    2.   paid the applicable taxes on the property; and

    3.   claimed the property under a duly registered deed.

Answer "Yes" or "No."

Answer: _____

COMMENT

When to use. PJC 301.3 should be used to submit a claim under the five-year adverse possession statute. This claim may be raised either affirmatively or defensively. The burden of proof rests with the party raising the adverse possession claim or defense.

Source of question and instructions. PJC 301.3 is derived from Tex. Civ. Prac. & Rem. Code §§ 16.021, 16.025; *see also BP America Production Co. v. Marshall,*

342 S.W.3d 59, 70–72 (Tex. 2011) (describing claim of right); *Tran v. Macha*, 213 S.W.3d 913, 914–15 (Tex. 2006) (discussing claim of right); *Calfee v. Duke*, 544 S.W.2d 640, 642 (Tex. 1976) (same); *Orsborn v. Deep Rock Oil Corp.*, 267 S.W.2d 781 (Tex. 1954) (discussing hostile claim of right); *Villarreal v. Guerra*, 446 S.W.3d 404, 410 (Tex. App.—San Antonio 2014, pet. denied) (defining the test for hostility); *Taub v. Houston Pipeline Co.*, 75 S.W.3d 606, 626 (Tex. App.—Texarkana 2002, pet. denied) (same); *see also Natural Gas Pipeline Co. of America v. Pool*, 124 S.W.3d 188, 198 (Tex. 2003) (discussing claim of right); *Rhodes v. Cahill*, 802 S.W.2d 643, 645 (Tex. 1990) (same).

Broad-form submission.   Submission of adverse possession elements in one question is proper. *Pinchback v. Hockless*, 158 S.W.2d 997, 1003 (Tex. 1942); *Davis v. Dowlen*, 136 S.W.2d 900, 905 (Tex. App.—Beaumont 1939, writ dism'd judgm't cor.). The entire time period over which adverse possession is claimed should be submitted in a single question. *Pinchback*, 158 S.W.2d at 1002.

Forged deeds/quitclaim deeds.   The five-year adverse possession statute "does not apply to a claim based on a forged deed or a deed executed under a forged power of attorney." Tex. Civ. Prac. & Rem. Code § 16.025(b). A quitclaim deed will not support an adverse possession claim under the five-year statute. *Porter v. Wilson*, 389 S.W.2d 650, 654–55 (Tex. 1965).

Possession of mineral estate.   Adverse possession of the surface estate results in adverse possession of the mineral estate unless the two estates have been severed. *Grissom v. Anderson*, 79 S.W.2d 619, 621 (Tex. 1935). Once severed from the surface estate, the mineral estate may be acquired only by adverse possession of the mineral estate and not by adverse possession of the surface estate. *Pool*, 124 S.W.3d at 192–93, 198; *Thedford v. Union Oil Co. of California*, 3 S.W.3d 609, 615 (Tex. App.—Dallas 1999, pet. denied); *Barfield v. Holland*, 844 S.W.2d 759, 767 (Tex. App.—Tyler 1992, writ denied); *Watkins v. Certain-Teed Products Corp.*, 231 S.W.2d 981, 985 (Tex. App.—Amarillo 1950, no writ). The severed mineral estate can be adversely possessed only by drilling and production operations for the statutory period of time. *Pool*, 124 S.W.3d at 193; *Sun Operating Ltd. Partnership v. Oatman*, 911 S.W.2d 749, 757 (Tex. App.—Amarillo 1995, writ denied); *Barfield*, 844 S.W.2d at 767; *Webb v. British American Oil Producing Co.*, 281 S.W.2d 726, 734 (Tex. App.—Eastland 1955, writ ref'd n.r.e.). The surface owner's possession of the severed surface estate is not adverse to the owner of the mineral estate. *Grissom*, 79 S.W.2d at 621. When the claim is made to a severed mineral estate, the definition of "adverse possession" may be modified as follows:

> "Adverse possession" means an actual and visible appropriation of real property by drilling and producing oil and gas, commenced and continued under a claim of right that is inconsistent with and hostile to the claim of another person.

Continuity of possession.   Possession is "continuous" as long as (1) any temporary breaks in possession by the claimant are reasonable under the circumstances and (2) the claimant did not intend to abandon possession. *Grayson v. Dunn*, 581 S.W.2d 785, 788 (Tex. App.—Waco 1979) (citing *Dunn v. Taylor*, 113 S.W. 265, 267 (Tex. 1908)). Where there is a break in the continuity of possession, the claimant must show that possession was resumed within a reasonable time. *Hardy v. Bumpstead*, 41 S.W.2d 226 (Tex. Comm'n App. 1931). If continuity of possession is a disputed issue, an additional instruction may be included in the question.

Tacking.   "To satisfy a limitations period, peaceable and adverse possession does not need to continue in the same person, but there must be privity of estate between each holder and his successor." Tex. Civ. Prac. & Rem. Code § 16.023; *Estrada v. Cheshire*, 470 S.W.3d 109, 124–26 (Tex. App.—Houston [1st Dist.] 2015, pet. denied); *Treviño v. Treviño*, 64 S.W.3d 166, 172 (Tex. App.—San Antonio 2001, no pet.); *First National Bank of Marshall v. Beavers*, 602 S.W.2d 327, 329 (Tex. App.—Texarkana 1980, no writ). If possessory periods are tacked, consider whether modification of the question (or additional questions) and an additional instruction are required.

Property identification and definition.   In this question or the general instructions of the charge, the real property in question should be defined, including the specific surface or mineral estate at issue:

> "Property" means the [*insert definition, description, or identification*].

Accrual.   "The structure of the adverse possession statute indicates that the 'cause of action' refers to the suit to recover real property held by another in peaceable and adverse possession." *Marshall*, 342 S.W.3d at 73. *See* Tex. Civ. Prac. & Rem. Code § 16.024. The cause of action accrues when the adverse possession begins. *Marshall*, 342 S.W.3d at 73; *see also Horton v. Crawford*, 10 Tex. 382, 390–91 (1853); *Waddy v. City of Houston*, 834 S.W.2d 97, 103 (Tex. App.—Houston [1st Dist.] 1992, writ denied); *Woolaver v. Texaco, Inc.*, 638 S.W.2d 153, 155 (Tex. App.—Fort Worth 1982, writ ref'd n.r.e.); *Crow v. Payne*, 242 S.W.2d 824, 825 (Tex. App.—Amarillo 1951, no writ). For a claim to have accrued, the jury must find that possession began more than five years before the cause of action was filed.

Multiple limitations questions.   If multiple limitations questions will be submitted, consider whether the phrase "For this question" should precede any definition to clarify the requirements between statutes.

Repudiation of title requirement.   Other than by the fifteen-year combined limitations period in Tex. Civ. Prac. & Rem. Code § 16.0265, a cotenant may not adversely possess against another cotenant in the absence of repudiation of the relationship or ouster. *See King Ranch, Inc. v. Chapman*, 118 S.W.3d 742, 756 (Tex. 2003); *Todd v. Bruner*, 365 S.W.2d 155, 160–61 (Tex. 1963); *see also Marshall*, 342

S.W.3d at 70–72; *Hardaway v. Nixon*, 544 S.W.3d 402, 409 (Tex. App.—San Antonio 2017, pet. denied). For additional discussion, see PJC 301.1. The same is true with a permissive holdover tenant. *See Pool*, 124 S.W.3d at 194 (" '[P]ossession cannot be considered adverse until the tenancy has been repudiated, and notice of such repudiation has been brought home to the titleholder.' But . . . actual notice of repudiation is not required. Rather, notice can be inferred, or there can be constructive notice.") (citing *Tex-Wis Co. v. Johnson*, 534 S.W.2d 895 (Tex. 1976)). "Whether there has been a repudiation of a nonpossessory cotenant's title is a question of fact [but] when the pertinent facts are undisputed, repudiation may be established as a matter of law." *King Ranch, Inc.*, 118 S.W.3d at 756; *see also Marshall*, 342 S.W.3d at 70–72. For additional discussion, see PJC 301.1.

When repudiation is disputed, an additional instruction may be required. *See, e.g., Dyer v. Cotton*, 333 S.W.3d 703, 711–13 (Tex. App.—Houston [1st Dist.] 2010, no pet.); *Bell v. Lyon*, 635 S.W.2d 586, 589–90 (Tex. App.—Houston [14th Dist.] 1982, writ ref'd n.r.e.). The court in *Dyer* affirmed submission of the following instruction in a suit between cotenants:

> [T]he possession by an owner of an interest in property will be presumed to be his right as a co-owner. The possession, to be adverse to the other owner, or owners, must be of such acts as to amount to an ouster of the other owner, or owners, and must be of such an unequivocal nature and so distinctly hostile to the others' rights that the intention to claim the property is clear and unmistakable.

Dyer, 333 S.W.3d at 711; *see also Todd*, 365 S.W.2d at 159–60. Although mere possession does not generally suffice, one exception may be when possession and assertion of a claim by one cotenant is so long-continued, at least in the absence of a claim by the nonpossessory cotenant, that it puts the nonpossessory cotenant on constructive notice of the repudiation. *Tex-Wis Co.*, 534 S.W.2d at 901 (jury may infer notice of repudiation from a cotenant's long-continued possession and absence of claim by the titleholder). *But see Hardaway*, 544 S.W.3d at 409–10 (cotenant's summary judgment burden on notice of repudiation not satisfied "based on an inference or presumption arising from long-continued possession and absence of a claim" without evidence of other unequivocal, hostile acts taken to disseize other cotenants).

Acknowledgment of title. Acknowledgment of title in another may defeat an adverse possession claim if made before limitations title ripens but not after. But a possessor's acknowledgment of title in another after the limitation period may tend to show that the possession was not adverse. *Bruni v. Vidaurri*, 166 S.W.2d 81, 88 (Tex. 1942). Whether an adverse claimant's conduct or statement constitutes an acknowledgment of title in another is a question of fact. *Kinder Morgan North Texas Pipeline, L.P. v. Justiss*, 202 S.W.3d 427, 439 (Tex. App.—Texarkana 2006, no pet.); *Bell*, 635

S.W.2d at 590. If acknowledgment is a disputed fact issue, an additional question or instruction may be necessary.

Attorney's fees.   Tex. Civ. Prac. & Rem. Code § 16.034(a)(1) provides for the recovery of attorney's fees by a record title holder in a suit for possession of real property, if successful against another party claiming adverse possession of the property. If the court finds that the adverse possessor's claim was groundless and made in bad faith, the court *shall* award costs and reasonable attorney's fees. Tex. Civ. Prac. & Rem. Code § 16.034(a)(1). Without such a finding, the court *may* award costs and reasonable fees. Tex. Civ. Prac. & Rem. Code § 16.034(a)(2). The statute imposes demand requirements. Tex. Civ. Prac. & Rem. Code § 16.034(b)–(c). The amount of reasonable attorney's fees is generally a fact issue. *See Transcontinental Insurance Co. v. Crump*, 330 S.W.3d 211, 229–32 (Tex. 2010); *City of Garland v. Dallas Morning News*, 22 S.W.3d 351, 367 (Tex. 2000); *Bocquet v. Herring*, 972 S.W.2d 19, 21 (Tex. 1998); *RDG Partnership v. Long*, 350 S.W.3d 262, 277–78 (Tex. App.—San Antonio 2011, no pet.); *Cullins v. Foster*, 171 S.W.3d 521, 536 (Tex. App.—Houston [14th Dist.] 2005, pet. denied). For a question on and additional discussion of attorney's fees, see PJC 313.33.

PJC 301.4   Question and Instructions on Adverse Possession—
               Ten-Year Limitations Period

QUESTION _____

Did [*Don Davis/Paul Payne*] hold the property in peaceable and adverse possession for a period of at least ten years before [*date cause of action was filed*]?

"Peaceable possession" means possession of real property that is continuous and is not interrupted by an adverse suit to recover the property.

"Adverse possession" means an actual and visible appropriation of real property, commenced and continued under a claim of right that is inconsistent with and hostile to the claim of another person.

"Claim of right" means an intention to claim the real property as one's own to the exclusion of all others.

A claim of right is hostile only if either (1) it provides notice, either actual or by implication, of a hostile claim of right to the true owner; or (2) the acts performed on the real property, and the use made of the real property, were of such a nature and character that would reasonably notify the true owner of the real property that a hostile claim is being asserted to the property.

[*For this question,*] To establish peaceable and adverse possession, a claimant must also have cultivated, used, or enjoyed the property.

Answer "Yes" or "No."

Answer: _____

COMMENT

When to use.   PJC 301.4 should be used to submit a claim under the ten-year adverse possession statute if the party claims adverse possession and cultivation, use, or enjoyment of the property. This claim may be raised either affirmatively or defensively. The burden of proof rests with the party raising the adverse possession claim or defense.

Source of question and instructions.   PJC 301.4 is derived from Tex. Civ. Prac. & Rem. Code §§ 16.021, 16.026; *see also BP America Production Co. v. Marshall*, 342 S.W.3d 59, 70–72 (Tex. 2011) (describing claim of right); *Tran v. Macha*, 213 S.W.3d 913, 914–15 (Tex. 2006) (discussing claim of right); *Calfee v. Duke*, 544 S.W.2d 640, 642 (Tex. 1976) (same); *Orsborn v. Deep Rock Oil Corp.*, 267 S.W.2d

781 (Tex. 1954) (discussing hostile claim of right); *Villarreal v. Guerra*, 446 S.W.3d 404, 410 (Tex. App.—San Antonio 2014, pet. denied) (defining the test for hostility); *Taub v. Houston Pipeline Co.*, 75 S.W.3d 606, 626 (Tex. App.—Texarkana 2002, pet. denied) (same); *see also Natural Gas Pipeline Co. of America v. Pool*, 124 S.W.3d 188, 198 (Tex. 2003) (discussing claim of right); *Rhodes v. Cahill*, 802 S.W.2d 643, 645 (Tex. 1990) (same).

Broad-form submission.   Submission of adverse possession elements in one question is proper. *Pinchback v. Hockless*, 158 S.W.2d 997, 1003 (Tex. 1942); *Davis v. Dowlen*, 136 S.W.2d 900, 905 (Tex. App.—Beaumont 1939, writ dism'd judgm't cor.). The entire time period over which adverse possession is claimed should be submitted in a single question. *Pinchback*, 158 S.W.2d at 1002.

No title instrument.   Peaceable and adverse possession under Tex. Civ. Prac. & Rem. Code § 16.026 without a title instrument is limited to 160 acres, including improvements, unless the number of acres actually enclosed exceeds 160, in which case the peaceable and adverse possession extends to the real property actually enclosed.

With title instrument.   Under Tex. Civ. Prac. & Rem. Code § 16.026(c), a possessor's claim may extend to the boundaries specified in any duly registered deed or other memorandum of title that fixes the boundaries of the adversely possessed tract of land.

Enclosed or adjacent land.   In a case involving fenced acreage, one or more additional instructions may be required. Tex. Civ. Prac. & Rem. Code §§ 16.031, 16.032. If the record owner is in actual possession of any part of the land to which he holds record title, the adverse possessor claiming under Tex. Civ. Prac. & Rem. Code § 16.031(b) can claim only the land actually enclosed. *See Coleman v. Waddell*, 249 S.W.2d 912, 913 (Tex. 1952).

Casual fence vs. designed enclosure.   Texas courts distinguish between "casual fences" and fences that "designedly enclose" an area. *Rhodes*, 802 S.W.2d at 646. If the fence existed before possession was taken of the land and the possessor fails to demonstrate the purpose for which it was erected, then the fence is a "casual fence." *Rhodes*, 802 S.W.2d at 646; *Orsborn*, 267 S.W.2d at 786. Repairing or maintaining a casual fence, even for the express purpose of keeping the claimant's animals within the enclosed area, generally does not change a casual fence into a designed enclosure. *McDonnold v. Weinacht*, 465 S.W.2d 136, 142–43 (Tex. 1971). However, an adverse possessor may substantially modify a casual fence so as to change its character to a designed enclosure, and such evidence will support a jury finding of adverse possession. *Rhodes*, 802 S.W.2d at 646; *Butler v. Hanson*, 455 S.W.2d 942, 945–46 (Tex. 1970). If the character of the fence is in dispute, an additional question or instruction may be necessary.

Possession of mineral estate. Adverse possession of the surface estate results in adverse possession of the mineral estate unless the two estates have been severed. *Grissom v. Anderson*, 79 S.W.2d 619, 621 (Tex. 1935). Once severed from the surface estate, the mineral estate may be acquired only by adverse possession of the mineral estate and not by adverse possession of the surface estate. *Pool*, 124 S.W.3d at 192–93, 198; *Thedford v. Union Oil Co. of California*, 3 S.W.3d 609, 615 (Tex. App.—Dallas 1999, pet. denied); *Barfield v. Holland*, 844 S.W.2d 759, 767 (Tex. App.—Tyler 1992, writ denied); *Watkins v. Certain-Teed Products Corp.*, 231 S.W.2d 981, 985 (Tex. App.—Amarillo 1950, no writ). The severed mineral estate can be adversely possessed only by drilling and production operations for the statutory period of time. *Pool*, 124 S.W.3d at 193; *Sun Operating Ltd. Partnership v. Oatman*, 911 S.W.2d 749, 757 (Tex. App.—Amarillo 1995, writ denied); *Barfield*, 844 S.W.2d at 767; *Webb v. British American Oil Producing Co.*, 281 S.W.2d 726, 734 (Tex. App.—Eastland 1955, writ ref'd n.r.e.). The surface owner's possession of the severed surface estate is not adverse to the owner of the mineral estate. *Grissom*, 79 S.W.2d at 621. When the claim is made to a severed mineral estate, the definition of "adverse possession" may be modified as follows:

> "Adverse possession" means an actual and visible appropriation of real property by drilling and producing oil and gas, commenced and continued under a claim of right that is inconsistent with and hostile to the claim of another person.

Continuity of possession. Possession is "continuous" as long as (1) any temporary breaks in possession by the claimant are reasonable under the circumstances and (2) the claimant did not intend to abandon possession. *Grayson v. Dunn*, 581 S.W.2d 785, 788 (Tex. App.—Waco 1979) (citing *Dunn v. Taylor*, 113 S.W. 265, 267 (Tex. 1908)). Where there is a break in the continuity of possession, the claimant must show that possession was resumed within a reasonable time. *Hardy v. Bumpstead*, 41 S.W.2d 226 (Tex. Comm'n App. 1931). If continuity of possession is a disputed issue, an additional instruction may be included in the question.

Tacking. "To satisfy a limitations period, peaceable and adverse possession does not need to continue in the same person, but there must be privity of estate between each holder and his successor." Tex. Civ. Prac. & Rem. Code § 16.023; *Estrada v. Cheshire*, 470 S.W.3d 109, 124–26 (Tex. App.—Houston [1st Dist.] 2015, pet. denied); *Treviño v. Treviño*, 64 S.W.3d 166, 172 (Tex. App.—San Antonio 2001, no pet.); *First National Bank of Marshall v. Beavers*, 602 S.W.2d 327, 329 (Tex. App.—Texarkana 1980, no writ). If possessory periods are tacked, consider whether modification of the question (or additional questions) and an additional instruction are required.

Property identification and definition. In this question or the general instructions of the charge, the real property in question should be defined, including the specific surface or mineral estate at issue:

"Property" means the [*insert definition, description, or identification*].

Accrual.   "The structure of the adverse possession statute indicates that the 'cause of action' refers to the suit to recover real property held by another in peaceable and adverse possession." *Marshall*, 342 S.W.3d at 73. *See* Tex. Civ. Prac. & Rem. Code § 16.024. The cause of action accrues when the adverse possession begins. *Marshall*, 342 S.W.3d at 73; *see also Horton v. Crawford*, 10 Tex. 382, 390–91 (1853); *Waddy v. City of Houston*, 834 S.W.2d 97, 103 (Tex. App.—Houston [1st Dist.] 1992, writ denied); *Woolaver v. Texaco, Inc.*, 638 S.W.2d 153, 155 (Tex. App.—Fort Worth 1982, writ ref'd n.r.e.); *Crow v. Payne*, 242 S.W.2d 824, 825 (Tex. App.—Amarillo 1951, no writ). For a claim to have accrued, the jury must find that possession began more than ten years before the cause of action was filed.

Multiple limitations questions.   If multiple limitations questions will be submitted, consider whether the phrase "For this question" should precede any definition to clarify the requirements between statutes.

Repudiation of title requirement.   Other than by the fifteen-year combined limitations period in Tex. Civ. Prac. & Rem. Code § 16.0265, a cotenant may not adversely possess against another cotenant in the absence of repudiation of the relationship or ouster. *See King Ranch, Inc. v. Chapman*, 118 S.W.3d 742, 756 (Tex. 2003); *Todd v. Bruner*, 365 S.W.2d 155, 160–61 (Tex. 1963); *see also Marshall*, 342 S.W.3d at 70–72; *Hardaway v. Nixon*, 544 S.W.3d 402, 409 (Tex. App.—San Antonio 2017, pet. denied). For additional discussion, see PJC 301.1. The same is true with a permissive holdover tenant. *See Pool*, 124 S.W.3d at 194 (" '[P]ossession cannot be considered adverse until the tenancy has been repudiated, and notice of such repudiation has been brought home to the titleholder.' But . . . actual notice of repudiation is not required. Rather, notice can be inferred, or there can be constructive notice.") (citing *Tex-Wis Co. v. Johnson*, 534 S.W.2d 895 (Tex. 1976)). "Whether there has been a repudiation of a nonpossessory cotenant's title is a question of fact [but] when the pertinent facts are undisputed, repudiation may be established as a matter of law." *King Ranch, Inc.*, 118 S.W.3d at 756; *see also Marshall*, 342 S.W.3d at 70–72. For additional discussion, see PJC 301.1.

When repudiation is disputed, an additional instruction may be required. *See, e.g., Dyer v. Cotton*, 333 S.W.3d 703, 711–13 (Tex. App.—Houston [1st Dist.] 2010, no pet.); *Bell v. Lyon*, 635 S.W.2d 586, 589–90 (Tex. App.—Houston [14th Dist.] 1982, writ ref'd n.r.e.). The court in *Dyer* affirmed submission of the following instruction in a suit between cotenants:

> [T]he possession by an owner of an interest in property will be presumed to be his right as a co-owner. The possession, to be adverse to the other owner, or owners, must be of such acts as to amount to an ouster of the other owner, or owners, and must be of such an unequivocal nature and so distinctly hos-

tile to the others' rights that the intention to claim the property is clear and unmistakable.

Dyer, 333 S.W.3d at 711; *see also Todd*, 365 S.W.2d at 159–60. Although mere possession does not generally suffice, one exception may be when possession and assertion of a claim by one cotenant is so long-continued, at least in the absence of a claim by the nonpossessory cotenant, that it puts the nonpossessory cotenant on constructive notice of the repudiation. *Tex-Wis Co.*, 534 S.W.2d at 901 (jury may infer notice of repudiation from a cotenant's long-continued possession and absence of claim by the titleholder). *But see Hardaway*, 544 S.W.3d at 409–10 (cotenant's summary judgment burden on notice of repudiation not satisfied "based on an inference or presumption arising from long-continued possession and absence of a claim" without evidence of other unequivocal, hostile acts taken to disseize other cotenants).

Acknowledgment of title. Acknowledgment of title in another may defeat an adverse possession claim if made before limitations title ripens but not after. But a possessor's acknowledgment of title in another after the limitation period may tend to show that the possession was not adverse. *Bruni v. Vidaurri*, 166 S.W.2d 81, 88 (Tex. 1942). Whether an adverse claimant's conduct or statement constitutes an acknowledgment of title in another is a question of fact. *Kinder Morgan North Texas Pipeline, L.P. v. Justiss*, 202 S.W.3d 427, 439 (Tex. App.—Texarkana 2006, no pet.); *Bell*, 635 S.W.2d at 590. If acknowledgment is a disputed fact issue, an additional question or instruction may be necessary.

Attorney's fees. Tex. Civ. Prac. & Rem. Code § 16.034(a)(1) provides for the recovery of attorney's fees by a record title holder in a suit for possession of real property, if successful against another party claiming adverse possession of the property. If the court finds that the adverse possessor's claim was groundless and made in bad faith, the court *shall* award costs and reasonable attorney's fees. Tex. Civ. Prac. & Rem. Code § 16.034(a)(1). Without such a finding, the court *may* award costs and reasonable fees. Tex. Civ. Prac. & Rem. Code § 16.034(a)(2). The statute imposes demand requirements. Tex. Civ. Prac. & Rem. Code § 16.034(b)–(c). The amount of reasonable attorney's fees is generally a fact issue. *See Transcontinental Insurance Co. v. Crump*, 330 S.W.3d 211, 229–32 (Tex. 2010); *City of Garland v. Dallas Morning News*, 22 S.W.3d 351, 367 (Tex. 2000); *Bocquet v. Herring*, 972 S.W.2d 19, 21 (Tex. 1998); *RDG Partnership v. Long*, 350 S.W.3d 262, 277–78 (Tex. App.—San Antonio 2011, no pet.); *Cullins v. Foster*, 171 S.W.3d 521, 536 (Tex. App.—Houston [14th Dist.] 2005, pet. denied). For a question on and additional discussion of attorney's fees, see PJC 313.33.

PJC 301.5   **Question and Instructions on Adverse Possession—
                   Twenty-Five-Year Limitations Period**

QUESTION _____

Did [*Don Davis/Paul Payne*] hold the property in peaceable and adverse possession for a period of at least twenty-five years before [*date cause of action was filed*]?

"Peaceable possession" means possession of real property that is continuous and is not interrupted by an adverse suit to recover the property.

"Adverse possession" means an actual and visible appropriation of real property, commenced and continued under a claim of right that is inconsistent with and hostile to the claim of another person.

"Claim of right" means an intention to claim the real property as one's own to the exclusion of all others.

A claim of right is hostile only if either (1) it provides notice, either actual or by implication, of a hostile claim of right to the true owner; or (2) the acts performed on the real property, and the use made of the real property, were of such a nature and character that would reasonably notify the true owner of the real property that a hostile claim is being asserted to the property.

[*For this question,*] To establish peaceable and adverse possession, a claimant must also have cultivated, used, or enjoyed the property.

Answer "Yes" or "No."

Answer: _____

COMMENT

When to use. PJC 301.5 should be used to submit a claim under the twenty-five-year adverse possession statute if the party claims adverse possession and cultivation, use, or enjoyment of the property, regardless of whether the person is or has been under a legal disability. This claim may be raised either affirmatively or defensively. The burden of proof rests with the party raising the adverse possession claim or defense.

Source of question and instructions. PJC 301.5 is derived from Tex. Civ. Prac. & Rem. Code §§ 16.021, 16.027; *see also BP America Production Co. v. Marshall*, 342 S.W.3d 59, 70–72 (Tex. 2011) (describing claim of right); *Tran v. Macha*, 213 S.W.3d 913, 914–15 (Tex. 2006) (discussing claim of right); *Calfee v. Duke*, 544

S.W.2d 640, 642 (Tex. 1976) (same); *Orsborn v. Deep Rock Oil Corp.*, 267 S.W.2d 781 (Tex. 1954) (discussing hostile claim of right); *Villarreal v. Guerra*, 446 S.W.3d 404, 410 (Tex. App.—San Antonio 2014, pet. denied) (defining the test for hostility); *Taub v. Houston Pipeline Co.*, 75 S.W.3d 606, 626 (Tex. App.—Texarkana 2002, pet. denied) (same); *see also Natural Gas Pipeline Co. of America v. Pool*, 124 S.W.3d 188, 198 (Tex. 2003) (discussing claim of right); *Rhodes v. Cahill*, 802 S.W.2d 643, 645 (Tex. 1990) (same).

Broad-form submission.   Submission of adverse possession elements in one question is proper. *Pinchback v. Hockless*, 158 S.W.2d 997, 1003 (Tex. 1942); *Davis v. Dowlen*, 136 S.W.2d 900, 905 (Tex. App.—Beaumont 1939, writ dism'd judgm't cor.). The entire time period over which adverse possession is claimed should be submitted in a single question. *Pinchback*, 158 S.W.2d at 1002.

Casual fence vs. designed enclosure.   Texas courts distinguish between "casual fences" and fences that "designedly enclose" an area. *Rhodes*, 802 S.W.2d at 646. If the fence existed before possession was taken of the land and the possessor fails to demonstrate the purpose for which it was erected, then the fence is a "casual fence." *Rhodes*, 802 S.W.2d at 646; *Orsborn*, 267 S.W.2d at 786. Repairing or maintaining a casual fence, even for the express purpose of keeping the claimant's animals within the enclosed area, generally does not change a casual fence into a designed enclosure. *McDonnold v. Weinacht*, 465 S.W.2d 136, 142–43 (Tex. 1971). However, an adverse possessor may substantially modify a casual fence so as to change its character to a designed enclosure, and such evidence will support a jury finding of adverse possession. *Rhodes*, 802 S.W.2d at 646; *Butler v. Hanson*, 455 S.W.2d 942, 945–46 (Tex. 1970). If the character of the fence is in dispute, an additional question or instruction may be necessary.

Possession of mineral estate.   Adverse possession of the surface estate results in adverse possession of the mineral estate unless the two estates have been severed. *Grissom v. Anderson*, 79 S.W.2d 619, 621 (Tex. 1935). Once severed from the surface estate, the mineral estate may be acquired only by adverse possession of the mineral estate and not by adverse possession of the surface estate. *Pool*, 124 S.W.3d at 192–93, 198; *Thedford v. Union Oil Co. of California*, 3 S.W.3d 609, 615 (Tex. App.—Dallas 1999, pet. denied); *Barfield v. Holland*, 844 S.W.2d 759, 767 (Tex. App.—Tyler 1992, writ denied); *Watkins v. Certain-Teed Products Corp.*, 231 S.W.2d 981, 985 (Tex. App.—Amarillo 1950, no writ). The severed mineral estate can be adversely possessed only by drilling and production operations for the statutory period of time. *Pool*, 124 S.W.3d at 193; *Sun Operating Ltd. Partnership v. Oatman*, 911 S.W.2d 749, 757 (Tex. App.—Amarillo 1995, writ denied); *Barfield*, 844 S.W.2d at 767; *Webb v. British American Oil Producing Co.*, 281 S.W.2d 726, 734 (Tex. App.—Eastland 1955, writ ref'd n.r.e.). The surface owner's possession of the severed surface estate is not adverse to the owner of the mineral estate. *Grissom*, 79 S.W.2d at 621. When the claim is made to a severed mineral estate, the definition of "adverse possession" may be modified as follows:

> "Adverse possession" means an actual and visible appropriation of real property by drilling and producing oil and gas, commenced and continued under a claim of right that is inconsistent with and hostile to the claim of another person.

Continuity of possession. Possession is "continuous" as long as (1) any temporary breaks in possession by the claimant are reasonable under the circumstances and (2) the claimant did not intend to abandon possession. *Grayson v. Dunn*, 581 S.W.2d 785, 788 (Tex. App.—Waco 1979) (citing *Dunn v. Taylor*, 113 S.W. 265, 267 (Tex. 1908)). Where there is a break in the continuity of possession, the claimant must show that possession was resumed within a reasonable time. *Hardy v. Bumpstead*, 41 S.W.2d 226 (Tex. Comm'n App. 1931). If continuity of possession is a disputed issue, an additional instruction may be included in the question.

Tacking. "To satisfy a limitations period, peaceable and adverse possession does not need to continue in the same person, but there must be privity of estate between each holder and his successor." Tex. Civ. Prac. & Rem. Code § 16.023; *Estrada v. Cheshire*, 470 S.W.3d 109, 124–26 (Tex. App.—Houston [1st Dist.] 2015, pet. denied); *Treviño v. Treviño*, 64 S.W.3d 166, 172 (Tex. App.—San Antonio 2001, no pet.); *First National Bank of Marshall v. Beavers*, 602 S.W.2d 327, 329 (Tex. App.—Texarkana 1980, no writ). If possessory periods are tacked, consider whether modification of the question (or additional questions) and an additional instruction are required.

Property identification and definition. In this question or the general instructions of the charge, the real property in question should be defined, including the specific surface or mineral estate at issue:

> "Property" means the [*insert definition, description, or identification*].

Accrual. "The structure of the adverse possession statute indicates that the 'cause of action' refers to the suit to recover real property held by another in peaceable and adverse possession." *Marshall*, 342 S.W.3d at 73. *See* Tex. Civ. Prac. & Rem. Code § 16.024. The cause of action accrues when the adverse possession begins. *Marshall*, 342 S.W.3d at 73; *see also Horton v. Crawford*, 10 Tex. 382, 390–91 (1853); *Waddy v. City of Houston*, 834 S.W.2d 97, 103 (Tex. App.—Houston [1st Dist.] 1992, writ denied); *Woolaver v. Texaco, Inc.*, 638 S.W.2d 153, 155 (Tex. App.—Fort Worth 1982, writ ref'd n.r.e.); *Crow v. Payne*, 242 S.W.2d 824, 825 (Tex. App.—Amarillo 1951, no writ). For a claim to have accrued, the jury must find that possession began more than twenty-five years before the cause of action was filed.

Multiple limitations questions.   If multiple limitations questions will be submitted, consider whether the phrase "For this question" should precede any definition to clarify the requirements between statutes.

Repudiation of title requirement.   Other than by the fifteen-year combined limitations period in Tex. Civ. Prac. & Rem. Code § 16.0265, a cotenant may not adversely possess against another cotenant in the absence of repudiation of the relationship or ouster. *See King Ranch, Inc. v. Chapman*, 118 S.W.3d 742, 756 (Tex. 2003); *Todd v. Bruner*, 365 S.W.2d 155, 160–61 (Tex. 1963); *see also Marshall*, 342 S.W.3d at 70–72; *Hardaway v. Nixon*, 544 S.W.3d 402, 409 (Tex. App.—San Antonio 2017, pet. denied). For additional discussion, see PJC 301.1. The same is true with a permissive holdover tenant. *See Pool*, 124 S.W.3d at 194 (" '[P]ossession cannot be considered adverse until the tenancy has been repudiated, and notice of such repudiation has been brought home to the titleholder.' But . . . actual notice of repudiation is not required. Rather, notice can be inferred, or there can be constructive notice.") (citing *Tex-Wis Co. v. Johnson*, 534 S.W.2d 895 (Tex. 1976)). "Whether there has been a repudiation of a nonpossessory cotenant's title is a question of fact [but] when the pertinent facts are undisputed, repudiation may be established as a matter of law." *King Ranch, Inc.*, 118 S.W.3d at 756; *see also Marshall*, 342 S.W.3d at 70–72. For additional discussion, see PJC 301.1.

When repudiation is disputed, an additional instruction may be required. *See, e.g., Dyer v. Cotton*, 333 S.W.3d 703, 711–13 (Tex. App.—Houston [1st Dist.] 2010, no pet.); *Bell v. Lyon*, 635 S.W.2d 586, 589–90 (Tex. App.—Houston [14th Dist.] 1982, writ ref'd n.r.e.). The court in *Dyer* affirmed submission of the following instruction in a suit between cotenants:

> [T]he possession by an owner of an interest in property will be presumed to be his right as a co-owner. The possession, to be adverse to the other owner, or owners, must be of such acts as to amount to an ouster of the other owner, or owners, and must be of such an unequivocal nature and so distinctly hostile to the others' rights that the intention to claim the property is clear and unmistakable.

Dyer, 333 S.W.3d at 711; *see also Todd*, 365 S.W.2d at 159–60. Although mere possession does not generally suffice, one exception may be when possession and assertion of a claim by one cotenant is so long-continued, at least in the absence of a claim by the nonpossessory cotenant, that it puts the nonpossessory cotenant on constructive notice of the repudiation. *Tex-Wis Co.*, 534 S.W.2d at 901 (jury may infer notice of repudiation from a cotenant's long-continued possession and absence of claim by the titleholder). *But see Hardaway*, 544 S.W.3d at 409–10 (cotenant's summary judgment burden on notice of repudiation not satisfied "based on an inference or presumption arising from long-continued possession and absence of a claim" without evidence of other unequivocal, hostile acts taken to disseize other cotenants).

Acknowledgment of title. Acknowledgment of title in another may defeat an adverse possession claim if made before limitations title ripens but not after. But a possessor's acknowledgment of title in another after the limitation period may tend to show that the possession was not adverse. *Bruni v. Vidaurri*, 166 S.W.2d 81, 88 (Tex. 1942). Whether an adverse claimant's conduct or statement constitutes an acknowledgment of title in another is a question of fact. *Kinder Morgan North Texas Pipeline, L.P. v. Justiss*, 202 S.W.3d 427, 439 (Tex. App.—Texarkana 2006, no pet.); *Bell*, 635 S.W.2d at 590. If acknowledgment is a disputed fact issue, an additional question or instruction may be necessary.

Attorney's fees. Tex. Civ. Prac. & Rem. Code § 16.034(a)(1) provides for the recovery of attorney's fees by a record title holder in a suit for possession of real property, if successful against another party claiming adverse possession of the property. If the court finds that the adverse possessor's claim was groundless and made in bad faith, the court *shall* award costs and reasonable attorney's fees. Tex. Civ. Prac. & Rem. Code § 16.034(a)(1). Without such a finding, the court *may* award costs and reasonable fees. Tex. Civ. Prac. & Rem. Code § 16.034(a)(2). The statute imposes demand requirements. Tex. Civ. Prac. & Rem. Code § 16.034(b)–(c). The amount of reasonable attorney's fees is generally a fact issue. *See Transcontinental Insurance Co. v. Crump*, 330 S.W.3d 211, 229–32 (Tex. 2010); *City of Garland v. Dallas Morning News*, 22 S.W.3d 351, 367 (Tex. 2000); *Bocquet v. Herring*, 972 S.W.2d 19, 21 (Tex. 1998); *RDG Partnership v. Long*, 350 S.W.3d 262, 277–78 (Tex. App.—San Antonio 2011, no pet.); *Cullins v. Foster*, 171 S.W.3d 521, 536 (Tex. App.—Houston [14th Dist.] 2005, pet. denied). For a question on and additional discussion of attorney's fees, see PJC 313.33.

PJC 301.6   Question and Instructions on Adverse Possession with Recorded Instrument—Twenty-Five-Year Limitations Period

QUESTION _____

Did [*Don Davis/Paul Payne*] hold the property in peaceable and adverse possession for a period of at least twenty-five years before [*date cause of action was filed*]?

"Peaceable possession" means possession of real property that is continuous and is not interrupted by an adverse suit to recover the property.

"Adverse possession" means an actual and visible appropriation of real property, commenced and continued under a claim of right that is inconsistent with and hostile to the claim of another person.

"Claim of right" means an intention to claim the real property as one's own to the exclusion of all others.

A claim of right is hostile only if either (1) it provides notice, either actual or by implication, of a hostile claim of right to the true owner; or (2) the acts performed on the real property, and the use made of the real property, were of such a nature and character that would reasonably notify the true owner of the real property that a hostile claim is being asserted to the property.

[*For this question,*] To establish peaceable and adverse possession, [*Don Davis/Paul Payne*] must have held the property—

1.   in good faith; and

2.   under a deed or other instrument purporting to convey the property that is recorded in the deed records of the county where any part of the property is located.

Answer "Yes" or "No."

Answer: _____

COMMENT

When to use.   PJC 301.6 should be used to submit a claim under the twenty-five-year adverse possession statute when the claimant holds a recorded instrument. This claim may be raised either affirmatively or defensively. The burden of proof rests with the party raising the adverse possession claim or defense.

Source of question and instructions.   PJC 301.6 is derived from Tex. Civ. Prac. & Rem. Code §§ 16.021, 16.028; *see also BP America Production Co. v. Marshall*, 342 S.W.3d 59, 70–72 (Tex. 2011) (describing claim of right); *Tran v. Macha*, 213 S.W.3d 913, 914–15 (Tex. 2006) (discussing claim of right); *Calfee v. Duke*, 544 S.W.2d 640, 642 (Tex. 1976) (same); *Orsborn v. Deep Rock Oil Corp.*, 267 S.W.2d 781 (Tex. 1954) (discussing hostile claim of right); *Villarreal v. Guerra*, 446 S.W.3d 404, 410 (Tex. App.—San Antonio 2014, pet. denied) (defining the test for hostility); *Taub v. Houston Pipeline Co.*, 75 S.W.3d 606, 626 (Tex. App.—Texarkana 2002, pet. denied) (same); *see also Natural Gas Pipeline Co. of America v. Pool*, 124 S.W.3d 188, 198 (Tex. 2003) (discussing claim of right); *Rhodes v. Cahill*, 802 S.W.2d 643, 645 (Tex. 1990) (same).

Broad-form submission.   Submission of adverse possession elements in one question is proper. *Pinchback v. Hockless*, 158 S.W.2d 997, 1003 (Tex. 1942); *Davis v. Dowlen*, 136 S.W.2d 900, 905 (Tex. App.—Beaumont 1939, writ dism'd judgm't cor.). The entire time period over which adverse possession is claimed should be submitted in a single question. *Pinchback*, 158 S.W.2d at 1002.

Casual fence vs. designed enclosure.   Texas courts distinguish between "casual fences" and fences that "designedly enclose" an area. *Rhodes*, 802 S.W.2d at 646. If the fence existed before possession was taken of the land and the possessor fails to demonstrate the purpose for which it was erected, then the fence is a "casual fence." *Rhodes*, 802 S.W.2d at 646; *Orsborn*, 267 S.W.2d at 786. Repairing or maintaining a casual fence, even for the express purpose of keeping the claimant's animals within the enclosed area, generally does not change a casual fence into a designed enclosure. *McDonnold v. Weinacht*, 465 S.W.2d 136, 142–43 (Tex. 1971). However, an adverse possessor may substantially modify a casual fence so as to change its character to a designed enclosure, and such evidence will support a jury finding of adverse possession. *Rhodes*, 802 S.W.2d at 646; *Butler v. Hanson*, 455 S.W.2d 942, 945–46 (Tex. 1970). If the character of the fence is in dispute, an additional question or instruction may be necessary.

Possession of mineral estate.   Adverse possession of the surface estate results in adverse possession of the mineral estate unless the two estates have been severed. *Grissom v. Anderson*, 79 S.W.2d 619, 621 (Tex. 1935). Once severed from the surface estate, the mineral estate may be acquired only by adverse possession of the mineral estate and not by adverse possession of the surface estate. *Pool*, 124 S.W.3d at 192–93, 198; *Thedford v. Union Oil Co. of California*, 3 S.W.3d 609, 615 (Tex. App.—Dallas 1999, pet. denied); *Barfield v. Holland*, 844 S.W.2d 759, 767 (Tex. App.—Tyler 1992, writ denied); *Watkins v. Certain-Teed Products Corp.*, 231 S.W.2d 981, 985 (Tex. App.—Amarillo 1950, no writ). The severed mineral estate can be adversely possessed only by drilling and production operations for the statutory period of time. *Pool*, 124 S.W.3d at 193; *Sun Operating Ltd. Partnership v. Oatman*, 911 S.W.2d 749, 757 (Tex. App.—Amarillo 1995, writ denied); *Barfield*, 844 S.W.2d at 767; *Webb v.*

British American Oil Producing Co., 281 S.W.2d 726, 734 (Tex. App.—Eastland 1955, writ ref'd n.r.e.). The surface owner's possession of the severed surface estate is not adverse to the owner of the mineral estate. *Grissom*, 79 S.W.2d at 621. When the claim is made to a severed mineral estate, the definition of "adverse possession" may be modified as follows:

> "Adverse possession" means an actual and visible appropriation of real property by drilling and producing oil and gas, commenced and continued under a claim of right that is inconsistent with and hostile to the claim of another person.

Continuity of possession.   Possession is "continuous" as long as (1) any temporary breaks in possession by the claimant are reasonable under the circumstances and (2) the claimant did not intend to abandon possession. *Grayson v. Dunn*, 581 S.W.2d 785, 788 (Tex. App.—Waco 1979) (citing *Dunn v. Taylor*, 113 S.W. 265, 267 (Tex. 1908)). Where there is a break in the continuity of possession, the claimant must show that possession was resumed within a reasonable time. *Hardy v. Bumpstead*, 41 S.W.2d 226 (Tex. Comm'n App. 1931). If continuity of possession is a disputed issue, an additional instruction may be included in the question.

Tacking.   "To satisfy a limitations period, peaceable and adverse possession does not need to continue in the same person, but there must be privity of estate between each holder and his successor." Tex. Civ. Prac. & Rem. Code § 16.023; *Estrada v. Cheshire*, 470 S.W.3d 109, 124–26 (Tex. App.—Houston [1st Dist.] 2015, pet. denied); *Treviño v. Treviño*, 64 S.W.3d 166, 172 (Tex. App.—San Antonio 2001, no pet.); *First National Bank of Marshall v. Beavers*, 602 S.W.2d 327, 329 (Tex. App.—Texarkana 1980, no writ). If possessory periods are tacked, consider whether modification of the question (or additional questions) and an additional instruction are required.

Property identification and definition.   In this question or the general instructions of the charge, the real property in question should be defined, including the specific surface or mineral estate at issue:

> "Property" means the [*insert definition, description, or identification*].

Accrual.   "The structure of the adverse possession statute indicates that the 'cause of action' refers to the suit to recover real property held by another in peaceable and adverse possession." *Marshall*, 342 S.W.3d at 73. *See* Tex. Civ. Prac. & Rem. Code § 16.024. The cause of action accrues when the adverse possession begins. *Marshall*, 342 S.W.3d at 73; *see also Horton v. Crawford*, 10 Tex. 382, 390–91 (1853); *Waddy v. City of Houston*, 834 S.W.2d 97, 103 (Tex. App.—Houston [1st Dist.] 1992, writ denied); *Woolaver v. Texaco, Inc.*, 638 S.W.2d 153, 155 (Tex. App.—Fort Worth 1982, writ ref'd n.r.e.); *Crow v. Payne*, 242 S.W.2d 824, 825 (Tex. App.—Amarillo 1951, no writ). For a claim to have accrued, the jury must find that possession began more than twenty-five years before the cause of action was filed.

Multiple limitations questions.   If multiple limitations questions will be submitted, consider whether the phrase "For this question" should precede any definition to clarify the requirements between statutes.

Repudiation of title requirement.   Other than by the fifteen-year combined limitations period in Tex. Civ. Prac. & Rem. Code § 16.0265, a cotenant may not adversely possess against another cotenant in the absence of repudiation of the relationship or ouster. *See King Ranch, Inc. v. Chapman*, 118 S.W.3d 742, 756 (Tex. 2003); *Todd v. Bruner*, 365 S.W.2d 155, 160–61 (Tex. 1963); *see also Marshall*, 342 S.W.3d at 70–72; *Hardaway v. Nixon*, 544 S.W.3d 402, 409 (Tex. App.—San Antonio 2017, pet. denied). For additional discussion, see PJC 301.1. The same is true with a permissive holdover tenant. *See Pool*, 124 S.W.3d at 194 (" '[P]ossession cannot be considered adverse until the tenancy has been repudiated, and notice of such repudiation has been brought home to the titleholder.' But . . . actual notice of repudiation is not required. Rather, notice can be inferred, or there can be constructive notice.") (citing *Tex-Wis Co. v. Johnson*, 534 S.W.2d 895 (Tex. 1976)). "Whether there has been a repudiation of a nonpossessory cotenant's title is a question of fact [but] when the pertinent facts are undisputed, repudiation may be established as a matter of law." *King Ranch, Inc.*, 118 S.W.3d at 756; *see also Marshall*, 342 S.W.3d at 70–72. For additional discussion, see PJC 301.1.

When repudiation is disputed, an additional instruction may be required. *See, e.g., Dyer v. Cotton*, 333 S.W.3d 703, 711–13 (Tex. App.—Houston [1st Dist.] 2010, no pet.); *Bell v. Lyon*, 635 S.W.2d 586, 589–90 (Tex. App.—Houston [14th Dist.] 1982, writ ref'd n.r.e.). The court in *Dyer* affirmed submission of the following instruction in a suit between cotenants:

> [T]he possession by an owner of an interest in property will be presumed to be his right as a co-owner. The possession, to be adverse to the other owner, or owners, must be of such acts as to amount to an ouster of the other owner, or owners, and must be of such an unequivocal nature and so distinctly hostile to the others' rights that the intention to claim the property is clear and unmistakable.

Dyer, 333 S.W.3d at 711; *see also Todd*, 365 S.W.2d at 159–60. Although mere possession does not generally suffice, one exception may be when possession and assertion of a claim by one cotenant is so long-continued, at least in the absence of a claim by the nonpossessory cotenant, that it puts the nonpossessory cotenant on constructive notice of the repudiation. *Tex-Wis Co.*, 534 S.W.2d at 901 (jury may infer notice of repudiation from a cotenant's long-continued possession and absence of claim by the titleholder). *But see Hardaway*, 544 S.W.3d at 409–10 (cotenant's summary judgment burden on notice of repudiation not satisfied "based on an inference or presumption arising from long-continued possession and absence of a claim" without evidence of other unequivocal, hostile acts taken to disseize other cotenants).

Acknowledgment of title.   Acknowledgment of title in another may defeat an adverse possession claim if made before limitations title ripens but not after. But a possessor's acknowledgment of title in another after the limitation period may tend to show that the possession was not adverse. *Bruni v. Vidaurri*, 166 S.W.2d 81, 88 (Tex. 1942). Whether an adverse claimant's conduct or statement constitutes an acknowledgment of title in another is a question of fact. *Kinder Morgan North Texas Pipeline, L.P. v. Justiss*, 202 S.W.3d 427, 439 (Tex. App.—Texarkana 2006, no pet.); *Bell*, 635 S.W.2d at 590. If acknowledgment is a disputed fact issue, an additional question or instruction may be necessary.

Attorney's fees.   Tex. Civ. Prac. & Rem. Code § 16.034(a)(1) provides for the recovery of attorney's fees by a record title holder in a suit for possession of real property, if successful against another party claiming adverse possession of the property. If the court finds that the adverse possessor's claim was groundless and made in bad faith, the court *shall* award costs and reasonable attorney's fees. Tex. Civ. Prac. & Rem. Code § 16.034(a)(1). Without such a finding, the court *may* award costs and reasonable fees. Tex. Civ. Prac. & Rem. Code § 16.034(a)(2). The statute imposes demand requirements. Tex. Civ. Prac. & Rem. Code § 16.034(b)–(c). The amount of reasonable attorney's fees is generally a fact issue. *See Transcontinental Insurance Co. v. Crump*, 330 S.W.3d 211, 229–32 (Tex. 2010); *City of Garland v. Dallas Morning News*, 22 S.W.3d 351, 367 (Tex. 2000); *Bocquet v. Herring*, 972 S.W.2d 19, 21 (Tex. 1998); *RDG Partnership v. Long*, 350 S.W.3d 262, 277–78 (Tex. App.—San Antonio 2011, no pet.); *Cullins v. Foster*, 171 S.W.3d 521, 536 (Tex. App.—Houston [14th Dist.] 2005, pet. denied). For a question on and additional discussion of attorney's fees, see PJC 313.33.

PJC 302.1   Injury to Real Property from Oil and Gas Operations (Comment)

Disputes involving injury to real property in connection with oil and gas operations may arise from lease provisions, excessive or negligent use of the surface by the mineral estate owner, nuisance, trespass, or breach of statutory duty. *See* Patrick H. Martin & Bruce M. Kramer, 1 *Williams & Meyers, Oil and Gas Law* § 218.10 (2014). Generally, the mineral owner has the right to enter the surface estate and use as much of the surface as is reasonably necessary to remove the minerals without compensating the surface owner. *Moser v. U.S. Steel Corp.*, 676 S.W.2d 99 (Tex. 1984); *Humble Oil & Refining Co. v. Williams*, 420 S.W.2d 133, 134 (Tex. 1967).

This general rule of reasonable use of the surface without compensation has been extended to surface rights, including water, conveyed separately from the remainder of the surface estate. *See Coyote Lake Ranch, LLC v. City of Lubbock*, 498 S.W.3d 53, 64 (Tex. 2016). For an exception to the general rule that surface owners need not be compensated for reasonable and necessary use, see *Moser*, 676 S.W.2d at 103.

Breach of lease and breach of implied duties are treated in chapter 303 of this volume. Other disputes asserting damage to real property, if supported by the facts, can include unreasonable use, failure to accommodate, trespass, nuisance, or negligence. See PJC 302.2–302.4 for questions on unreasonable use, failure to accommodate, and trespass.

For questions on injuries to persons and for questions and instructions on nuisance, see the current edition of State Bar of Texas, *Texas Pattern Jury Charges—General Negligence, Intentional Personal Torts & Workers' Compensation* ch. 12.

PJC 302.2   **Question and Instruction on Unreasonable Use of Surface Estate**

QUESTION _____

Did *Larry Lessee* use more of the [*surface estate*] than was reasonably necessary?

Larry Lessee had the right to use the surface of the land in a manner reasonably necessary for exploration, extraction, or production of minerals.

Answer "Yes" or "No."

Answer: _____

COMMENT

When to use.   PJC 302.2 can be used in cases of alleged excessive, unreasonable, or negligent use of the surface estate by the party with the right to develop the minerals. The practitioner may also wish to use PJC 302.4, the simple trespass question, with an appropriate instruction on the mineral owner's right to use of the surface estate. *See Brown v. Lundell*, 344 S.W.2d 863, 866 (Tex. 1961). This question may also be modified for use in cases in which the party with the right to develop minerals seeks damages because the lessor or surface owner has interfered with that right. *See Ball v. Dillard*, 602 S.W.2d 521, 523 (Tex. 1980); *Brown*, 344 S.W.2d at 866. The owner of rights in groundwater conveyed separately from the remainder of the surface estate may also make reasonable use of the surface in the valid exercise of such rights. *Coyote Lake Ranch, LLC v. City of Lubbock*, 498 S.W.3d 53, 64 (Tex. 2016).

Source of question and instruction.   PJC 302.2 is derived from *Merriman v. XTO Energy, Inc.*, 407 S.W.3d 244, 249 (Tex. 2013); *Moser v. U.S. Steel Corp.*, 676 S.W.2d 99, 103 (Tex. 1984); *Sun Oil Co. v. Whitaker*, 483 S.W.2d 808, 810–11 (Tex. 1972); *Getty Oil Co. v. Jones*, 470 S.W.2d 618, 621–23, 627–28 (Tex. 1971); and *Brown*, 344 S.W.2d at 866.

Defining surface estate.   Depending on the facts and circumstances of the case, the parties may need to include an appropriate definition of the surface estate. *See Lightning Oil Co. v. Anadarko E&P Onshore, LLC*, 520 S.W.3d 39 (Tex. 2017); *Coyote Lake Ranch, LLC*, 498 S.W.3d at 64; *Moser*, 676 S.W.2d at 102; *Getty Oil Co.*, 470 S.W.2d at 621–23.

Negligent use of surface estate.   A claim may be based on negligent use of the surface, rather than unreasonable use of the surface. *Brown*, 344 S.W.2d at 865, 866 ("[I]f the lessee negligently and unnecessarily damages the lessor's land, either surface or subsurface, his liability to the lessor is no different from what it would be under the same circumstances to an adjoining landowner."); *see also Crosstex North Texas Pipeline, L.P. v. Gardiner*, 505 S.W.3d 580, 614 (Tex. 2016) (duty owed is "duty to do what a person of ordinary prudence in the same or similar circumstances would have done"); *Humble Oil & Refining Co. v. Williams*, 420 S.W.2d 133, 134 (Tex. 1967) ("A person who seeks to recover from the lessee for damages to the surface has the burden of alleging and proving either specific acts of negligence or that more of the land was used by the lessee than was reasonably necessary."). For basic negligence questions, see the current edition of State Bar of Texas, *Texas Pattern Jury Charges—General Negligence, Intentional Personal Torts & Workers' Compensation*, ch. 4.

PJC 302.3 **Question and Instruction on Accommodation Doctrine**

QUESTION _____

Did *Larry Lessee* fail to accommodate *Suzie Surface Owner*'s existing use of the surface of the land in question?

Larry Lessee failed to accommodate an existing use of the surface if—

1. *Larry Lessee*'s use of the surface completely precluded or substantially impaired *Suzie Surface Owner*'s existing use; and

2. there was no reasonable alternative method available to *Suzie Surface Owner* on the land in question by which the existing use could be continued; and

3. there were alternative reasonable, customary, and industry-accepted methods available to *Larry Lessee* on the land in question that would have allowed recovery of the minerals and also allowed *Suzie Surface Owner* to continue the existing use.

Answer "Yes" or "No."

Answer: _____

COMMENT

When to use. PJC 302.3 should be used when a surface owner claims that the party with the right to develop minerals has failed to accommodate an existing use of the surface subject to the lease of the land in question. This question should be used when "existing use" is not a disputed fact. In cases in which "existing use" is in dispute, a predicate question may be needed.

Source of question and instruction. PJC 302.3 is derived from *Merriman v. XTO Energy, Inc.*, 407 S.W.3d 244, 249 (Tex. 2013); *see also Coyote Lake Ranch, LLC v. City of Lubbock*, 498 S.W.3d 53, 64–65 (Tex. 2016) (applying doctrine to severed groundwater estate); *Tarrant County Water Control & Improvement District No. One v. Haupt, Inc.*, 854 S.W.2d 909, 911 (Tex. 1993); *Sun Oil Co. v. Whitaker*, 483 S.W.2d 808 (Tex. 1972); and *Getty Oil Co. v. Jones*, 470 S.W.2d 618, 622–23 (Tex. 1971).

Alternative submission. In *Getty Oil Co.*, the Texas Supreme Court recognized that a "single or a multiple issue submission may be in order depending on the facts and circumstances in a given situation." *Getty Oil Co.*, 470 S.W.2d at 628 (recognizing the evidence and circumstances were such that an initial inquiry was proper regarding element 2 above); *see also Merriman*, 407 S.W.3d at 249 (holding that if surface owner carries burden on first two elements, he must "further prove" third element). Thus, this question may be submitted as a single question or as multiple questions, depending on the facts and circumstances of the case.

Severed groundwater estate.   In *Coyote Lake Ranch*, the Texas Supreme Court applied the three-element accommodation doctrine to a severed groundwater estate. 498 S.W.3d at 64–65. PJC 302.3 should be modified as necessary to submit the doctrine as applied to severed groundwater estates. *See, e.g., Coyote Lake Ranch, LLC*, 498 S.W.3d at 64–65 (groundwater owner must show in element 3 "methods to access and produce the water").

PJC 302.4   Question and Instruction on Trespass

QUESTION _____

Did *Don Davis* trespass on *Paul Payne*'s property?

"Trespass" means [*an entry on/use of*] the property of another without having consent or authorization of the owner. To constitute trespass, [*entry on/use of*] another's property need not be in person but may be made [*by causing or permitting a thing to cross the boundary of the property/by a use of the property that is in excess of that reasonably necessary to extract and produce the minerals*].

Answer "Yes" or "No."

Answer: _____

COMMENT

When to use.   PJC 302.4 is appropriate in cases involving an unauthorized physical entry on property (including continued use after authorization lapses, such as continued production of minerals after lease termination), causing or permitting a thing to cross the boundary of the property, or use of the property in excess of that reasonably necessary to extract and produce minerals. *Brown v. Lundell*, 344 S.W.2d 863, 866 (Tex. 1961) (uses of the surface in excess of those reasonably necessary to explore for and produce minerals may be considered a trespass); *Gregg v. Delhi-Taylor Oil Corp.*, 344 S.W.2d 411, 416 (Tex. 1961) (entry on another's land need not be in person but may be made by causing or permitting a thing to cross the boundary of the premises). The definition may need to be modified to fit the type of trespass at issue. *See Crosstex North Texas Pipeline, L.P. v. Gardiner*, 505 S.W.3d 580, 603 n.17 (Tex. 2016). There is no cause of action for trespass against cotenants. *Byrom v. Pendley*, 717 S.W.2d 602 (Tex. 1986). For a discussion distinguishing nuisance from trespass, see *Crosstex North Texas Pipeline, L.P.*, 505 S.W.3d at 603 n.17. See the current edition of State Bar of Texas, *Texas Pattern Jury Charges—General Negligence, Intentional Personal Torts & Workers' Compensation* ch. 12 for a discussion on private nuisance.

Source of question and instruction.   PJC 302.4 is derived from *Environmental Processing Systems, L.C. v. FPL Farming, Ltd.*, 457 S.W.3d 414 (Tex. 2015), and *Brown*, 344 S.W.2d at 866.

Physical and subsurface trespass.   For trespass claims other than those resulting in production, see the recent discussion of physical trespass in *Lightning Oil Co. v. Anadarko E&P Onshore, LLC*, 520 S.W.3d 39 (Tex. 2017); *Environmental Processing Systems, L.C. v. FPL Farming, Ltd.*, 457 S.W.3d 414 (Tex. 2015); and *FPL Farming,*

Ltd. v. Environmental Processing Systems, L.C., 351 S.W.3d 306 (Tex. 2011). The Texas Supreme Court has not determined the validity of deep subsurface trespass claims. *See Environmental Processing Systems, L.C. v. FPL Farming, Ltd.*, 457 S.W.3d 414 (Tex. 2015); *Coastal Oil & Gas Corp. v. Garza Energy Trust*, 268 S.W.3d 1 (Tex. 2008); *Railroad Commission of Texas v. Manziel*, 361 S.W.2d 560 (Tex. 1962); *FPL Farming, Ltd. v. Environmental Processing Systems, L.C.*, 383 S.W.3d 274, 280 (Tex. App.—Beaumont 2012, rev'd on other grounds).

In *Coastal Oil & Gas Corp.*, the Texas Supreme Court held that recovery for drainage is barred by the rule of capture when proppant from a fracture treatment on a legal well crosses subsurface lease lines and results in flow of gas to another owner's tract. *Coastal Oil & Gas Corp.*, 268 S.W.3d at 12–13. The opinion left open the question whether a fracture originating at an illegal well would be actionable and expressly declined to decide the broader issue of whether subsurface hydraulic fracturing (also known as fracking) can ever give rise to an action for trespass. *Coastal Oil & Gas Corp.*, 268 S.W.3d at 12–13.

PJC 302.5   Question and Instruction on Affirmative Good-Faith Defense to Trespass

If you answered "Yes" to Question _____ [*302.4*], then answer the following question. Otherwise, do not answer the following question.

QUESTION _____

Did [*Don Davis*] trespass in good faith?

A person acts in good faith when that person does so with both an honest and a reasonable belief in the superiority of that person's title.

Answer "Yes" or "No."

Answer: _____

COMMENT

When to use.   PJC 302.5 is appropriate as an affirmative defense in cases involving drilling of or production from wells that are not authorized (e.g., not subject to a valid oil and gas lease, because of a surveying dispute, or a lease that has terminated) and, if applicable, should be conditionally submitted after PJC 302.4.

Source of question and instruction.   PJC 302.5 is derived from *Gulf Production Co. v. Spear*, 84 S.W.2d 452, 457 (Tex. Comm'n App. 1935), and *Mayfield v. Benavides*, 693 S.W.2d 500, 504 (Tex. App.—San Antonio 1985, writ ref'd n.r.e.).

[PJC 302.6 and 302.7 are reserved for expansion.]

PJC 302.8   **Question and Instruction on Statutory Waste**

QUESTION _____

Did [*Don Davis*] commit waste of [*oil/gas*] [*on/from/of*] *Paul Payne*'s [*property/production*]?

Waste includes the following:

> *[Insert applicable forms of waste in dispute.]*

Answer "Yes" or "No."

Answer: _____

COMMENT

When to use.   PJC 302.8 should be used when the plaintiff seeks a remedy for statutory waste.

Source of question and instruction.   PJC 302.8 is based on Tex. Nat. Res. Code §§ 85.045–.046, 85.321–.322.

> A party who owns an interest in property or production that may be damaged by another party violating the provisions of this chapter that were formerly part of Chapter 26, Acts of the 42nd Legislature . . . as amended, or another law of this state prohibiting waste or a valid rule or order of the commission may sue for and recover damages and any other relief to which he may be entitled at law or in equity.

Tex. Nat. Res. Code § 85.321. Section 85.321 creates a private cause of action for waste under chapter 85 or other laws and for violations of valid rules and orders of the Railroad Commission. *Exxon Corp. v. Emerald Oil & Gas Co.*, 331 S.W.3d 419, 422–23 (Tex. 2010). The cause of action does not extend to subsequent lessees against prior lessees. *Emerald Oil & Gas Co.*, 331 S.W.3d at 424–25. PJC 302.8 addresses statutory waste.

Statutory definition.   The Natural Resources Code provides that waste includes, among other things, the following:

> (1)   operation of any oil well or wells with an inefficient gas-oil ratio and the commission may determine and prescribe by order the permitted gas-oil ratio for the operation of oil wells;

> (2)   drowning with water a stratum or part of a stratum that is capable of producing oil or gas or both in paying quantities;

(3)   underground waste or loss, however caused and whether or not the cause of the underground waste or loss is defined in this section;

(4)   permitting any natural gas well to burn wastefully;

(5)   creation of unnecessary fire hazards;

(6)   physical waste or loss incident to or resulting from drilling, equipping, locating, spacing, or operating a well or wells in a manner that reduces or tends to reduce the total ultimate recovery of oil or gas from any pool;

(7)   waste or loss incident to or resulting from the unnecessary, inefficient, excessive, or improper use of the reservoir energy, including the gas energy or water drive, in any well or pool; however, it is not the intent of this section or the provisions of this chapter that were formerly a part of Chapter 26, Acts of the 42nd Legislature, 1st Called Session, 1931, as amended, to require repressuring of an oil pool or to require that the separately owned properties in any pool be unitized under one management, control, or ownership;

(8)   surface waste or surface loss, including the temporary or permanent storage of oil or the placing of any product of oil in open pits or earthen storage, and other forms of surface waste or surface loss including unnecessary or excessive surface losses, or destruction without beneficial use, either of oil or gas;

(9)   escape of gas into the open air in excess of the amount necessary in the efficient drilling or operation of the well from a well producing both oil and gas;

(10)   production of oil in excess of transportation or market facilities or reasonable market demand, and the commission may determine when excess production exists or is imminent and ascertain the reasonable market demand; or

(11)   surface or subsurface waste of hydrocarbons, including the physical or economic waste or loss of hydrocarbons in the creation, operation, maintenance, or abandonment of an underground hydrocarbon storage facility.

Tex. Nat. Res. Code § 85.046. This list may not be exclusive. *See Exxon Corp. v. Miesch*, 180 S.W.3d 299, 318–19 (Tex. App.—Corpus Christi–Edinburg 2005), *aff'd in part, rev'd in part on other grounds*, 348 S.W.3d 194 (Tex. 2011) (citing *Railroad Commission v. Shell Oil Co.*, 206 S.W.2d 235, 240 (Tex. 1947), and noting that it discussed similar language in precursor statute regarding production, storage, or transportation as "sweeping language . . . by which all waste in the handling of oil and gas was declared unlawful"); *see also Railroad Commission*, 206 S.W.2d at 294 (noting "among other things" precludes a narrowing of the statutory list and thus the term "waste" has an ordinarily and generally accepted meaning: "Whatever the dictates of reason, fairness, and good judgment under all the facts would lead one to conclude is a wasteful practice in the production, storage or transportation of oil and gas, must be held to have been denounced by the legislature as unlawful."). "[T]he code prohibits all waste of oil or gas." *Miesch*, 180 S.W.3d at 319 (rejecting argument that "the natural resources code only prohibits waste in the 'production, storage, or transportation' of oil or gas" and holding complaint of waste in plugging prohibited by statute).

The question and instruction should be modified based on the facts of the case to include the forms of waste that are at issue and in dispute.

Statutory defense.   In any cause of action brought under section 85.321 or otherwise "alleging waste to have been caused by an act or omission of a lease owner or operator, it shall be a defense that the lease owner or operator was acting as a reasonably prudent operator would act under the same or similar facts and circumstances." Tex. Nat. Res. Code § 85.321; *see also Emerald Oil & Gas Co.*, 331 S.W.3d at 422. See PJC 302.9 for a question and instruction on reasonably prudent operator.

Negligent waste or destruction.   In addition to statutory waste, an operator owes "due care to avoid the negligent waste or destruction of the minerals imbedded in [the] oil and gas-bearing strata." *Elliff v. Texon Drilling Co.*, 210 S.W.2d 558, 563 (Tex. 1948). A royalty or mineral owner is entitled to damages that will reasonably compensate the injured party for negligent waste or production, including damage to a reservoir underlying an oil and gas lease. *See Elliff*, 210 S.W.2d at 563; *see also Coastal Oil & Gas Corp. v. Garza Energy Trust*, 268 S.W.3d 1, 37 (Tex. 2008) (Willett, J., concurring) (recognizing longstanding claim for negligent damage to a common reservoir that reduces recoveries or constitutes waste); *HECI Exploration Co. v. Neel*, 982 S.W.2d 881, 890 (Tex. 1999). "A royalty owner may sue for its own damages without the joinder or permission of the lessee." *HECI Exploration Co.*, 982 S.W.2d at 890. Section 85.321 does not exclude common law rights for the same harms. *See Forest Oil Corp. v. El Rucio Land & Cattle Co.*, 518 S.W.3d 422, 429 (Tex. 2017).

Common-law waste of reversioner's or remainderman's interest.   In addition to statutory waste and negligent waste or destruction, an action exists for common-law waste of a reversioner's or remainderman's interest. The general rule is that "royalties and bonuses . . . are corpus which is to be preserved for the remaindermen." *Clyde v. Hamilton*, 414 S.W.2d 434, 439 (Tex. 1967).

> Ordinarily a life tenant who dissipates the corpus of an estate is liable to the remaindermen for waste. Waste is defined as "permanent harm to real property committed by tenants for life or for years, not justified as a reasonable exercise of ownership and enjoyment by the possessory tenant and resulting in a reduction in value of the interest of the reversioner or remainderman."

Moore v. Vines, 474 S.W.2d 437, 439 (Tex. 1971) (citing 1 *American Law of Property* § 2.16e (1952)); *see also McGill v. Johnson*, 799 S.W.2d 673, 676–77 (Tex. 1990); *Clyde*, 414 S.W.2d at 439. A claim of waste may include unauthorized destruction or severance of minerals on or from the land or injury resulting from a failure to exercise reasonable care in preserving the property. *See, e.g., Moore*, 474 S.W.2d at 440 (involving oil and gas lease executed after death of testator); *Erickson v. Rocco*, 433 S.W.2d 746, 751 (Tex. App.—Houston [14th Dist.] 1968, writ ref'd n.r.e.) (analyzing claim of waste for injury to reversionary deed of trust interest allegedly resulting from a failure to exercise reasonable care in preserving property). Exceptions to the general waste rule exist, e.g., the open mines doctrine and a will or other contract that authorizes the opening of, or receipt of proceeds on, leases executed after the testator's death. *See, e.g., Phillips v. Ivy*, 160 S.W.3d 91, 94 (Tex. App.—Waco 2004, pet. denied); *Singleton v. Donalson*, 117 S.W.3d 516, 518 (Tex. App.—Beaumont 2003, pet. denied).

Damages.   For statutory waste, the measure of damages may differ by the form of waste at issue. For unrecovered minerals from a plaintiff's land, the measure for a removal done in good faith is "the fair market value of the minerals less the defendant's cost of bringing them to the surface." *Miesch*, 180 S.W.3d at 324. If a bad-faith removal, the measure is the minerals' enhanced value. *Miesch*, 180 S.W.3d at 324; *see also Karrell v. West*, 616 S.W.2d 692, 697 (Tex. App.—Fort Worth 1981), *writ ref'd n.r.e.*, 628 S.W.2d 48 (Tex. 1982) (per curiam) (measures of damage for bad-faith removal is the "enhanced value of the product when and where it is finally converted, without any deductions of expenses incurred, or for any value he might have added to the minerals by his labor") (quoting *Dahlstrom Corp. v. Martin*, 582 S.W.2d 159, 161 (Tex. App.—Houston [1st Dist.] 1979, writ ref'd n.r.e.). "[I]f a destroyed well can be reproduced and the reproduction costs do not exceed the value of the well, the plaintiff can recover damages for the cost of reproducing and equipping the well." *Miesch*, 180 S.W.3d at 325 (involving plugged wells). Other measures may exist as well. *Miesch*, 180 S.W.3d at 326 (affirming lost bonus payment); *see also HECI Exploration Co.*, 982 S.W.2d at 890 ("[A] royalty interest has a reasonable market value that can be adversely affected by the loss of otherwise recoverable reserves that are burdened with royalty obligations."); *Elliff*, 210 S.W.2d at 560, 563 (affirming recovery for negligent damage to surface and wasted minerals from and under land).

PJC 302.9   **Question and Instruction on Reasonably Prudent Operator Defense to Statutory Waste Claim**

If you answered "Yes" to Question _____ [*302.8*], then answer the following question. Otherwise, do not answer the following question.

QUESTION _____

Did [*Don Davis*] act as a reasonably prudent operator with respect to the conduct described in Question _____ [*302.8*]?

A "reasonably prudent operator" means an operator of ordinary prudence acting with ordinary diligence under the same or similar circumstances, having due regard for the interests of both *Don Davis* and *Paul Payne*.

Answer "Yes" or "No."

Answer: _____

COMMENT

When to use.   PJC 302.9 should be used as a defense to a cause of action brought under Tex. Nat. Res. Code § 85.321 if the lease owner or operator claims to have been acting as a reasonably prudent operator. See PJC 302.8.

Source of question and instruction.   This question is derived from *Amoco Production Co. v. Alexander*, 622 S.W.2d 563, 567–68 (Tex. 1981); *Cabot Corp. v. Brown*, 754 S.W.2d 104 (Tex. 1987); and *Hurd Enterprises, Ltd. v. Bruni*, 828 S.W.2d 101, 109 (Tex. App.—San Antonio 1992, writ denied).

CHAPTER 303   LESSOR-LESSEE ISSUES

PJC 303.1   Claims for Breach of Lease Provisions (Comment)

An oil and gas lease, in addition to being a conveyance of real property, contains covenants and conditions that must be interpreted under the same rules that apply to other contracts. *Hitzelberger v. Samedan Oil Corp.*, 948 S.W.2d 497, 503 (Tex. App.— Waco 1997, writ denied). If the oil and gas lease is unambiguous, courts seek to determine and enforce the intention of the parties as expressed in the lease. *Heritage Resources, Inc. v. NationsBank*, 939 S.W.2d 118, 121 (Tex. 1996).

Disputes concerning breach of express and implied lease covenants are covered in PJC 303.1 through 303.12, and disputes concerning breach of lease conditions are covered in PJC 303.13 through 303.25. The appropriate remedy for breach of covenants generally is damages, whereas the remedy for breach of lease conditions is termination. *See Shell Oil Co. v. Stansbury*, 401 S.W.2d 623 (Tex. App.—Beaumont), *writ ref'd n.r.e.*, 410 S.W.2d 187 (Tex. 1966); *see also Texas Oil & Gas Corp. v. Vela*, 429 S.W.2d 866, 875 (Tex. 1968). Furthermore, because an oil and gas lease is a contract as well as a conveyance, an action for breach of either an express or implied covenant sounds in contract rather than in tort. Therefore, punitive damages are not recoverable. *Amoco Production Co. v. Alexander*, 622 S.W.2d 563, 571 (Tex. 1981).

The pattern jury charges in this chapter focus on two common claims for breach of express lease covenants: (1) failure to properly pool and (2) failure to properly pay royalty. Both claims are considered breaches of the lease, because the right to pool and the method for calculating royalty are terms provided in the lease. For disputes involving the breach of other express or implied covenants, the jury charges should conform to the lease language or implied duty at issue. Additionally, disputes concerning breach of express and implied lease covenants could be affected by division orders and the Texas Division Order Statute. Tex. Nat. Res. Code § 91.402; *Exxon Corp. v. Middleton*, 613 S.W.2d 240 (Tex. 1981); *Ohrt v. Union Gas Corp.*, 398 S.W.3d 315 (Tex. App.—Corpus Christi–Edinburg 2012, pet. denied).

For additional questions and instructions regarding contract claims and defenses that may be applicable to disputes involving the breach of the lease, see chapters 305 and 312 of this volume.

PJC 303.2   Question on Breach of Express Pooling Provision

QUESTION _____

Did *Larry Lessee* fail to pool in accordance with the terms of the lease?

The lease provides [*insert express lease provision*].

Answer "Yes" or "No."

Answer: _____

COMMENT

When to use.   PJC 303.2 should be used when the lessor claims the lessee has breached the express terms of the pooling provisions of the lease. The right to pool must be expressly granted in the lease and may be exercised only to the extent stipulated in the lease.

Source of question.   PJC 303.2 is derived from *Samson Exploration, LLC v. T.S. Reed Properties, Inc.*, 521 S.W.3d 766 (Tex. 2017); *Coastal Oil & Gas Corp. v. Garza Energy Trust*, 268 S.W.3d 1, 21 n.68 (Tex. 2008) (citing *Southeastern Pipe Line Co. v. Tichacek*, 997 S.W.2d 166, 170 (Tex. 1999)); and *Jones v. Killingsworth*, 403 S.W.2d 325, 327 (Tex. 1965).

Remedies.   When a lessee fails to pool in accordance with the terms of the lease, courts view the pooling as ineffective from the beginning and grant remedies to reflect that fact. *Tittizer v. Union Gas Corp.*, 171 S.W.3d 857 (Tex. 2005) (holding lessee's declaration of retroactive pooling improper in light of express terms of pooling clause); *Jones*, 403 S.W.2d 325 (holding lessee could not maintain lease by forming pooled unit that did not comply with express terms of pooling clause). For a question on damages for breach of express pooling provisions, see PJC 313.9.

PJC 303.3   Question and Instruction on Good-Faith Pooling

QUESTION _____

Did *Larry Lessee* fail to pool the lease in good faith?

When exercising the pooling authority granted in the lease, *Larry Lessee* failed to pool the lease in good faith if *he* failed to act as a reasonably prudent operator would have acted under the same or similar circumstances, taking into account the interests of both *Larry Lessee* and *Paul Payne*.

Answer "Yes" or "No."

Answer: _____

COMMENT

When to use.   PJC 303.3 should be used when the plaintiff claims the lessee has failed to pool in good faith. The exercise of the express right to pool is subject to an implied duty to pool in "good faith." *Coastal Oil & Gas Corp. v. Garza Energy Trust*, 268 S.W.3d 1, 21 (Tex. 2008); *Southeastern Pipe Line Co. v. Tichacek*, 997 S.W.2d 166, 171 (Tex. 1999). This duty requires the lessee to act in fairness and good faith when exercising the pooling authority, as would a reasonably prudent operator under the same or similar circumstances, taking into account the interests of both the lessee and the lessor. *Circle Dot Ranch, Inc. v. Sidwell Oil & Gas, Inc.*, 891 S.W.2d 342, 346 (Tex. App.—Amarillo 1995, writ denied); *Elliott v. Davis*, 553 S.W.2d 223, 226–27 (Tex. App.—Amarillo 1977, writ ref'd n.r.e.) (quoting Eugene Kuntz, *The Law of Oil and Gas* § 48.3, p. 218 (1972)). The requirement of good faith in exercising pooling authority does not change the relationship between the lessee and lessor into that of an agent or fiduciary. *Vela v. Pennzoil Producing Co.*, 723 S.W.2d 199, 206 (Tex. App.—San Antonio 1986, writ ref'd n.r.e.); *Elliott*, 553 S.W.2d at 226–27.

Source of question and instruction.   PJC 303.3 is derived from *Circle Dot Ranch, Inc.*, 891 S.W.2d at 346, and *Elliott*, 553 S.W.2d at 226–27 (quoting Kuntz, at § 48.3, p. 218).

Good-faith pooling duty.   Lessors have challenged the lessee's exercise of the pooling authority based on a variety of facts, including (1) drawing boundaries of a pooled unit to perpetuate as many leases as possible rather than to accomplish a permissible pooling goal, *Elliott*, 553 S.W.2d at 227; (2) gerrymandering of pooled unit boundaries, *Circle Dot Ranch, Inc.*, 891 S.W.2d at 347; (3) express statements that pooled unit boundaries have been drawn to maintain leases, *Amoco v. Underwood*, 558 S.W.2d 509, 512–13 (Tex. App.—Eastland 1977, writ ref'd n.r.e.); (4) pooling an undrilled tract shortly before the end of the primary term, *Circle Dot Ranch, Inc.*, 891

S.W.2d at 347; *Elliott*, 553 S.W.2d at 227; (5) failure to consider geological factors in forming the pooled unit, *Elliott*, 553 S.W.2d at 227; (6) the absence of plans for additional development and pooling portions of leases with smaller royalties with a well-site lease that has ample acreage to support the well, *Underwood*, 558 S.W.2d at 511–12; and (7) exclusion of productive acreage located near the well and inclusion of unproductive acreage or of acreage which is probably not within the well's drainage pattern, *Elliott*, 553 S.W.2d at 226 (refusal by Texas Railroad Commission to approve pooled acreage as a unit to be assigned to well is not, in itself, determinative of question of good faith); *Circle Dot Ranch, Inc.*, 891 S.W.2d at 347.

Remedies.   If the jury finds the lessee has breached its duty to pool in good faith, the pooling is "canceled and held for naught" as to the lessor's lease. *Underwood*, 558 S.W.2d at 511. The lessor also may be entitled to damages measured by the lessor's undiluted royalty on the well's production from the date of initial production through the date of trial, assuming that the well is located on and producing from the lessor's lease.

PJC 303.4   Question on Breach of Express Royalty Provision

QUESTION _____

Did *Larry Lessee* fail to pay a royalty in accordance with the terms of the lease?

The lease provides [*insert express lease provision*].

Answer "Yes" or "No."

Answer: _____

COMMENT

When to use.   PJC 303.4 should be used when the lessor claims the lessee has breached express royalty provisions in the lease.

Source of question.   PJC 303.4 is derived from *Yzaguirre v. KCS Resources, Inc.*, 53 S.W.3d 368 (Tex. 2001), and *Exxon Corp. v. Middleton*, 613 S.W.2d 240 (Tex. 1981).

Royalty.   Leases typically contain express provisions governing the lessee's royalty-payment obligation. These clauses contain language dictating how the royalty is to be paid, including language regarding what, when, where, and how to value production for royalty purposes. Disputes arising under the express provisions of the lease generally involve disagreements regarding the volume or measurement of production, the value of production, and whether any improper deductions have been taken before the calculation of royalty. In all instances, however, the express language of the lease determines the lessee's royalty obligation to the lessor. *See, e.g., Sowell v. Natural Gas Pipeline Co. of America*, 789 F.2d 1151, 1155 (5th Cir. 1986) (royalty calculated in a manner other than market value or amounts realized). Other clauses, such as pooling and proportionate reduction clauses, may affect the royalty payment obligation. *See Samson Exploration, LLC v. T.S. Reed Properties, Inc.*, 521 S.W.3d 766 (Tex. 2017). Therefore, jury questions must be modified to reflect the express lease royalty obligation in dispute.

Lease forms typically provide different royalty provisions for oil and gas. Oil royalty clauses often provide that lessees may pay royalty "in kind" or, at the lessee's option, base payments on "the market price . . . prevailing in the field." As commentators have noted, oil royalty provisions have not been as extensively litigated as the gas clause for a variety of reasons, including the complicated regulatory provisions and physical differences that affect gas sales contracts. Ernest E. Smith & Jacqueline Lang Weaver, 1 *Texas Law of Oil and Gas* § 4.6 [E] (2d ed. 2013).

Royalty on gas has historically been valued on the basis of either (1) the "amount realized" or (2) the "market value." Often both of these royalty-valuation standards are found in the same lease form, and they will apply depending on where the gas is sold. A frequently litigated gas royalty clause provides as follows: "The royalties to be paid by Lessee are: . . . on gas . . . produced and sold or used off the premises . . . the market value at the well of one-eighth of the gas so sold or used, provided that on gas sold at the wells the royalty shall be one-eighth of the amount realized from such sale." *See, e.g., Yzaguirre*, 53 S.W.3d 368; *Exxon Corp.*, 613 S.W.2d 240. The definitions of "market value," "proceeds received," and "amounts realized" have been established by Texas case law. Therefore, when submitting a question regarding breach of express provisions to pay royalty, absent an express definition in the lease, an instruction on any established legal definition of the applicable term should be included.

Postproduction costs.   Another issue that may arise is whether improper deductions have been taken from the royalty amount before calculation of the royalty. Generally, the lessor's royalty interest bears no costs of drilling and production or bringing the product to the surface but will bear its proportionate share of production and severance taxes, transportation, marketing, compression, processing, and gathering costs, unless the lease provides otherwise. Reasonable postproduction costs may be deducted from the proceeds of a sale that occurs "down-stream" or beyond the well in order to "net back" to the well the amounts realized from the sale or to determine market value at the well. *See Burlington Resources v. Texas Crude*, 573 S.W.3d 198 (Tex. 2019) (holding as first impression that phrase "into the pipeline" required owner of overriding royalty to bear share of postproduction costs); *Chesapeake Exploration, L.L.C. v. Hyder*, 483 S.W.3d 870 (Tex. 2016); *French v. Occidental Permian Ltd.*, 440 S.W.3d 1 (Tex. 2014); *Judice v. Mewbourne Oil Co.*, 939 S.W.2d 133, 135 (Tex. 1996); *Heritage Resources, Inc. v. NationsBank*, 939 S.W.2d 118, 122–23 (Tex. 1996); *see also Holbein v. Austral Oil Co.*, 609 F.2d 206, 209 (5th Cir. 1980); *Martin v. Glass*, 571 F. Supp. 1406, 1410 (N.D. Tex. 1983), *aff'd*, 736 F.2d 1524 (5th Cir. 1984); *Cartwright v. Cologne Production Co.*, 182 S.W.3d 438, 444–46 (Tex. App.—Corpus Christi–Edinburg 2006, pet. denied).

Broad-form submission.   PJC 303.4 is a broad-form submission and should be submitted with the appropriate instructions and conditional questions on damages for the specific issues in dispute. For further discussion, see PJC 314.2 regarding broad-form issues and the *Casteel* doctrine.

PJC 303.5   **Question on Untimely Payment of Proceeds of Production under Natural Resources Code**

QUESTION _____

Did *Larry Lessee* fail to pay *Paul Payne* proceeds due on production within [*specify number of days in lease or under Texas Natural Resources Code*] days of production?

Answer "Yes" or "No."

Answer: _____

COMMENT

When to use. A question on whether royalty payments have been timely made usually will arise under one of two circumstances: (1) the lease at issue contains an express provision stating the time for payment or (2) an action has been brought under Tex. Nat. Res. Code §§ 91.401–.408, which sets out a statutory time for payment. Because most standard-form royalty clauses do not provide a time period for making royalty payments, the instruction for claims brought under leases that do not provide a period for payment of royalty should conform to sections 91.401–.408. If a lease contains express provisions governing the timely payment of royalties, the instruction should be modified to reflect the terms of the lease. If there is a fact question regarding a good-faith title dispute or if the date of payment is in dispute, an additional question will be needed.

For a question on breach of the express royalty provision, see PJC 303.4.

Source of question. Under Tex. Nat. Res. Code §§ 91.401–.408, a payor must pay to the payee the proceeds received from the sale of oil or gas production on or before 120 days after the end of the month of first sale of production from the well and no later than 60 days for oil or 90 days for gas after the end of the calendar month in which the production is sold in subsequent months. If payments are not made within these time periods, the payments are not timely, and the payee must pay interest on the payment at the rate provided in the statute. Tex. Nat. Res. Code § 91.403(a). The time period set out in this question or instruction should conform either to the express lease terms or the statutory requirements, whichever is appropriate. *See ConocoPhillips Co. v. Koopmann*, 547 S.W.3d 858 (Tex. 2018). See *Anadarko E&P Co., L.P. v. Clear Lake Pines, Inc.*, No. 03-04-00600-CV, 2005 WL 1583506 (Tex. App.—Austin July 7, 2005, no pet.), for a discussion on whether "the owner of the right to produce under an oil or gas lease or pooling order" or the "the first purchaser" qualifies as a payor under Tex. Nat. Res. Code §§ 91.401–.408.

In addition to specifying time periods for payment, Tex. Nat. Res. Code § 91.404 requires the payee to give the payor written notice by mail of the failure to pay timely as a prerequisite to suing the payor for nonpayment.

Defenses.   Tex. Nat. Res. Code § 91.402(b) allows the lessee to suspend royalty payments under certain situations, including the existence of a title dispute that would affect the distribution of payments. See PJC 312.17 for a question on defenses.

Other proceeds.   In addition to royalties, Tex. Nat. Res. Code §§ 91.401–.408 apply to other oil or gas proceeds or the interest on those proceeds.

PJC 303.6   Question on Location of Sale

QUESTION _____

Was the gas at issue sold [*on/off*] *Paul Payne*'s leased premises?

Answer "Yes" or "No."

Answer: _____

COMMENT

When to use.   PJC 303.6 should be used when the location of sale is at issue under the express terms of the lease. Historically, gas royalty lease clauses value royalty on the basis of either (1) the "amount realized," sometimes referred to as proceeds, provided the gas was sold at the well or on the lease; or (2) market value at the well for gas produced and sold or used off the lease. *See, e.g., Yzaguirre v. KCS Resources, Inc.*, 53 S.W.3d 368 (Tex. 2001); *Exxon Corp. v. Middleton*, 613 S.W.2d 240 (Tex. 1981).

When the dispute involves these types of clauses, one of the two bracketed options should be chosen, with the burden of proof placed on the plaintiff. The jury's response will determine whether the "amount realized" or the "market value at the well" standard governs the lessee's royalty obligation to the lessor. In all instances, however, the express language of the lease determines the lessee's royalty obligation. *See, e.g., Sowell v. Natural Gas Pipeline Co. of America*, 789 F.2d 1151, 1155 (5th Cir. 1986) (royalty calculated in a manner other than market value or amounts realized). Therefore, jury questions regarding the location of sale must be modified to reflect the express terms in dispute.

PJC 303.7   Question and Instruction on Implied Duty to Reasonably Market Production (Proceeds/Amount Realized Royalty Provision)

QUESTION _____

Did *Larry Lessee* fail to reasonably market the [*oil/gas*] produced from *Paul Payne*'s lease?

"Reasonably market" means to market the production with due diligence and to obtain the best price reasonably possible as would a reasonably prudent operator acting with ordinary diligence under the same or similar circumstances, having due regard for the interests of both *Larry Lessee* and *Paul Payne*.

Answer "Yes" or "No."

Answer: _____

COMMENT

When to use.   PJC 303.7 should be used when the issue is whether the lessee acted prudently in marketing the production. The duty to market production by obtaining the best price reasonably possible is included within the implied covenant of management and administration of the leasehold estate. *Cabot Corp. v. Brown*, 754 S.W.2d 104, 106 (Tex. 1987) (citing Richard W. Hemingway, *Law of Oil and Gas* § 8.9(C) (2d ed. 1983)). A covenant to reasonably market the production as to price is not implied when the lessor's royalty is based on market value at the well. *Yzaguirre v. KCS Resources, Inc.*, 53 S.W.3d 368, 373 (Tex. 2001). See PJC 303.10 on implied covenants.

Source of question and instruction.   PJC 303.7 is derived from *Cabot Corp.*, 754 S.W.2d at 106. *See also Union Pacific Resources Group, Inc. v. Hankins*, 111 S.W.3d 69 (Tex. 2003); *Yzaguirre*, 53 S.W.3d 368; *Amoco Production Co. v. Alexander*, 622 S.W.2d 563, 568 (Tex. 1981); *Amoco Production Co. v. First Baptist Church of Pyote*, 611 S.W.2d 610 (Tex. 1980).

PJC 303.8   Question and Instructions on Breach of Express Market Value Royalty Provision

QUESTION _____

Did *Larry Lessee* fail to pay *Paul Payne* a royalty based on the market value at the well for [*gas/other product*] produced from *Paul Payne*'s lease?

"Market value" is the price a willing seller not obligated to sell can obtain from a willing buyer not obligated to buy.

[Include the following if comparable sales are available.]

Market value at the well may be determined by comparable sales. A "comparable sale" is one that is comparable in time, quality, quantity, and availability of marketing outlets.

[Include the following if comparable sales are not available.]

Market value at the well may be determined by subtracting reasonable post-production costs from the market value at the point of sale.

Answer "Yes" or "No."

Answer: _____

COMMENT

When to use.   PJC 303.8 should be used when a party seeks royalties under an express market value royalty provision. If the dispute includes whether the gas or other product was sold on or off the leased premises, see PJC 303.6.

Source of question and instructions.   PJC 303.8 is derived from *French v. Occidental Permian Ltd.*, 440 S.W.3d 1 (Tex. 2014) (holding royalty owners required to share in removal of carbon dioxide as part of netback calculation to determine market value); *Heritage Resources, Inc. v. NationsBank*, 939 S.W.2d 118, 122 (Tex. 1996); *Exxon Corp. v. Middleton*, 613 S.W.2d 240, 246–47 (Tex. 1981); and *Texas Oil & Gas Corp. v. Hagen*, 683 S.W.2d 24, 28 (Tex. App.—Texarkana 1984), *dismissed as moot*, 760 S.W.2d 960 (Tex. 1988). For another definition of "market value" see the current edition of State Bar of Texas, *Texas Pattern Jury Charges—General Negligence, Intentional Personal Torts & Workers' Compensation* PJC 31.3.

Determining market value.   Comparable sales is the preferred method to use when determining market value. *Heritage Resources, Inc.*, 939 S.W.2d at 122. When the lease requires valuation at the well but comparable sales at the well are not readily available, the market value at the well can be determined by subtracting reasonable postproduction costs from the market value at the point of sale (the netback method). *Heritage Resources, Inc.*, 939 S.W.2d at 122. Postproduction costs include transporting the gas to the market and processing the gas to make it marketable. *Heritage Resources, Inc.*, 939 S.W.2d at 122. In such circumstances, the question will have to be modified to fit the facts of the case. If there is a fact dispute about whether there are comparable sales at the well, the dispute should be resolved by submission to the jury. Market value is also defined in the Texas division order statute and in the Texas Tax Code. Tex. Nat. Res. Code § 91.402(i); Tex. Tax Code § 201.101.

Modification depending on lease terms. If the lease provision requires valuation at some place other than at the well (e.g., at the point of sale or point of transfer to a nonaffiliated third party) or if it provides for a different method of valuation (e.g., highest index price), the question and instruction should be altered to be consistent with the lease terms.

PJC 303.9 Question and Instruction on Unreasonable Deduction of Postproduction Costs

QUESTION _____

Did *Larry Lessee* take [*an*] unreasonable deduction[*s*] from the royalty payable under *Paul Payne*'s lease?

A deduction is unreasonable if it is in excess of a reasonable amount of postproduction costs. Postproduction costs can include taxes, treatment costs, gathering costs, marketing costs, compression costs, and transportation costs.

Answer "Yes" or "No."

Answer: _____

COMMENT

When to use. PJC 303.9 should be used when the plaintiff claims deductions from the royalty are unreasonable.

Source of question and instruction. PJC 303.9 is derived from *Burlington Resources v. Texas Crude*, 573 S.W.3d 198 (Tex. 2019) (holding as first impression that phrase "into the pipeline" required owner of overriding royalty to bear share of postproduction costs); *Heritage Resources, Inc. v. NationsBank*, 939 S.W.2d 118, 122 (Tex. 1996), and *Martin v. Glass*, 571 F. Supp. 1406, 1410 (N.D. Tex. 1983), *aff'd*, 736 F.2d 1524 (5th Cir. 1984). *See also Cartwright v. Cologne Production Co.*, 182 S.W.3d 438 (Tex. App.—Corpus Christi–Edinburg 2006, pet. denied).

Postproduction costs and the calculation of royalty. Royalty is commonly defined as the landowner's share of production, free of the expenses of production. The lessee is entitled to deduct reasonable postproduction costs, such as taxes, treatment costs to render the gas marketable, and compression, transportation, gathering, and marketing costs in calculating the royalty due under the lease. *Martin*, 571 F. Supp at 1410. Compression costs may or may not be deductible, depending on whether the compression is necessary for production purposes or for transportation purposes. *Martin*, 571 F. Supp at 1410. The instruction should be modified to reflect any lease provisions that specify the costs that may or may not be deducted, but note that when the lease provides for the royalty to be based on market value at the well, and deductions are an integral part in reaching that valuation, contrary lease language may not be effective. *See Heritage Resources, Inc.*, 939 S.W.2d at 122.

PJC 303.10   Implied Covenants (Comment)

The doctrine of implied covenants developed early in Texas case law. *See W.T. Waggoner Estate v. Sigler Oil Co.*, 19 S.W.2d 27, 29–31 (Tex. 1929); *Freeport Sulphur Co. v. American Sulphur Royalty Co.*, 6 S.W.2d 1039, 1041–42 (Tex. 1928); *Grubb v. McAfee*, 212 S.W. 464, 465 (Tex. 1919). Implied covenants must be complementary but not contrary to the express provisions of the lease.

> A covenant will not be implied unless it appears from the express terms of the contract that "it was so clearly within the contemplation of the parties that they deemed it unnecessary to express it," and therefore they omitted to do so, or "it must appear that it is necessary to infer such a covenant in order to effectuate the full purpose of the contract as a whole as gathered from the written instrument."

HECI Exploration Co. v. Neel, 982 S.W.2d 881, 888 (Tex. 1998) (quoting *Danciger Oil & Refining Co. of Texas v. Powell*, 154 S.W.2d 632, 635 (Tex. 1941)). Accordingly, "there is no implied covenant when the oil and gas lease expressly covers the subject matter of an implied covenant." *Yzaguirre v. KCS Resources, Inc.*, 53 S.W.3d 368, 373 (Tex. 2001).

The landmark supreme court case describing implied covenants in the oil and gas lease is *Amoco Production Co. v. Alexander*, 622 S.W.2d 563 (Tex. 1981). In that case, the Texas Supreme Court grouped the implied covenants into three broad categories according to the factual basis of the dispute between the lessor and lessee as follows: (1) covenant to develop the premises; (2) covenant to protect the leasehold, which includes the duty to protect against drainage; and (3) covenant to manage and administer the lease, which includes the duty to market. *Amoco Production Co.*, 622 S.W.2d at 567. See PJC 303.7 for a question on the implied duty to market.

Amoco also identifies the standard by which a lessee's conduct under these implied covenants will be measured. The general duty of the lessee is to conduct operations as would a reasonably prudent operator to carry out the purposes of the oil and gas lease. *Amoco Production Co.*, 622 S.W.2d at 567–68. This standard is often described as the "reasonably prudent operator standard" and is defined as "what a reasonably prudent operator would do under the same or similar circumstances." *Amoco Production Co.*, 622 S.W.2d at 567–68. Absent evidence of some special relationship between the lessor and the lessee, or some duty explicit in the language of the lease, the lessee does not owe a fiduciary duty to the lessor. *Hurd Enterprises, Ltd. v. Bruni*, 828 S.W.2d 101, 108–09 (Tex. App.—San Antonio 1992, writ denied) (citing *Texas Oil & Gas Corp. v. Hagen*, 31 Tex. Sup. Ct. J. 140, 142, 1987 WL 47847 (Dec. 16, 1987), *op. withdrawn, case settled*, 760 S.W.2d 960 (Tex. 1988)).

PJC 303.11   **Question and Instructions on Breach of Implied Covenant to Protect against Drainage**

QUESTION _____

Did *Larry Lessee* fail to prevent substantial drainage from *Paul Payne*'s lease?

Larry Lessee failed to prevent substantial drainage from a lease under *his* control if *he* failed to act as a reasonably prudent operator would under the same or similar circumstances with a reasonable expectation of profit.

A "reasonably prudent operator" means an operator of ordinary prudence acting with ordinary diligence under the same or similar circumstances, having due regard for the interests of both *Larry Lessee* and *Paul Payne*.

Answer "Yes" or "No."

Answer: _____

COMMENT

When to use.   PJC 303.11 should be used when the plaintiff is suing for failure to protect against drainage.

Source of question and instruction.   PJC 303.11 is derived from *Coastal Oil & Gas Corp. v. Garza Energy Trust*, 268 S.W.3d 1, 17 n.57 (Tex. 2008); *Kerr-McGee Corp. v. Helton*, 133 S.W.3d 245, 249–53 (Tex. 2004); *Southeastern Pipe Line Co. v. Tichacek*, 997 S.W.2d 166, 170 (Tex. 1999); *Amoco Production Co. v. Alexander*, 622 S.W.2d 563, 567 n.1 (Tex. 1981); *Circle Dot Ranch, Inc. v. Sidwell Oil & Gas, Inc.*, 891 S.W.2d 342, 346 (Tex. App.—Amarillo 1995, writ denied); *Good v. TXO Production Corp.*, 763 S.W.2d 59, 61 (Tex. App.—Amarillo 1988, writ ref'd n.r.e.); *Vela v. Pennzoil Producing Co.*, 723 S.W.2d 199, 206 (Tex. App.—San Antonio 1986, writ ref'd n.r.e.); and *Elliott v. Davis*, 553 S.W.2d 223, 226–27 (Tex. App.—Amarillo 1977, writ ref'd n.r.e.) (citing Eugene Kuntz, *The Law of Oil and Gas* § 48.3, p. 218 (1972)); *see also* Ernest E. Smith & Jacqueline Lang Weaver, 1 *Texas Law of Oil and Gas* § 5.3 A.1. (2d ed. 2013).

Common lessee.   For a discussion regarding the circumstances in which the lessee is the same on both leases, see *Amoco Production Co.*, 622 S.W.2d at 569, and *Shell Oil Co. v. Stansbury*, 410 S.W.2d 187 (Tex. 1967). The implied covenant to protect a lease from drainage extends not only to a localized occurrence across the lease line but also to field-wide drainage. *Amoco Production Co.*, 622 S.W.2d at 568.

Reasonably prudent operator. The reasonably prudent operator is the standard for measuring the lessee's performance of the duty to protect from drainage. The key issues are the actions the lessor claims the lessee should have taken to protect the lease from substantial drainage and whether those actions could be undertaken by the lessee with a reasonable expectation of profit. *See Amoco Production Co.*, 622 S.W.2d at 568 (citing *Clifton v. Koontz*, 325 S.W.2d 684, 695–96 (Tex. 1959)). The Texas Supreme Court noted in *Amoco* that the duty to protect against drainage encompasses any act a reasonably prudent operator would perform to protect the lease from drainage, including "(1) drilling replacement wells, (2) re-working existing wells, (3) drilling additional wells, (4) seeking field-wide regulatory action, (5) seeking Rule 37 exceptions from the Railroad Commission, (6) seeking voluntary unitization, or (7) seeking other available administrative relief." *Amoco Production Co.*, 622 S.W.2d at 568. However, none of these duties arises unless "such an amount of oil can be recovered to equal the cost of administrative expenses, drilling or re-working and equipping a protection well, producing and marketing the oil, and yield to the lessee a reasonable expectation of profit." *Amoco Production Co.*, 622 S.W.2d at 568.

PJC 303.12   **Question and Instruction on Breach of Implied Covenant to Develop**

QUESTION _____

Did *Larry Lessee* fail to drill additional wells on the lease that a reasonably prudent operator would have drilled?

The lessee has a duty to drill all wells that a reasonably prudent operator would drill under the same or similar circumstances, with a reasonable expectation of profit. This duty to drill extends both to already producing formations or strata and also to formations or strata other than the formations or strata from which production is being obtained, but which in reasonable probability exist and are known to be capable of production.

A "reasonably prudent operator" means an operator of ordinary prudence acting with ordinary diligence under the same or similar circumstances, having due regard for the interests of both *Larry Lessee* and *Paul Payne*.

Answer "Yes" or "No."

Answer: _____

COMMENT

When to use.   PJC 303.12 should be used when the plaintiff is suing for failure to reasonably develop after production has been obtained from the leased premises.

Source of question and instruction.   PJC 303.12 is derived from *Sun Exploration & Production Co. v. Jackson*, 783 S.W.2d 202, 204 (Tex. 1989), and *Clifton v. Koontz*, 325 S.W.2d 684, 695 (Tex. 1959).

Reasonably prudent operator.   Under the implied covenant of reasonable development, a lessee is generally obligated to drill whatever wells on the lease that a reasonably prudent operator would drill. While the lessee can fulfill the duty to reasonably develop the lease by other actions besides drilling, drilling a well is most often the action that the plaintiff claims should have occurred. However, a reasonably prudent operator is not required to drill a well unless there is a reasonable expectation of profit in the drilling. *Clifton*, 325 S.W.2d at 695. Whether there is a reasonable expectation of profit is usually a matter for expert testimony. In this respect, the development well that the plaintiff alleges should have been drilled is virtually indistinguishable from the "protection well" under the drainage covenant discussed at PJC 303.11; both are wells that a reasonable and prudent operator would have drilled with a reasonable expectation of profit. In the question, the jury is asked about "additional wells" as opposed to a general question about "development." While either phrase could be used depending on the facts of the particular case, this "additional wells" language, a direct quote from *Clifton*, is used here because in certain situations a jury might be confused by a question that asks only whether the lease has been "properly developed." An alleged failure to drill either a development well or an exploratory well, or both, should be submitted in a "development" question. *Sun Exploration & Production Co.*, 783 S.W.2d at 204.

PJC 303.13   Lease Termination (Comment)

In Texas, the term or habendum clause of a typical oil, gas, or mineral lease provides that the lease will last "so long as" there is production from the leased premises. The "so long as" language creates a fee simple determinable interest in the mineral estate in the lessee and a possibility of reverter in the lessor. *Natural Gas Pipeline Co. of America v. Pool*, 124 S.W.3d 188, 192 (Tex. 2002). The lessee's possessory interest is "determinable" because it may terminate and revert to the lessor upon the occurrence of conditions specified in the lease. *Pool*, 124 S.W.3d 188; *Stephens County v. Mid-Kansas Oil & Gas Co.*, 254 S.W. 290, 295 (Tex. 1923). Courts have addressed the differences between covenants and conditions in oil and gas leases. *See Rogers v. Ricane Enterprises*, 772 S.W.2d 76, 79 (Tex. 1989); *Freeman v. Magnolia Petroleum Co.*, 171 S.W.2d 339, 341–42 (Tex. 1943); *Blackmon v. XTO Energy, Inc.*, 276 S.W.3d 600, 605 (Tex. App.—Waco 2008, pet. denied); *Hitzelberger v. Samedan Oil Corp.*, 948 S.W.2d 497, 506 (Tex. App.—Waco 1997, pet. denied). Typically, the habendum clause creates two terms: (1) the primary term, which lasts for a set number of years, and (2) the secondary term, which endures as long as there is production. Unless defined otherwise by the lease, the term "production" in the habendum clause means "production in paying quantities." *Clifton v. Koontz*, 325 S.W.2d 684, 692 (Tex. 1959).

During the primary term, leases frequently provide for the payment of delay rentals, which are due annually. A lessee's failure to properly pay delay rentals triggers a terminating condition of the lease. *Humble Oil & Refining Co. v. Harrison*, 205 S.W.2d 355, 360 (Tex. 1947). At the end of the primary term, a nonproducing lease terminates unless it is perpetuated by a savings clause, which serves as constructive production. *Watson v. Rochmill*, 155 S.W.2d 783, 784 (Tex. 1941); *see also Krabbe v. Anadarko Petroleum Corp.*, 46 S.W.3d 308, 315 (Tex. App.—Amarillo 2001, pet. denied). Typical savings clauses include the following:

1.   *dry hole clauses:* these clauses save a lease if, after having drilled a dry hole, the lessee begins drilling or reworking operations within the time specified in the lease;

2.   *operations clauses:* these clauses save a lease if the lessee has commenced operations before the end of the primary term; two types of operations clauses are common:

    a.   a "well completion" clause, which requires the lessee to complete the same well it commenced before the end of the primary term, and

    b.   a "continuous operations" clause, which saves the lease even if the lessee commences an additional well;

3.   *cessation of production clauses:* these clauses save a lease if the operator commences additional drilling or reworking within a specified number of days after production has ceased;

4.   *force majeure clauses:* these clauses excuse the lessee's nonperformance of obligations in the lease; and

5.   *shut-in royalty clauses:* these clauses apply to gas wells "capable of producing in paying quantities."

Additionally, pooling can act as a savings clause because production from anywhere on a pooled unit constitutes production from leases properly pooled in the unit. See PJC 303.2 and 303.3 on pooling.

In addition to these express savings clauses, Texas courts have created other savings doctrines. For example, regarding delay rentals, courts have allowed lessees to rely on equitable doctrines to excuse their noncompliance with the terms of the delay rental clause. *Humble Oil & Refining Co.*, 205 S.W.2d at 361; *Brannon v. Gulf States Energy Corp.*, 562 S.W.2d 219, 222 (Tex. 1977). In the event of a total cessation of production, Texas courts have applied the temporary cessation of production doctrine, but only if the lease does not contain an express "cessation of production" clause. *See Watson*, 155 S.W.2d at 784; *Krabbe*, 46 S.W.3d at 315. In addition, a lessee may assert defenses to avoid lease termination. See chapter 312 of this volume on defenses.

The following pattern jury charges are based on court opinions addressing whether the habendum clause or a particular savings clause has been satisfied so as to prevent lease termination. The fact issues raised by such cases commonly include whether drilling operations were commenced timely or whether they continued without cessation. In determining whether a lessee has complied with a savings clause, Texas courts generally require strict compliance with the language of the clause. *See Rogers v. Osborn*, 261 S.W.2d 311 (Tex. 1953); *Hydrocarbon Management, Inc. v. Tracker Exploration, Inc.*, 861 S.W.2d 427 (Tex. App.—Amarillo 1993, no writ). For that reason, the jury charges should be modified to reflect the particular requirements of the clause at issue.

PJC 303.14   Question on Failure to Tender Delay Rental Payment

QUESTION _____

Did *Larry Lessee* fail to pay or tender a delay rental payment as provided in the lease?

The lease provides [*insert express lease provision*].

Answer "Yes" or "No."

Answer: _____

COMMENT

When to use.   PJC 303.14 should be used when the dispute stems from the lessor's claim that the lease terminated due to the lessee's failure to properly pay delay rentals according to the terms of the lease.

Source of question.   PJC 303.14 is derived from *Humble Oil & Refining Co. v. Harrison*, 205 S.W.2d 355, 361 (Tex. 1947) (lessee's failure to comply with terms of delay rental payment resulted in lease termination), and *W.T. Waggoner Estate v. Sigler Oil Co.*, 19 S.W.2d 27 (Tex. 1929) (failure to drill or to pay delay rental resulted in lease termination).

PJC 303.15   Question and Instruction on Failure to Commence Operations before End of Primary Term

QUESTION _____

Did *Larry Lessee* fail to [*commence/engage in*] drilling or reworking operations on or before [*date primary term expired*]?

"Drilling or reworking operations" means actual work or operations in which an ordinarily competent operator, under the same or similar circumstances, would engage in a good-faith effort with due diligence to cause a well or wells to produce oil or gas in paying quantities.

Answer "Yes" or "No."

Answer: _____

COMMENT

When to use.   PJC 303.15 should be used when there is a fact issue about whether the lessee's activity before the expiration of the primary term satisfied express lease requirements, generally found in an operations savings clause, that the lessee commence operations.

Source of question.   PJC 303.15 is derived from *Ridge Oil Co. v. Guinn Investments, Inc.*, 148 S.W.3d 143, 158–60 (Tex. 2004); *Rogers v. Osborn*, 261 S.W.2d 311, 314 (Tex. 1953); *Valence Operating Co. v. Anadarko Petroleum Corp.*, 303 S.W.3d 435, 441 (Tex. App.—Texarkana 2010, no pet.); *Bargsley v. Pryor Petroleum Corp.*, 196 S.W.3d 823, 826–27 (Tex. App.—Eastland 2006, pet. denied); *Utley v. Marathon Oil Co.*, 31 S.W.3d 274, 278–79 (Tex. App.—Waco 2000, no writ); and *Cox v. Stowers*, 786 S.W.2d 102, 105 (Tex. App.—Amarillo 1990, no writ).

What constitutes drilling operations.   In *Ridge Oil Co.*, 148 S.W.3d 143, the supreme court recognized that the staking of a well and obtaining a drilling permit, without further activity, were not "operations" as a matter of law. *Ridge Oil Co.*, 148 S.W.3d at 158–59. However, the court also discussed several cases in which acts, including making a well location, bringing equipment to the location, digging pits, drilling water wells, and erecting a derrick, followed by continuous operations, constituted "operations." *See Ridge Oil Co.*, 148 S.W.3d at 158–59. PJC 303.15 should be modified if "operations" are defined in the lease. For a discussion of whether the dispute should be submitted to the jury, see *Valence Operating Co.*, 303 S.W.3d at 440–41.

PJC 303.16   Question and Instruction on Failure to Commence Operations after Cessation of Production

QUESTION _____

Did *Larry Lessee* fail to commence additional drilling or reworking operations within [*indicate number of days specified in lease*] days after the well ceased to produce [*oil/gas*] [*in paying quantities*]?

"Drilling or reworking operations" means actual work or operations in which an ordinarily competent operator, under the same or similar circumstances, would engage in a good-faith effort with due diligence to cause a well or wells to produce oil or gas in paying quantities.

Answer "Yes" or "No."

Answer: _____

COMMENT

When to use. PJC 303.16 should be used when the lease specifies a period of time of nonproduction after which the lease terminates unless the lessee commences additional operations. Such language is generally found in a "cessation of production" savings clause. The cessation may be actual physical cessation or cessation in paying quantities. *Clifton v. Koontz*, 325 S.W.2d 684, 690 (Tex. 1959); *Bachler v. Rosenthal*, 798 S.W.2d 646, 648–49 (Tex. App.—Austin 1990, writ denied). For questions and instructions on cessation of production in paying quantities, see PJC 303.20. The above question and its instructions should conform to the language of the lease regarding the applicable time period, the event from which the time period is measured, any limitation on the applicability of the savings clause (e.g., whether the operation must be before the discovery of oil or gas or whether production ceased after the discovery of oil or gas), and any specific definitions of the operations required. *See, e.g., Stanolind Oil & Gas Co. v. Newman Bros. Drilling Co.*, 305 S.W.2d 169 (Tex. 1957); *Rogers v. Osborn*, 261 S.W.2d 311 (Tex. 1953). Finally, further instructions or additional questions may be needed to determine what actions constitute "drilling operations" or "reworking operations" if such terms are defined in the lease.

Source of question and instruction. PJC 303.16 is derived from *Ridge Oil Co. v. Guinn Investments, Inc.*, 148 S.W.3d 143, 158–60 (Tex. 2004); *Rogers*, 261 S.W.2d at 314; *Crystal River Oil & Gas, LLC v. Patton*, 510 S.W.3d 226 (Tex. App.—Eastland 2016, no pet.); *Valence Operating Co. v. Anadarko Petroleum Corp.*, 303 S.W.3d 435, 441 (Tex. App.—Texarkana 2010, no pet.); *Bargsley v. Pryor Petroleum Corp.*, 196 S.W.3d 823 (Tex. App.—Eastland 2006, pet. denied); *Utley v. Marathon Oil Co.*, 31

S.W.3d 274, 278–79 (Tex. App.—Waco 2000, no writ); and *Cox v. Stowers*, 786 S.W.2d 102, 105 (Tex. App.—Amarillo 1990, no writ).

PJC 303.17   **Question and Instruction on Failure to Prosecute
                  Operations without Cessation**

QUESTION _____

Did *Larry Lessee* fail to prosecute drilling or reworking operations without
cessation of more than [*indicate number of days specified in lease*] consecutive
days?

"Drilling or reworking operations" means actual work or operations in
which an ordinarily competent operator, under the same or similar circumstances, would engage in a good-faith effort with due diligence to cause a well
or wells to produce oil or gas in paying quantities.

Answer "Yes" or "No."

Answer: _____

COMMENT

When to use.   PJC 303.17 should be used when there is a dispute regarding
whether the lessee prosecuted its operations diligently and in a good-faith attempt to
establish commercial production as required by the express terms of a lease savings
clause. This language generally appears in an "operations" savings clause. However
the question and its instructions should conform to the language of the lease regarding
the applicable time period, the event from which the time period is measured, any limitation on the applicability of the clause (e.g., whether the operation must be before the
discovery of oil or gas or whether production ceased after the discovery of oil or gas),
and any specific definitions of the operations required. *See, e.g., Stanolind Oil & Gas
Co. v. Newman Bros. Drilling Co.*, 305 S.W.2d 169 (Tex. 1957).

Source of question and instruction.   PJC 303.17 is derived from *Ridge Oil Co. v.
Guinn Investments, Inc.*, 148 S.W.3d 143, 158–60 (Tex. 2004); *Rogers v. Osborn*, 261
S.W.2d 311, 313–14 (Tex. 1953); *Valence Operating Co. v. Anadarko Petroleum
Corp.*, 303 S.W.3d 435, 441 (Tex. App.—Texarkana 2010, no pet.); *Bargsley v. Pryor
Petroleum Corp.*, 196 S.W.3d 823, 826–28 (Tex. App.—Eastland 2006, pet. denied);
Utley v. Marathon Oil Co., 31 S.W.3d 274, 278–79 (Tex. App.—Waco 2000, no writ);
and *Cox v. Stowers*, 786 S.W.2d 102, 105 (Tex. App.—Amarillo 1990, no writ).

PJC 303.18   Question and Instruction on Failure to Commence Operations after Completion of Dry Hole

QUESTION _____

Did *Larry Lessee* fail to commence additional drilling or reworking operations within [*indicate number of days specified in lease*] days after the [*prior*] well was completed as a dry hole?

"Drilling or reworking operations" means actual work or operations in which an ordinarily competent operator, under the same or similar circumstances, would engage in a good-faith effort with due diligence to cause a well or wells to produce oil or gas in paying quantities.

Answer "Yes" or "No."

Answer: _____

COMMENT

When to use.   PJC 303.18 should be used when the lessee is relying on the dry hole clause to maintain the lease. This question must conform to the language of the lease regarding the applicable time period and the event from which the time period is measured, such as the completion of a dry hole or other reasons for cessation of operations. Additionally, the controlling oil and gas lease may limit the applicability of the clause (e.g., whether the operation must be before the discovery of oil or gas or whether production ceased after the discovery of oil or gas). *See, e.g., Rogers v. Osborn*, 261 S.W.2d 311, 313–14 (Tex. 1953); *Stanolind Oil & Gas Co. v. Newman Bros. Drilling Co.*, 305 S.W.2d 169, 174–75 (Tex. 1957). Finally, further instructions, revised instructions, or additional questions may be needed if underlying facts are in dispute.

Source of question and instructions.   PJC 303.18 is derived from *Rogers*, 261 S.W.2d at 313–14; *Valence Operating Co. v. Anadarko Petroleum Corp.*, 303 S.W.3d 435, 441 (Tex. App.—Texarkana 2010, no pet.); *Utley v. Marathon Oil Co.*, 31 S.W.3d 274, 278–79 (Tex. App.—Waco 2000, no writ); *Cox v. Stowers*, 786 S.W.2d 102, 105 (Tex. App.—Amarillo 1990, no writ); *Whelan v. R. Lacy Inc.*, 251 S.W.2d 175, 176 (Tex. App.—Texarkana 1952, writ ref'd n.r.e.) (recognizing that operations require diligence); *Phillips Petroleum v. Rudd*, 226 S.W.2d 464, 466 (Tex. App.—Texarkana 1949, no writ); and *Geier-Jackson, Inc. v. James*, 160 F. Supp. 524, 529 (E.D. Tex. 1958). For examples of what might constitute "drilling operations" or "reworking operations," *see Bargsley v. Pryor Petroleum Corp.*, 196 S.W.3d 823, 826–28 (Tex. App.—Eastland 2006, pet. denied).

PJC 303.19   Question on Cessation of Production

QUESTION _____

Did production of [*oil/gas*] from the lease in question cease?

Answer "Yes" or "No."

Answer: _____

COMMENT

When to use. PJC 303.19 should be used when there is a dispute about whether there has been a complete cessation of production of oil or gas, rather than a cessation of production in "paying quantities." (See PJC 303.20 for questions and instructions on cessation of production in paying quantities). Complete cessation is generally in issue when the lessee is relying on a "cessation of production" savings clause. *See Ridenour v. Herrington*, 47 S.W.3d 117, 121–22 (Tex. App.—Waco 2001, pet. denied); *Bachler v. Rosenthal*, 798 S.W.2d 646, 649–50 (Tex. App.—Austin 1990, writ denied) (holding that reasonably prudent operator test for paying quantities is not applicable with a physical cessation of production).

Source of question. PJC 303.19 is derived from *Watson v. Rochmill*, 155 S.W.2d 783, 784 (Tex. 1941), and *Bachler*, 798 S.W.2d at 649–50.

Cessation on pooled units. Absent specific language in the lease to the contrary, the lessor must show that all wells located on the land covered by the lease or pooled therewith ceased to produce, because generally production on one tract will operate to perpetuate the lease as to all tracts covered by or pooled with the lease. *Matthews v. Sun Oil Co.*, 425 S.W.2d 330, 333 (Tex. 1968); *Southland Royalty Co. v. Humble Oil & Refining Co.*, 249 S.W.2d 914, 916 (Tex. 1952); *Sabre Oil & Gas Corp. v. Gibson*, 72 S.W.3d 812, 818–19 (Tex. App.—Eastland 2002, pet. denied).

Date of cessation of production. If the jury answers "Yes" to PJC 303.19, see PJC 303.21 for a question regarding the date of the cessation.

PJC 303.20   Question and Instructions on Cessation of Production in Paying Quantities

PJC 303.20A   Question and Instruction on Cessation of Production in Paying Quantities

QUESTION _____

Did the lease cease to produce [*oil/gas*] in paying quantities?

A lease ceases to produce in paying quantities when production on the lease fails to yield a return in excess of operating and marketing costs over a reasonable period of time. A lease is producing in paying quantities even though drilling and equipment costs may never be repaid and the undertaking as a whole may ultimately result in a loss.

"Operating and marketing costs" include expenses such as taxes, overhead charges, labor, repair, depreciation on salvageable equipment, and periodic expenditures that were allocated to the well and that were used on the well in order to produce or keep it producing. You shall not consider any costs or expenses incurred in connection with the original drilling or the reworking of the well.

"Overhead charges" do not include administrative costs that would continue whether or not the well is producing.

"Depreciation on salvageable equipment" does not represent bookkeeping depreciation; rather, it is the actual physical depreciation in the salvage value of on-location production equipment as the result of continued operations.

Do not consider any capital expenses in determining whether the production from the well over a reasonable period of time yields a profit after deducting operating and marketing costs. "Capital expenses" means one-time investment expenses, such as drilling and equipping costs.

Answer "Yes" or "No."

Answer: _____

PJC 303.20B   Question and Instruction on Continued Production by Reasonably Prudent Operator

If you answered "Yes" to Question _____ [*303.20A*], then answer the following question. Otherwise, do not answer the following question.

QUESTION _____

Do you find that, under all the relevant circumstances, a reasonably prudent operator would not continue, for the purpose of making a profit and not merely for speculation, to operate the lease in the manner in which it was operated?

In deciding whether a prudent operator would not continue, for profit and not merely for speculation, to operate the lease in the manner in which it was operated, you must take into consideration all factors that would influence a reasonably prudent operator. Some of the factors include—

 1. the depletion of the reservoir and the price for which the lessee is able to sell his produce;

 2. the relative profitableness of other wells in the area;

 3. the operating and marketing costs of the lease;

 4. the lessee's net profit;

 5. the lease provisions;

 6. a reasonable period of time under the circumstances; and

 7. whether or not the lessee is holding the lease merely for speculative purposes.

Answer "Yes" or "No."

Answer: _____

COMMENT

When to use. PJC 303.20 should be used when the issue is whether a lease has terminated for failure to produce in paying quantities.

Source of question and instruction. PJC 303.20 is derived from *BP America Production Co. v. Laddex, Ltd.*, 513 S.W.3d 476 (Tex. 2017); *Skelly Oil Co. v. Archer*, 356 S.W.2d 774, 780–82 (Tex. 1961); *Clifton v. Koontz*, 325 S.W.2d 684, 691 (Tex. 1959); *Evans v. Gulf Oil Corp.*, 840 S.W.2d 500, 503 (Tex. App.—Corpus Christi–Edinburg 1992, writ denied); and *Pshigoda v. Texaco, Inc.*, 703 S.W.2d 416, 418 (Tex. App.—Amarillo 1986, writ ref'd n.r.e.).

Burden of proof in paying quantities case. Note that the burden of proof in a paying quantities case is on the lessor who alleges a failure to produce in paying quantities. *See Bargsley v. Pryor Petroleum Corp.*, 196 S.W.3d 823, 829 (Tex. App.—Eastland 2006, no writ).

Date of cessation of production.   If the jury answers "Yes" to both PJC 303.20A and 303.20B, see PJC 303.21 for a question regarding the date of the cessation.

PJC 303.21   Question on Date of Cessation of Production

QUESTION _____

On what date do you find that production [*ceased/ceased to produce in paying quantities*]?

Answer with a date in the blank below.

Answer: _____

COMMENT

When to use.   PJC 303.21 should be used to determine the date of cessation if the jury answers "Yes" to PJC 303.19 or 303.20A and 303.20B, and the nature of the dispute requires a determination of the date when the lease ceased to produce or produce in paying quantities. *Clifton v. Koontz*, 325 S.W.2d 684, 691 (Tex. 1959).

Source of question.   PJC 303.21 is derived from *Clifton*, 325 S.W.2d at 691.

PJC 303.22   **Question and Instruction on Temporary Cessation of Production**

QUESTION _____

Was the cessation of production of [*oil/gas*] from the lease in question temporary?

A cessation of production of oil or gas is temporary if the lessee acts with diligence to remedy the cessation and resumes production in a reasonable time.

Answer "Yes" or "No."

Answer: _____

COMMENT

When to use.   PJC 303.22 should be used if it has been determined that the cause of the cessation of production is a valid excuse under the temporary cessation of production doctrine. If the validity of the excuse is not determinable as a matter of law, an additional question or a modification of the question may be needed for the jury to determine that fact dispute. The above question is not appropriate when the lease contains an express "cessation of production" clause. *Ridenour v. Herrington*, 47 S.W.3d 117, 121–22 (Tex. App.—Waco 2001, pet. denied).

Source of question and instruction.   PJC 303.22 is derived from *Ridge Oil Co. v. Guinn Investments, Inc.*, 148 S.W.3d 143, 158 (Tex. 2004), and *Watson v. Rochmill*, 155 S.W.2d 783, 784 (Tex. 1941).

Scope of the temporary cessation of production doctrine.   Earlier cases suggested that the temporary cessation of production doctrine was limited to situations in which the cessation was the result of mechanical breakdown of equipment used in conjunction with the well, a sudden stoppage of production from the well, or the like or was unforeseen and unavoidable. *See, e.g., Amoco Production Co. v. Braslau*, 561 S.W.2d 805 (Tex. 1978); *Midwest Oil Corp. v. Winsauer*, 323 S.W.2d 944 (Tex. 1959); *Watson*, 155 S.W.2d at 784; *Scarborough v. New Domain Oil & Gas Co.*, 276 S.W. 331 (Tex. App.—El Paso 1925, writ dism'd). However, the Texas Supreme Court clarified that the doctrine is not so limited. *Ridge Oil Co.*, 148 S.W.3d at 151–52. The cause of the cessation need not be a sudden stoppage or a mechanical breakdown, nor must the cessation be unforeseeable and unavoidable. *Ridge Oil Co.*, 148 S.W.3d at 151–52. Instead, a variety of circumstances may qualify as a valid excuse under the doctrine, including situations in which the stoppage was voluntary, foreseeable, or avoidable. *Ridge Oil Co.*, 148 S.W.3d at 151–52. Whether a cause constitutes a valid excuse may be determined as a matter of law. *See, e.g., Winsauer*, 323 S.W.2d at 948. However, the validity of an excuse could also present a fact question. *See Braslau*, 561 S.W.2d at 806, 809–10 (affirming trial court's fact findings on temporary cessation, diligence, and resumption of production in reasonable time); *see also Ridge Oil Co.*, 148 S.W.3d at 151–52 (not requiring unforeseeable and unavoidable for valid excuse); *Natural Gas Pipeline Co. of America v. Pool*, 124 S.W.3d 188, 203–10 (Tex. 2003) (Jefferson, J., dissenting) (discussing history and purpose of temporary cessation of production doctrine and potential issues for the fact finder). If the doctrine applies to the cause of cessation, the lessee is entitled to a reasonable time in which to exercise diligence to remedy the defect and resume production. *Watson*, 155 S.W.2d at 784.

PJC 303.23   Question on Failure to Tender Shut-In

QUESTION _____

Did *Larry Lessee* fail to pay or tender a shut-in royalty payment as provided in the lease?

The lease provides [*insert express lease provision*].

Answer "Yes" or "No."

Answer: _____

COMMENT

When to use.   PJC 303.23 should be used when the lessee is relying on an express shut-in royalty clause to avoid lease termination. This question should be modified to reflect the language in the clause at issue and will require appropriate instructions defining the applicable provisions of the lease.

Source of question.   PJC 303.23 is derived from *BP America Production Co. v. Red Deer Resources, LLC*, 526 S.W.3d 389 (Tex. 2017); *Skelly Oil Co. v. Harris*, 352 S.W.2d 950, 953 (Tex. 1962); *Gulf Oil Corp. v. Reid*, 337 S.W.2d 267, 271 (Tex. 1960); *Blackmon v. XTO Energy, Inc.*, 276 S.W.3d 600, 605–07 (Tex. App.—Waco 2008, no pet.); *Hydrocarbon Management, Inc. v. Tracker Exploration, Inc.*, 861 S.W.2d 427, 431, 432 (Tex. App.—Amarillo 1993, no writ); *Mayers v. Sanchez-O'Brien Minerals Corp.*, 670 S.W.2d 704, 709 (Tex. App.—San Antonio 1984, writ refused n.r.e.); and *Duke v. Sun Oil Co.*, 320 F.2d 853, 858–59 (5th Cir. 1963).

PJC 303.24   **Question and Instruction on Determining Whether Well Qualifies as Shut-In Well**

QUESTION _____

Was the shut-in well on the leased premises [*or lands pooled therewith*] capable of producing [*oil/gas*] in paying quantities?

"Capable of producing in paying quantities" means:

    1.   the well, when turned on, does not need additional equipment, repairs, or pipeline facilities to produce and market oil or gas; and

    2.   over a reasonable period of time, the proceeds from the mineral produced by the well can generate a profit, however small, over current operating expenses, without regard to whether those profits ever repay the original drilling costs.

Answer "Yes" or "No."

Answer: _____

COMMENT

When to use. PJC 303.24 should be used when there is a dispute regarding whether the well or wells in question were capable of production for purposes of the shut-in clause. The instruction should be conformed to the language of the lease in issue and to the relevant time that the well ceased to produce.

Source of question and instruction. PJC 303.24 is derived from *BP America Production Co. v. Red Deer Resources, LLC*, 526 S.W.3d 389 (Tex. 2017); *Anadarko Petroleum Corp. v. Thompson*, 94 S.W.3d 550, 558 (Tex. 2002) (citing *Hydrocarbon Management, Inc. v. Tracker Exploration, Inc.*, 861 S.W.2d 427, 434 (Tex. App.— Amarillo 1993, no writ)), and *Clifton v. Koontz*, 325 S.W.2d 684, 690–91 (Tex. 1959).

Capable of producing in paying quantities. Unless the lease provides otherwise, a mineral lease that does not have a well capable of producing in paying quantities may not be perpetuated merely by payment of shut-in royalties. *Red Deer Resources, LLC*, 526 S.W.3d at 396–98; *Hydrocarbon Management, Inc.*, 861 S.W.2d at 432–33; *Kidd v. Hoggett*, 331 S.W.2d 515, 519 (Tex. App.—San Antonio 1959, writ ref'd n.r.e.); *see also Peveto v. Starkey*, 645 S.W.2d 770, 771 (Tex. 1982) (citing *Archer County v. Webb*, 338 S.W.2d 435 (1969)); *EnerQuest Oil & Gas v. Plains Exploration & Production Co.*, 981 F. Supp. 2d 575, 587 (W.D. Tex. 2013). "Capable of producing" means that the well will produce in paying quantities if the well is turned "on" and it begins flowing, without additional equipment or repair. *Red Deer*

Resources, LLC, 526 S.W.3d at 399. The time at which the well must be capable of producing in paying quantities may be affected by language in the lease. *Red Deer Resources, LLC*, 526 S.W.3d at 399–400.

PJC 303.25   Question on Force Majeure

QUESTION _____

Did [*insert claimed force majeure event*] [*prevent lessee from/result in les-see's failure to/cause lessee's delay in*] [*insert obligation, e.g., maintain(ing) production*]?

Answer "Yes" or "No."

Answer: _____

COMMENT

When to use.   PJC 303.25 should be used when there is a fact dispute regarding the application of the force majeure clause to avoid a lease obligation or termination. The specific terms in the force majeure clause will control. *Hydrocarbon Management, Inc. v. Tracker Exploration, Inc.*, 861 S.W.2d 427, 436 (Tex. App.—Amarillo 1993, no writ).

Source of question.   PJC 303.25 is derived from *Hydrocarbon Management, Inc.*, 861 S.W.2d at 436 (noting that "lease terms are controlling regarding force majeure, and common law rules merely fill in gaps left by lease"); *Moore v. Jet Stream Invest-ments, Ltd.*, 261 S.W.3d 412, 420 (Tex. App.—Texarkana 2008, pet. denied); and *Sun Operating Ltd. Partnership v. Holt*, 984 S.W.2d 277, 282–83 (Tex. App.—Amarillo 1998, writ denied).

Burden of proof.   The lessee has the burden to prove the affirmative defense of force majeure. *Sun Operating Ltd. Partnership*, 984 S.W.2d at 290 (citing *Hydrocar-bon Management, Inc.*, 861 S.W.2d at 436).

Other fact disputes.   The terms of the lease may impose requirements other than causation. If so, consider whether additional modification or other questions or instructions are required to resolve any factual dispute on those requirements. *See Rowan Cos. v. Transco Exploration Co.*, 679 S.W.2d 660, 662, 664 (Tex. App.—Hous-ton [1st Dist.] 1984, writ ref'd n.r.e.) (noting question on clause's reasonable control requirement submitted to jury but undisputed evidence established fire not in lessee's control; clause's notice requirement not submitted to jury to the extent clause made notice a condition precedent to invoking clause); *see also Moore*, 261 S.W.3d at 420 (discussing whether order to cease production prevented production if regulatory order not "beyond reasonable control" of lessee, in absence of contractual lack-of-control requirement). *Cf. Wolf Hollow I, L.P. v. El Paso Marketing, L.P.*, 409 S.W.3d 879, 885–87 (Tex. App.—Houston [14th Dist.] 2013) (noting when facts regarding cause and duration of each delivery were undisputed, legal question presented in appeal of summary judgment is "whether or not these are events of force majeure as described in the contract"), *rev'd on other grounds*, 450 S.W.3d 121 (Tex. 2014).

PJC 304.1   Breach of Executive Rights Duty (Comment)

The executive right is one of the real property rights incident to the mineral estate. It includes the exclusive right to explore for and develop the minerals as well as the exclusive right to execute mineral leases and other written agreements concerning the mineral estate. *Lesley v. Veterans Land Board*, 352 S.W.3d 479, 487 (Tex. 2011); *French v. Chevron U.S.A., Inc.*, 896 S.W.2d 795, 797 n.1 (Tex. 1995); *Altman v. Blake*, 712 S.W.2d 117, 118 (Tex. 1986). The executive right can be severed and owned separately from other incidents of mineral ownership in various ways and for a variety of reasons. *Lesley*, 352 S.W.3d at 487. It remains a property interest even if severed by conveyance from other interests in the minerals. *Day & Co. v. Texland Petroleum, Inc.*, 786 S.W.2d 667, 669 (Tex. 1990). An interest in the minerals severed from the executive right is a non-executive interest. A non-executive interest can be in the form of a nonparticipating mineral interest, as in *Lesley*, or a nonparticipating royalty interest, as in *KCM Financial LLC v. Bradshaw*, 457 S.W.3d 70 (Tex. 2015), and *In re Bass*, 113 S.W.3d 735, 745 (Tex. 2002). The Texas Supreme Court has imposed a duty on the owner of the executive rights in favor of the holders of non-executive interests. Because of the various transactions that can arise affecting non-executive mineral or royalty interests, as well as the different ways conflicts can arise, the court has stated that it is "difficult to determine precisely what duty the executive owes the non-executive interest." *Lesley*, 352 S.W.3d at 487–88.

The court has described the duty of the executive as "fiduciary," and it has long been characterized as a relationship "of trust," with a duty of "utmost fair dealing." *Lesley*, 352 S.W.3d at 490 (citing *Manges v. Guerra*, 673 S.W.2d 180, 183 (Tex. 1984)); *see also HECI Exploration Co. v. Neel*, 982 S.W.2d 881, 888 (Tex. 1998); *Andretta v. West*, 415 S.W.2d 638, 641 (Tex. 1967); *Schlittler v. Smith*, 101 S.W.2d 543, 544 (Tex. 1937). However, the executive's duty to the non-executive is not that of a true fiduciary. In *Texas Outfitters Limited, LLC v. Nicholson*, 572 S.W.3d 647 (Tex. 2019), the court described the executive rights duty as a "duty of utmost good faith and fair dealing" that does not require the executive to "subjugate his interests to those of the non-executive" but requires the executive to "acquire for the non-executive every benefit that he exacts for himself." *Texas Outfitters Limited, LLC*, 572 S.W.3d at 649, 652 (citing *KCM Financial LLC*, 457 S.W.3d at 81). While a traditional fiduciary is required to subordinate his interest to that of another, "the executive is not required to grant priority to the non-executive's interest." *KCM Financial LLC*, 457 S.W.3d at 81.

The complex nature of the executive's relationship to the non-executive often leads to conflict between their separate interests. The executive is allowed to resolve these conflicts without subordinating his rights to the non-executive but is prohibited from engaging in acts of self-dealing that "unfairly diminish[] the value of the non-executive interest." *KCM Financial LLC*, 457 S.W.3d at 82. "Thus, in ascertaining whether the executive breached its duty to the non-executive, the controlling inquiry is whether the executive engaged in acts of self-dealing that unfairly diminished the value of the non-executive interest." *KCM Financial LLC*, 457 S.W.3d at 82.

Actionable self-dealing "has most commonly been observed in situations where the executive employs a legal contrivance to benefit himself, a close familial relation, or both." *KCM Financial LLC*, 457 S.W.3d at 81; *see, e.g., Manges*, 673 S.W.2d at 183; *Luecke v. Wallace*, 951 S.W.2d 267 (Tex. App.—Austin 1997, no pet.); *Dearing, Inc. v. Spiller*, 824 S.W.2d 728 (Tex. App.—Fort Worth 1992, writ denied). Actionable self-dealing has been found when the executive, who also owned the surface estate, had knowledge that other undivided mineral owners leased their interest to a particular lessee, but refused to lease to that same lessee in order to reap the benefits of an "unburdened" surface estate. *Texas Outfitters Limited, LLC*, 572 S.W.3d at 657. Actionable self-dealing has also been observed when the executive attempts to deprive the non-executive of a term-limited interest. *Comanche Land & Cattle Co. v. Adams*, 688 S.W.2d 914, 916 (Tex. App.—Eastland 1985, no writ); *Kimsey v. Fore*, 593 S.W.2d 107, 112 (Tex. App.—Beaumont 1979, writ ref'd n.r.e.).

PJC 304.2   **Question and Instruction on Breach of Executive Rights Duty**

QUESTION _____

Did *Don Davis* fail to comply with *his* executive duty to *Paul Payne*?

Don Davis fails to comply with *his* executive duty if *he* engages in acts of self-dealing that unfairly diminish the value of *Paul Payne*'s [*royalty/mineral*] interests.

Answer "Yes" or "No."

Answer: _____

COMMENT

When to use.   PJC 304.2 is appropriate for use when a non-executive claims an executive has failed to comply with the duty owed to him.

Source of question and instruction.   The question and instruction are based on principles stated in *KCM Financial LLC v. Bradshaw*, 457 S.W.3d 70, 81–82 (Tex. 2015) (holding that the controlling inquiry is whether executive engaged in acts of self-dealing that unfairly diminished value of non-executive interest), and *Texas Outfitters Limited, LLC v. Nicholson*, 572 S.W.3d 647, 654 (Tex. 2019) (holding that the "controlling inquiry" stated in *KCM Financial LLC* applied whether challenged conduct consists of leasing or refusing to lease).

Modification of question.   The court has described the parameters of the executive duty as "'difficult to determine,' 'imprecise,' and unsusceptible to a 'bright line rule.'" *Texas Outfitters Limited, LLC*, 572 S.W.3d at 652 (citing *Lesley v. Veterans Land Board*, 352 S.W.3d 479, 488 (Tex. 2011); *KCM Financial LLC*, 457 S.W.3d at 74). "Evaluating compliance with the executive duty is rarely straightforward and is heavily dependent on the facts and circumstances." *Texas Outfitters Limited, LLC*, 572 S.W.3d at 653. This question and instruction may be modified to reflect the specific facts of the case. *See Texas Outfitters Limited, LLC*, 572 S.W.3d at 657; *KCM Financial LLC*, 457 S.W.3d at 74; *Lesley*, 352 S.W.3d at 487–88.

Actions that trigger duty.   Generally, the executive's duties to the non-executive are not triggered until some aspect of the executive rights is exercised. Such exercise occurs by executing a lease for the minerals in which the non-executive has an interest and also occurs in refusing to accept a lease offer. *See In re Bass*, 113 S.W.3d 735, 745 (Tex. 2002); *see also Texas Outfitters Limited, LLC*, 572 S.W.3d at 657. The duty may also be triggered by actions preventing mineral development. *See Lesley*, 352 S.W.3d at 491. The executive's inaction could violate the duty if, for example, a refusal to lease is arbitrary or motivated by the executive's self-interest to the non-executive's detriment. *Lesley*, 352 S.W.3d at 491.

Damages.   For a question on actual damages for breach of the executive rights duty, see PJC 313.16.

PJC 305.1   Oil and Gas Industry Contracts (Comment)

Contracts in the oil and gas industry are typically governed by general contract principles. Contracts specific to the oil and gas industry, other than the oil and gas lease, are described below and include joint operating agreements, farmout agreements, preferential right to purchase agreements, and areas of mutual interest agreements.

Disputes involving the agreements discussed below may be resolved with general contract principles. As such, the applicable questions and instructions provided in the current edition of State Bar of Texas, *Texas Pattern Jury Charges—Business, Consumer, Insurance & Employment* chapter 101 have been included in this chapter in their entirety. The corresponding defense questions have also been included in chapter 312 of this volume, and the corresponding damages questions have been included in chapter 313.

However, the express terms of an exculpatory clause in a joint operating agreement often require a finding of gross negligence or willful misconduct in order to impose liability for a breach. The terms and application of exculpatory clauses in joint operating agreements have been frequently litigated. For that reason, in addition to the questions generally applicable in contracts disputes, this chapter provides questions and instructions specific to the joint operating agreement that reflect case law requirements unique to joint operating agreement exculpatory clauses. In all circumstances, these questions and instructions must be modified as appropriate to fit the facts of each individual case.

Joint operating agreements. An "operating agreement" or "joint operating agreement" (often referred to as a "JOA") is an agreement for the exploration and development of a described area of land commonly defined as the "contract area." Under the JOA, a party is designated as the operator with the authority to conduct all operations in the contract area. The other parties to the JOA are designated as nonoperators, joint interest owners, or working interest owners. The agreement generally contains detailed provisions concerning drilling and production operations and responsibilities regarding expenses and accounting, for example, the accounting procedures of the Council of Petroleum Accountants Societies (COPAS). The JOA describes the authority of and restrictions placed on the operator. *See* Patrick H. Martin & Bruce M. Kramer, 8 *Williams and Meyers, Manual of Oil and Gas Terms* 528 (2014). The JOA generally sets forth the standard of care required of the operator.

There is no standard JOA; however, the American Association of Professional Landmen (AAPL) has published several versions of its standard form beginning in 1956, with revisions in 1977, 1982, and 1989. These AAPL forms are commonly used for Texas onshore oil and gas joint operations but often contain various modifications. Each of these forms is distinct, and legal precedent under one form may not apply to all the forms. *See, e.g., Reeder v. Wood County Energy, L.L.C.*, 395 S.W.3d 789 (Tex. 2012) (comparing exculpatory clauses under 1977 JOA, 1982 JOA, and 1989 JOA);

Valence Operating Co. v. Dorsett, 164 S.W.3d 656 (Tex. 2005) (interpreting modified 1977 AAPL Form 610 Model Form Operating Agreement's notice requirements affecting nonoperators' rights to consent to drilling operations).

Farmout agreements.   A "farmout agreement" is an agreement in which a lease owner agrees to assign a lease or some portion of it to another in exchange for specified drilling obligations. *See, e.g., Mengden v. Peninsula Production Co.*, 544 S.W.2d 643, 645 n.1 (Tex. 1976) (a primary characteristic of a farmout is obligation or right of assignee to drill one or more wells on assigned acreage as prerequisite to completion of transfer). The assignor may retain a share of the interest assigned, for example, an overriding royalty, back-in working interest, or production payment. Martin & Kramer, 2 *Williams & Meyers, Oil and Gas Law*, at § 432.

Preferential right to purchase agreements.   A "preferential right to purchase" is a right of one party to buy the interest of another, usually by matching the terms of a good-faith offer made by a third party. A preferential right to purchase may exist as an independent agreement between the parties or as a part of another agreement. In an oil and gas context, the preferential right to purchase is usually included as part of an operating agreement or farmout agreement. Other names for this type of agreement include "preference right," "preference right to purchase," "first privilege to purchase," "preemption," "preemptive right," "first right of refusal," "first refusal clause," and "right of first refusal." Martin & Kramer, 8 *Williams & Meyers, Manual of Oil and Gas Terms*, at 792.

Area of mutual interest agreements.   An "area of mutual interest" agreement or "AMI" is an agreement by which the parties attempt to describe a geographical area within which they agree to share certain leases or other interests acquired by any of them in the future. *See Westland Oil Development Corp. v. Gulf Oil Corp.*, 637 S.W.2d 903, 905 (Tex. 1982). While not contained in the body of any of the AAPL joint operating agreement forms, the parties often add an AMI to the JOA. *See* Martin & Kramer, 8 *Williams and Meyers, Manual of Oil and Gas Terms*, at 55.

This chapter also includes a question and instruction on reformation, which could be relevant for a variety of contract disputes when one party asserts that the document does not reflect the parties' agreement. Additionally, in recent years, reformation has been an issue in mineral and royalty deed disputes.

PJC 305.2 **Basic Question—Existence**

QUESTION _____

Did *Paul Payne* and *Don Davis* agree [*insert all disputed terms*]?

[*Insert instructions, if appropriate.*]

Answer "Yes" or "No."

Answer: _____

COMMENT

When to use. PJC 305.2 submits the issue of the existence of an agreement. It should be used if there is a dispute about the existence of an agreement or its terms and a specific factual finding is necessary to determine whether the agreement constitutes a legally binding contract. (See the discussion of consideration and essential terms below.) Usually PJC 305.2 will apply in cases involving oral agreements, oral modification of written agreements, and agreements based on several written instruments.

Broad-form submission. PJC 305.2 is a broad-form question designed to be accompanied by one or more appropriate instructions. Tex. R. Civ. P. 277 requires that "the court shall, whenever feasible, submit the cause upon broad-form questions." Tex. R. Civ. P. 277; *see Thota v. Young*, 366 S.W.3d 678, 689 (Tex. 2012) (rule 277's use of "whenever feasible" mandates broad-form submission in any or every instance in which it is capable of being accomplished). For further discussion, see PJC 314.2 regarding broad-form issues and the *Casteel* doctrine.

In some cases an even broader question that combines issues of both existence and breach of an agreement may be appropriate. For example:

Did *Don Davis* fail to comply with the agreement, if any?

In such a case, however, care should be taken that the submission does not ask the jury to decide questions of law, which must be determined by the court alone. *MCI Telecommunications Corp. v. Texas Utilities Electric Co.*, 995 S.W.2d 647, 650–51 (Tex. 1999) (construction of unambiguous contract is question of law for court).

Accompanying instructions. In most cases, the court should instruct the jury to consider the facts and circumstances surrounding the contract's execution. See PJC 305.4.

Essential terms. To be enforceable, a contract must be reasonably definite and certain. *T.O. Stanley Boot Co. v. Bank of El Paso*, 847 S.W.2d 218, 221 (Tex. 1992). Failure to agree on or include an essential term renders a contract unenforceable. *T.O.*

Stanley Boot Co., 847 S.W.2d at 221. The court should include in PJC 305.2 all disputed terms essential to create an enforceable agreement. A disputed nonessential term should also be included if it is the basis of the plaintiff's claim for damages.

Some omitted terms supplied by law. Some omitted terms will be supplied by application of law, and the failure to include those terms will not render the agreement invalid. See, e.g., PJC 305.11 (instruction on time of compliance) and 305.14 (instruction on price). In such cases it is not necessary to secure a jury finding on the parties' agreement to those terms, and they should not be included in PJC 305.2 unless their absence will be confusing to the jury. *See America's Favorite Chicken Co. v. Samaras*, 929 S.W.2d 617, 625 (Tex. App.—San Antonio 1996, writ denied). The circumstances of each case will determine whether it is appropriate to include instructions such as those contemplated by PJC 305.11 and 305.14.

Agreement contemplating further negotiations or writings. During negotiations, the parties may agree to some terms of the agreement with the expectation that other terms are to be agreed on later. Such an expectation may not prevent the agreement already made from being an enforceable agreement if the circumstances indicate that the parties intended to be bound. *Railroad Commission of Texas v. Gulf Energy Exploration Corp.*, 482 S.W.3d 559, 572–75 (Tex. 2016). In such a case, the basic issue submitted in PJC 305.2 should be modified to inquire whether the parties intended to bind themselves to an agreement that includes the terms initially agreed on. *Railroad Commission of Texas*, 482 S.W.3d 559. Case law suggests the following question:

> Did *Paul Payne* and *Don Davis* intend to bind themselves to an agreement that included the following terms:
>
> *[Insert disputed terms.]*

A similar issue is presented if the parties reach preliminary agreement on certain material terms yet also contemplate a future written document. Whether the parties intended to be bound in the absence of execution of the final written document is ordinarily a question of fact. *Foreca, S.A. v. GRD Development Co.*, 758 S.W.2d 744 (Tex. 1988). The *Foreca* opinion approves the following submission in such a case:

> Do you find that the writings of *September 2, 2001*, and *October 19, 2001*, constituted an agreement whereby [*insert disputed terms*]?

The court cited comment c to section 27 of the *Restatement (Second) of Contracts* (1981) as setting forth circumstances that may be helpful in determining whether a contract has been formed. *Foreca, S.A.*, 758 S.W.2d at 746 n.2. The court did not make it clear, however, whether these considerations should be included in the jury instructions.

PJC 305.3   Basic Question—Compliance (Non-JOA)

QUESTION _____

Did *Don Davis* fail to comply with *the agreement*?

[Insert instructions, if appropriate.]

Answer "Yes" or "No."

Answer: _____

COMMENT

When to use.   If breach is the only issue in dispute, no predicate is required. Otherwise, PJC 305.3 should be submitted predicated on an affirmative answer to PJC 305.2. For questions specifically addressing the joint operating agreement, see PJC 305.27 and 305.28.

Broad-form submission.   PJC 305.3 is a broad-form question designed to be accompanied by one or more appropriate instructions. Tex. R. Civ. P. 277 requires that "the court shall, whenever feasible, submit the cause upon broad-form questions." Tex. R. Civ. P. 277; *see Thota v. Young*, 366 S.W.3d 678, 689 (Tex. 2012) (rule 277's use of "whenever feasible" mandates broad-form submission in any or every instance in which it is capable of being accomplished). For further discussion, see PJC 314.2 regarding broad-form issues and the *Casteel* doctrine.

When a broad-form submission is not feasible, the cause may be submitted on more limited fact-specific questions, such as—

Did *Don Davis* fail *[insert alleged failure]*?

Disjunctive question for competing claims of material breach.   If both parties allege a breach of contract against one another, the court can ask the breach-of-contract question disjunctively, together with an appropriate instruction directing the jury to decide who committed the first material breach. *Mustang Pipeline Co. v. Driver Pipeline Co.*, 134 S.W.3d 195, 200 (Tex. 2004). An alternative way to submit competing claims of breach of an agreement is set forth below.

QUESTION 1

Did *Don Davis* fail to comply with *the agreement*?

[Insert instructions, if appropriate.]

Answer "Yes" or "No."

Answer: _____

QUESTION 2

Did *Paul Payne* fail to comply with *the agreement*?

[Insert instructions, if appropriate.]

Answer "Yes" or "No."

Answer: _____

If you answered "Yes" to both Question 1 and Question 2, then answer Question 3. Otherwise, do not answer Question 3.

QUESTION 3

Who failed to comply with *the agreement* first?

Answer *"Don Davis"* or *"Paul Payne."*

Answer: _____

The Committee believes that this conditional submission satisfies the supreme court's instruction in *Mustang Pipeline Co.*, 134 S.W.3d at 200, to have the jury determine which party breached first and thereby excuse performance by the other party. *See Mustang Pipeline Co.*, 134 S.W.3d at 200. The Committee recommends that any damages submission be predicated on a "Yes" answer to Question 1 or Question 2, but not on the answer to Question 3, which submits the defense of prior material breach. *National City Bank of Indiana v. Ortiz*, 401 S.W.3d 867, 883 n.11 (Tex. App.—Houston [14th Dist.] 2013, no pet.).

Material breach.   If the parties dispute whether the alleged breach is a material one, the court should insert any or all of the following instructions regarding materiality, as appropriate:

A failure to comply must be material. The circumstances to consider in determining whether a failure to comply is material include:

1.   the extent to which the injured party will be deprived of the benefit which he reasonably expected;

2.   the extent to which the injured party can be adequately compensated for the part of that benefit of which he will be deprived;

3.   the extent to which the party failing to perform or to offer to perform will suffer forfeiture;

4.   the likelihood that the party failing to perform or to offer to perform will cure his failure, taking into account the circumstances including any reasonable assurances;

5.   the extent to which the behavior of the party failing to perform or to offer to perform comports with standards of good faith and fair dealing.

See Mustang Pipeline Co., 134 S.W.3d at 199 (adopting *Restatement (Second) of Contracts* § 241 (1981)). See also PJC 312.2.

Integrated written document.   If the dispute arises from an integrated written document, a phrase identifying the agreement should be substituted for the words *the agreement. See Intercontinental Group Partnership v. KB Home Lone Star L.P.*, 295 S.W.3d 650, 652 n.5 (Tex. 2009) ("Did Intercontinental Group Partnership fail to comply with the Santa Clara Lot Contract?").

Implied terms.   If the alleged breach involves an omitted term, such as time of compliance, an additional instruction is necessary. See, e.g., PJC 305.11 and 305.14.

Interpretation.   Construction of an unambiguous term is an issue for the court. *Milner v. Milner*, 361 S.W.3d 615, 619 (Tex. 2012). If appropriate, an instruction should be included giving the jury the correct interpretation of that term. See PJC 305.8. If the court determines that a particular provision is ambiguous, an instruction on resolving that ambiguity should be included. See PJC 305.9.

Caveat.   Care must be taken to ensure that the question is appropriate under the facts of the particular case. Many contract disputes focus entirely on issues such as defenses, damages, promissory estoppel, quantum meruit, or agency, which are addressed in other parts of this volume. In such cases the parties may not need any form of PJC 305.3. If the only jury question is the validity of a defense, PJC 305.3 is not appropriate, and the instruction appropriate to that defense (e.g., PJC 312.1–312.13) may be rewritten as the question.

UCC good-faith obligation.   Every contract or duty governed by the Uniform Commercial Code imposes an obligation of good faith in its performance or enforcement. Tex. Bus. & Com. Code § 1.304 (Tex. UCC); *El Paso Natural Gas Co. v. Minco Oil & Gas, Inc.*, 8 S.W.3d 309, 313 (Tex. 1999). The failure to act in good faith under the UCC does not create an independent cause of action. *Northern Natural Gas Co. v. Conoco, Inc.*, 986 S.W.2d 603, 606 (Tex. 1998) (to be actionable, bad-faith conduct must relate to some aspect of performance under terms of contract).

Except as otherwise provided in chapter 5 of the Code, "'Good faith' . . . means honesty in fact and the observance of reasonable commercial standards of fair dealing." Tex. UCC § 1.201(b)(20).

If the transaction is covered by the Code, the following instruction would be appropriate to submit with the basic question:

> In addition to the language of the agreement, the law imposes on a party to a contract a duty to [*perform*] [*enforce*] [*perform or enforce*] the contract in good faith. In that connection, good faith means honesty in fact and the observance of reasonable commercial standards of fair dealing.

Depending on the pleadings and evidence in the particular case, the court may instruct on performance or enforcement or both.

If a party contends that the agreement defines the standards for good-faith performance, the jury should be instructed as follows:

> The parties to the agreement may by agreement determine the standards by which the performance of the obligation of good faith is to be measured if such standards are not manifestly unreasonable.

Tex. UCC § 1.302(b). The Committee is not aware of any Texas case supporting a departure from the language of section 1.302(b) (formerly section 1.102(c)).

Good and workmanlike manner. In some cases involving construction, repairs, and some services, there is an obligation to perform in a good and workmanlike manner. See the current edition of State Bar of Texas, *Texas Pattern Jury Charges—Business, Consumer, Insurance & Employment* PJC 102.12.

PJC 305.4   **Instruction on Formation of Agreement**

In deciding whether the parties reached an agreement, you may consider what they said and did in light of the surrounding circumstances, including any earlier course of dealing. You may not consider the parties' unexpressed thoughts or intentions.

COMMENT

When to use.   If appropriate, PJC 305.4 should be submitted with the question on the existence of a contract (PJC 305.2) to confine the jury's deliberations on the issue of contract formation to legally appropriate factors.

Source of instruction.   The supreme court has explained that the parties' intent expressed in the text should be "understood in light of the facts and circumstances surrounding the contract's execution." *Houston Exploration Co. v. Wellington Underwriting Agencies*, 352 S.W.3d 462, 469 (Tex. 2011). Surrounding circumstances include the commercial or other setting in which the contract was negotiated and facts that give a context to the transaction between the parties. *Houston Exploration Co.*, 352 S.W.3d at 469 (citing *Williston on Contracts* § 32.7 (4th ed. 1999)). However, "evidence of surrounding facts and circumstances . . . cannot be used to add, alter, or change the contract's agreed-to terms." *Barrow-Shaver Resources Co. v. Carrizo Oil & Gas, Inc.*, 590 S.W.3d 471, 485 (Tex. 2019).

Only what the parties "said and did, rather than the parties' subjective state of mind," may be considered. *Lindsey Construction, Inc. v. AutoNation Financial Services, LLC*, 541 S.W.3d 355, 363 (Tex. App.—Houston [14th Dist.] 2017, no pet.). An agreement may be implied from and evidenced by the parties' conduct in the light of the surrounding circumstances, including any earlier course of dealing. *McAllen Hospitals, L.P. v. Lopez*, 576 S.W.3d 389, 392 (Tex. 2019).

Generally, silence and inaction cannot be construed as an assent to an offer because "[s]ilence as to a material term differs from silence as to an immaterial or non-essential term." *Barrow-Shaver Resources Co.*, 590 S.W.3d at 481 ("Material and essential terms are those that the parties would consider 'vitally important ingredients' to their agreement.") (quoting *Fischer v. CTMI, L.L.C.*, 479 S.W.3d 231 (Tex. 2016)); *Texas Ass'n of Counties County Government Risk Management Pool v. Matagorda County*, 52 S.W.3d 128, 132 (Tex. 2000) (applying 2 *Williston on Contracts* § 6.49 (4th ed. 1999)). Contractual "terms need be definite and certain only as to the terms that are 'material and essential' to the agreement." *Barrow-Shaver Resources Co.*, 590 S.W.3d at 481 (citing *Fischer*, 479 S.W.3d at 237).

"Parol evidence rule" distinguished from "surrounding circumstances" evidence. The supreme court has provided the following guidance concerning the distinctions between parol evidence and surrounding circumstances:

> "[O]bjectively determinable facts and circumstances that contextualize the parties' transaction" may help clarify the parties' intent as expressed in the text of their written agreement. *URI*, [Inc. v. Kleberg County,] 543 S.W.3d [755], 757–58 [(Tex. 2018)]. The parol evidence rule prohibits us from relying on such evidence to "create ambiguity in the contract's text," *Community Health Systems Professional Services Corp. v. Hansen*, 525 S.W.3d 671, 688 (Tex. 2017), to "augment, alter, or contradict the terms of an unambiguous contract," *URI*, 543 S.W.3d at 757–58, to "show that the parties probably meant, or could have meant, something other than what their agreement stated," *Anglo-Dutch Petroleum International, Inc. v. Greenberg Peden, P.C.*, 352 S.W.3d 445, 451 (Tex. 2011), or to "make the language say what it unambiguously does not say," *[First Bank v.] Brumitt*, 519 S.W.3d [95,] 110 [(Tex. 2017)]. But evidence of surrounding circumstances may "aid the understanding of an unambiguous contract's language," "inform the meaning" of the language actually used, and "provide context that elucidates the meaning of the words employed." *URI*, 543 S.W.3d at 757–59.

Piranha Partners v. Neuhoff, 596 S.W.3d 740, 749 (Tex. 2020).

UCC article 2 cases. Tex. Bus. & Com. Code § 1.201(b)(3) (Tex. UCC) defines "agreement" and includes those factors that may be considered in determining the existence of an agreement. *See also* Tex. UCC § 1.303 (course of performance, course of dealing, and usage of trade), § 2.202 (final written expression: parol evidence), § 2.204 (formation in general).

PJC 305.5   Instruction on Authority

A party's conduct includes the conduct of another who acts with the party's authority or apparent authority.

Authority for another to act for a party must arise from the party's agreement that the other act on behalf and for the benefit of the party. If a party so authorizes another to perform an act, that other party is also authorized to do whatever else is proper, usual, and necessary to perform the act expressly authorized.

Apparent authority exists if a party (1) knowingly permits another to hold himself out as having authority or, (2) through lack of ordinary care, bestows on another such indications of authority that lead a reasonably prudent person to rely on the apparent existence of authority to his detriment. Only the acts of the party sought to be charged with responsibility for the conduct of another may be considered in determining whether apparent authority exists.

COMMENT

When to use.   PJC 305.5 may be appropriate if the evidence raises a question of express, implied, or apparent authority. It is to be used only to determine whether a party is contractually bound by the conduct of another. In common-law tort and statutory actions, where the issue is a party's vicarious liability for the wrongful conduct of another, different rules of law may apply.

Express authority.   Express authority arises from the principal's agreement that the agent act on the principal's behalf and for his benefit. *Clark's-Gamble, Inc. v. State*, 486 S.W.2d 840, 845 (Tex. App.—Amarillo 1972, writ ref'd n.r.e.) (upholding charge submission that an "agent is one who acts in behalf of another under the latter's authority and for the latter's benefit"); *see Gaines v. Kelly*, 235 S.W.3d 179, 183 (Tex. 2007) (an agent's authority to act on behalf of a principal depends on some communication by the principal to the agent).

Implied authority.   Implied authority arises by implication from a grant of express authority. A grant of express authority implies authority to do those acts proper, usual, and necessary to perform the act expressly authorized. *Nears v. Holiday Hospitality Franchising, Inc.*, 295 S.W.3d 787, 795 (Tex. App.—Texarkana 2009, no pet.).

Apparent authority.   Apparent authority, which is based partly on estoppel, may arise from two sources: first, from the principal's knowingly allowing an agent to claim authority; and second, from the principal's negligently bestowing on the agent such indications of authority that a reasonably prudent person is led to rely on the existence of that authority. *Gaines*, 235 S.W.3d at 182–84.

Because apparent authority is based on estoppel, the principal's conduct must be that which would lead a reasonably prudent person to believe that authority exists. *Gaines*, 235 S.W.3d at 182. A principal's full knowledge of all material facts is essential to establish a claim of apparent authority, and only the conduct of the principal is relevant for determining the existence of apparent authority. *Gaines*, 235 S.W.3d at 182.

If apparent authority is not an issue, the phrase "or apparent authority" should be deleted from the first paragraph of the instruction, along with the definition of apparent authority.

PJC 305.6   Instruction on Ratification

A party's conduct includes conduct of others that the party has ratified. Ratification may be express or implied.

Implied ratification occurs if a party, though he may have been unaware of unauthorized conduct taken on his behalf at the time it occurred, retains the benefits of the transaction involving the unauthorized conduct after he acquired full knowledge of the unauthorized conduct. Implied ratification results in the ratification of the entire transaction.

COMMENT

When to use.   PJC 305.6 may be appropriate if a party seeks to avoid liability on the basis that the act of a purported agent was unauthorized or if a party seeks to hold another responsible for unauthorized but ratified conduct.

Source of instruction.   The instruction is derived from *Land Title Co. v. F.M. Stigler, Inc.*, 609 S.W.2d 754 (Tex. 1980) (ratification occurs if principal retains benefits of transaction after full knowledge of unauthorized acts of person acting on principal's behalf). *See also Willis v. Donnelly*, 199 S.W.3d 262, 273 (Tex. 2006).

Timing of knowledge.   A principal may ratify the conduct whether he has knowledge of the transaction at the time he received the benefits or whether he gains such knowledge at a time after he receives the benefits. *Land Title Co.*, 609 S.W.2d at 756–57.

Not applicable to fraud.   PJC 305.6 does not apply in situations involving ratification of fraud.

PJC 305.7   Conditions Precedent (Comment)

Conditions precedent defined.   "A condition precedent may be either a condition to the formation of a contract or to an obligation to perform an existing agreement. Conditions may, therefore, relate either to the formation of contracts or to liability under them." *Hohenberg Bros. Co. v. George E. Gibbons & Co.*, 537 S.W.2d 1, 3 (Tex. 1976). "A condition precedent is an event that must happen or be performed before a right can accrue to enforce an obligation." *Centex Corp. v. Dalton*, 840 S.W.2d 952, 956 (Tex. 1992).

Conditions precedent to an obligation to perform are acts or events that are to occur after the contract is made and that must occur before there is a right to immediate performance and before there can be a breach of contractual duty. *Hohenberg Bros. Co.*, 537 S.W.2d at 3.

Creation of condition precedent.   Although no particular words are necessary to create a condition, terms such as "if," "provided that," and "on condition that" usually connote a condition rather than a covenant or promise. *Community Health Systems Professional Services Corp. v. Hansen*, 525 S.W.3d 671, 683 (Tex. 2017) (citing *Hohenberg Bros. Co.*, 537 S.W.2d at 3). Absent such a limiting clause, whether a provision represents a condition or a promise must be gathered from the contract as a whole and from the intent of the parties. *Temple-Eastex Inc. v. Addison Bank*, 672 S.W.2d 793, 798 (Tex. 1984); *Hohenberg Bros. Co.*, 537 S.W.2d at 3.

Conditions not favored.   To prevent forfeitures, courts are inclined to construe provisions as covenants rather than as conditions. *PAJ, Inc. v. Hanover Insurance Co.*, 243 S.W.3d 630, 636 (Tex. 2008).

PJC 305.8 Court's Construction of Provision of Agreement (Comment)

Court's construction should be included in charge. If the construction of a provision of the agreement is in dispute and the court resolves the dispute by interpreting the provision according to the rules of construction, the court should include that interpretation in submitting PJC 305.3.

Court's duty to interpret unambiguous contract. Whether a contract is ambiguous is a question of law. If a contract as written can be given a clear and definite legal meaning, it is not ambiguous as a matter of law. *Gilbert Texas Construction, L.P. v. Underwriters at Lloyd's London*, 327 S.W.3d 118, 133 (Tex. 2010). A contract is ambiguous if, after application of the pertinent rules of construction, it remains reasonably susceptible of more than one meaning, taking into consideration the circumstances present when the contract was executed. *Dynegy Midstream Services, L.P. v. Apache Corp.*, 294 S.W.3d 164, 168 (Tex. 2009); *Coker v. Coker*, 650 S.W.2d 391, 393–94 (Tex. 1983). The court may conclude that a contract is ambiguous in the absence of such a pleading by any party. *See URI, Inc. v. Kleberg County*, 543 S.W.3d 755, 763 (Tex. 2018) (a contract may be ambiguous even though the parties agree it is not); *Progressive County Mutual Insurance Co. v. Kelley*, 284 S.W.3d 805, 808–09 (Tex. 2009) (per curiam) (summary judgment appeal where supreme court concluded contract was ambiguous even though neither party asserted ambiguity); *see also Sage Street Associates v. Northdale Construction Co.*, 863 S.W.2d 438, 445 (Tex. 1993).

PJC 305.9   Instruction on Ambiguous Provisions

It is your duty to interpret the following language of the agreement:

[Insert ambiguous language.]

You must decide its meaning by determining the intent of the parties at the time of the agreement. Consider all the facts and circumstances surrounding the making of the agreement, the interpretation placed on the agreement by the parties, and the conduct of the parties.

COMMENT

When to use.   If the court determines that the contract contains ambiguous language, PJC 305.9 should accompany PJC 305.2 or 305.3. This instruction is appropriate to inform the jury of its duty to decide the meaning of ambiguous language.

See PJC 305.19 for a question and instruction on ambiguity to be used when a specific finding on the meaning of ambiguous language is sought and for an additional discussion on ambiguity.

Parties' interpretation given great weight.   The most significant rule of contractual interpretation is that great, if not controlling, weight should be given to the parties' interpretation. *See, e.g., Harris v. Rowe*, 593 S.W.2d 303, 306 (Tex. 1979). The court and the jury should assume that parties to a contract are in the best position to know what they intended by the language used. *Harris*, 593 S.W.2d at 306. One factor to be considered in determining the construction the parties placed on a contract is their conduct. *Consolidated Engineering Co. v. Southern Steel Co.*, 699 S.W.2d 188, 192–93 (Tex. 1985).

PJC 305.10   Trade Custom (Comment)

Instruction may be appropriate.   "When consideration of evidence as to industry custom and usage is appropriate, it is a question of fact for the jury, and it is the province of the jury to weigh witness credibility." *Barrow-Shaver Resources Co. v. Carrizo Oil & Gas, Inc.*, 590 S.W.3d 471, 485 (Tex. 2019). Such an instruction would be used to augment or modify PJC 305.2 or 305.3. It could inquire whether a particular custom or usage existed and, if it existed, whether the parties intended that it would affect a contract term. *Lambert v. H. Molsen & Co.*, 551 S.W.2d 151, 154 (Tex. App.—Waco 1977, writ ref'd n.r.e.) ("The [trial] court instructed the jury . . . that if it found . . . that the custom and usage actually existed, then it could be considered by the jury toward determining the parties' contractual intent."). The court in *Lambert* did not expressly approve the instruction used by the trial court, but the opinion does provide an example of the form of a trade-custom instruction. *See also Tennell v. Esteve Cotton Co.*, 546 S.W.2d 346, 354–55 (Tex. App.—Amarillo 1976, writ ref'd n.r.e.) (discussing submissions of instructions on trade); *Englebrecht v. W.D. Brannan & Sons, Inc.*, 501 S.W.2d 707 (Tex. App.—Amarillo 1973, no writ) (discussing submission of instructions on custom).

Evidence of trade custom may aid interpretation of ambiguous contract. Evidence of custom may be admitted to aid in the interpretation of a contract if the contract is ambiguous, imprecise, incomplete, or inconsistent, but such evidence is not admissible to contradict, restrict, or enlarge what otherwise needs no explanation. *Miller v. Gray*, 149 S.W.2d 582, 583–84 (Tex. 1941); *see Barrow-Shaver Resources Co.*, 590 S.W.3d at 485 ("[E]vidence of surrounding facts and circumstances, including evidence of industry custom and usage, cannot be used to add, alter, or change the contract's agreed-to terms.").

UCC article 2 cases.   Trade custom, course of dealing, and course of performance are relevant in determining the meaning of the agreement. *See* Tex. Bus. & Com. Code §§ 1.303, 2.202 (Tex. UCC).

PJC 305.11   Instruction on Time of Compliance

Compliance with an agreement must occur within a reasonable time under the circumstances unless the parties agreed that compliance must occur within a specified time and the parties intended compliance within such time to be an essential part of the agreement.

In determining whether the parties intended time of compliance to be an essential part of the agreement, you may consider the nature and purpose of the agreement and the facts and circumstances surrounding its making.

COMMENT

When to use.   PJC 305.11 is appropriate if a party contends that failure to comply by the date specified in the agreement constitutes a material breach, even though the agreement itself does not expressly state that time is of the essence. *See Kennedy Ship & Repair, L.P. v. Pham*, 210 S.W.3d 11, 19 (Tex. App.—Houston [14th Dist.] 2006, no pet.) ("Unless the contract expressly makes time of the essence, the issue is a fact question for the jury.").

UCC article 2 cases.   If the time for delivery or shipment is not specified in the contract, the time shall be reasonable. Tex. Bus. & Com. Code § 2.309(a) (Tex. UCC). "Whether a time for taking an action required by this title is reasonable depends on the nature, purpose, and circumstances of the action" and on any prior dealing between the parties. Tex. UCC § 1.205(a) & cmt. 2; *see also* Tex. UCC §§ 2.504, 2.601, 2.612.

PJC 305.12   Instruction on Offer and Acceptance

In attempting to reach an agreement, one party may specifically prescribe the time, manner, or other requirements for the other party's acceptance of the offer. If the offer is not accepted as prescribed, there is no agreement.

COMMENT

When to use.   PJC 305.12 submits a common offer-and-acceptance instruction and may be used in an appropriate case with PJC 305.2. The offeror can waive limitations on manner of acceptance, and the above instruction should be modified to incorporate waiver in an appropriate case. *See Padilla v. LaFrance*, 907 S.W.2d 454, 460 (Tex. 1995).

Acceptance by performance.   Under some circumstances performance of an act that the offeree is requested to promise to perform may constitute a valid acceptance. *Mid-Continent Casualty Co. v. Global Enercom Management, Inc.*, 323 S.W.3d 151, 157 (Tex. 2010) (citing *United Concrete Pipe Corp. v. Spin-Line Co.*, 430 S.W.2d 360, 364 (Tex. 1968)).

Time for acceptance.   If no time for acceptance of an offer is specified, the law implies a reasonable time. *Advantage Physical Therapy, Inc. v. Cruz*, 165 S.W.3d 21, 26 (Tex. App.—Houston [14th Dist.] 2005, no pet.) (citing *Valencia v. Garza*, 765 S.W.2d 893, 897 (Tex. App.—San Antonio 1989, no writ)).

PJC 305.13   Instruction on Withdrawal or Revocation of Offer

There is no agreement unless the party to whom an offer is made accepts it before knowing that the offer has been withdrawn.

COMMENT

When to use.   PJC 305.13 should be included with PJC 305.2 only if one party claims the offer was withdrawn before it was accepted.

Acceptance by performance.   Under some circumstances performance of an act that the offeree is requested to promise to perform may constitute a valid acceptance. *Mid-Continent Casualty Co. v. Global Enercom Management, Inc.*, 323 S.W.3d 151, 157 (Tex. 2010) (citing *United Concrete Pipe Corp. v. Spin-Line Co.*, 430 S.W.2d 360, 364 (Tex. 1968)).

Revocable or irrevocable offers.   Ordinarily, the party making an offer may revoke it anytime before the offeree accepts it in the manner prescribed. *See Bowles v. Fickas*, 167 S.W.2d 741, 742–43 (Tex. 1943); *Morgan v. Bronze Queen Management Co.*, 474 S.W.3d 701, 706 (Tex. App.—Houston [14th Dist.] 2014, no pet.). The offeror can effectively revoke an offer by doing some act inconsistent with the offer, but the offeree must have actual knowledge of the revocation. *Antwine v. Reed*, 199 S.W.2d 482, 485 (Tex. 1947). After making an irrevocable offer, however, the offeror cannot unilaterally vary or revoke it. *Wall v. Trinity Sand & Gravel Co.*, 369 S.W.2d 315, 317 (Tex. 1963). A common type of irrevocable offer is an option contract where the offer is supported by independent consideration.

UCC cases.   *See* Tex. Bus. & Com. Code § 2.206(b) (Tex. UCC).

PJC 305.14   Instruction on Price

If *Paul Payne* and *Don Davis* agreed to other essential terms but failed to specify price, it is presumed a reasonable price was intended.

COMMENT

When to use. PJC 305.14 should accompany PJC 305.2 or 305.3 in appropriate cases. *See Fischer v. CTMI, L.L.C.*, 479 S.W.3d 231, 241 (Tex. 2016) (law's presumption that parties intended a reasonable price is particularly strong when the agreement specifies a formula or other basis on which a reasonable price may be determined); *Sacks v. Haden*, 266 S.W.3d 447, 450 (Tex. 2008).

Source of instruction. The above instruction is derived from *Fischer*, 479 S.W.3d at 241, and *Sacks*, 266 S.W.3d at 450.

UCC cases. Tex. Bus. & Com. Code § 2.305(a) (Tex. UCC) states:

(a)   The parties if they so intend can conclude a contract for sale even though the price is not settled. In such a case the price is a reasonable price at the time for delivery if

    (1)   nothing is said as to price; or

    (2)   the price is left to be agreed by the parties and they fail to agree; or

    (3)   the price is to be fixed in terms of some agreed market or other standard as set or recorded by a third person or agency and it is not so set or recorded.

PJC 305.15   Consideration (Comment)

Consideration essential. Consideration is essential to a contract. *Unthank v. Rippstein*, 386 S.W.2d 134, 137 (Tex. 1964). Whether a particular matter constitutes adequate legal consideration is a question of law for the court. *Brownwood Ross Co. v. Maverick County*, 936 S.W.2d 42, 45 (Tex. App.—San Antonio 1996, no writ). The court's determination, however, may be based on facts found by the jury. *See, e.g., Houston Medical Testing Services v. Mintzer*, 417 S.W.3d 691, 695–96 (Tex. App.—Houston [14th Dist.] 2013, no pet.).

Burden of proof. In suits on a written contract, the burden of proof rests on the party alleging a lack of consideration. Tex. R. Civ. P. 94; *Simpson v. MBank Dallas, N.A.*, 724 S.W.2d 102, 107 (Tex. App.—Dallas 1987, writ ref'd n.r.e.). In actions on an oral contract, the burden is on the plaintiff to prove the existence of consideration. *Okemah Construction, Inc. v. Barkley-Farmer, Inc.*, 583 S.W.2d 458, 460 (Tex. App.—Houston [1st Dist.] 1979, no writ) (collecting cases).

Failure of consideration. The doctrine of failure of consideration does not involve issues relating to contract formation but is usually an affirmative defense based on a claim that the party seeking to recover on the contract has breached it in a manner sufficient to excuse the other party's noncompliance. *US Bank, N.A. v. Prestige Ford Garland Ltd. Partnership*, 170 S.W.3d 272, 279 (Tex. App.—Dallas 2005, no pet.). *See* Tex. R. Civ. P. 93, 94. For appropriate instructions, see PJC 312.2.

[PJC 305.16–305.18 are reserved for expansion.]

PJC 305.19   **Question and Instruction on Meaning of Ambiguous Provisions**

The following language is at issue:

[Insert ambiguous language.]

QUESTION _____

Did the parties mutually intend [*insert plaintiff's contention*]?

You must determine the intent of the parties at the time of the agreement. Consider all the facts and circumstances surrounding the making of the agreement, the interpretation placed on the agreement by the parties, and the conduct of the parties.

Answer "Yes" or "No."

Answer: _____

COMMENT

When to use.   PJC 305.19 should be used after the court determines the contract contains ambiguous language and a claimant seeks a specific finding on the meaning of that ambiguous language. If a counter-claimant seeks a different interpretation, this question can also be used with the burden on the counter-claimant. If findings on multiple interpretations are needed, the questions should be conditioned, or submitted alternatively, to avoid conflicting findings.

See PJC 305.9 for a jury instruction directing the jury to decide the meaning of ambiguous language.

The determination of whether a contract is ambiguous is a question of law for the court. *Endeavor Energy Resources, L.P. v. Discovery Operating, Inc.*, 554 S.W.3d 586, 601 (Tex. 2018); *J.M. Davidson, Inc. v. Webster*, 128 S.W.3d 223, 229 (Tex. 2003); *Coker v. Coker*, 650 S.W.2d 391, 394 (Tex. 1983). Whether the contract is ambiguous is determined by looking at the contract as a whole, in light of the circumstances present when the parties entered into the contract. *Universal Health Services, Inc. v. Renaissance Women's Group, P.A.*, 121 S.W.3d 742, 746 (Tex. 2003). A contract is ambiguous if it is susceptible of more than one reasonable interpretation. *North Shore Energy, L.L.C. v. Harkins*, 501 S.W.3d 598, 602 (Tex. 2016); *Frost National Bank v. L&F Distributors, Ltd.*, 165 S.W.3d 310, 312 (Tex. 2005) (per curiam). That the parties disagree about a contract's meaning does not render it ambiguous. *Endeavor*

Energy Resources, L.P., 554 S.W.3d at 601. See PJC 305.9 for an instruction on ambiguous provisions that may be used in appropriate circumstances.

An ambiguity creates a fact issue as to the parties' intent. *Barrow-Shaver Resources Co. v. Carrizo Oil & Gas, Inc.*, 590 S.W.3d 471, 480 (Tex. 2019); *Plains Exploration & Production Co. v. Torch Energy Advisors Inc.*, 473 S.W.3d 296, 305 (Tex. 2015); *Columbia Gas Transmission Corp. v. New Ulm Gas, Ltd.*, 940 S.W.2d 587, 589 (Tex. 1996). The court may conclude that a contract is ambiguous in the absence of such a pleading by any party. *See URI, Inc. v. Kleberg County*, 543 S.W.3d 755, 763 (Tex. 2018) (a contract may be ambiguous even though the parties agree it is not); *Progressive County Mutual Insurance Co. v. Kelley*, 284 S.W.3d 805, 808–09 (Tex. 2009) (per curiam) (summary judgment appeal where supreme court concluded contract was ambiguous even though neither party asserted ambiguity); *see also Sage Street Associates v. Northdale Construction Co.*, 863 S.W.2d 438, 445 (Tex. 1993).

Source of question. PJC 305.19 is derived in part from *Trinity Universal Insurance Co. v. Ponsford Bros.*, 423 S.W.2d 571, 575 (Tex. 1968), and *Recognition Communications, Inc. v. American Automobile Ass'n, Inc.*, 154 S.W.3d 878, 886–87 (Tex. App.—Dallas 2005, pet. denied).

Broad-form submission. PJC 305.19 is a broad-form question designed to be accompanied by one or more appropriate instructions. Tex. R. Civ. P. 277 requires that "the court shall, whenever feasible, submit the cause upon broad-form questions." Tex. R. Civ. P. 277; *see Thota v. Young*, 366 S.W.3d 678, 689 (Tex. 2012) (rule 277's use of "whenever feasible" mandates broad-form submission in any or every instance in which it is capable of being accomplished).

Intent must be understandable. Parties to a contract must express their intentions understandably. *See City of Houston v. Williams*, 353 S.W.3d 128, 138, 143–44 (Tex. 2011); *Montgomery County Hospital District v. Brown*, 965 S.W.2d 501, 502 (Tex. 1998). To be enforceable, a contract must be sufficiently certain to enable the court to determine the legal obligations of the parties. *T.O. Stanley Boot Co. v. Bank of El Paso*, 847 S.W.2d 218, 221 (Tex. 1992); *Bendalin v. Delgado*, 406 S.W.2d 897, 899 (Tex. 1966).

Parties' interpretation given great weight. The most significant rule of contractual interpretation is that great, if not controlling, weight should be given to the parties' interpretation. *See, e.g., Harris v. Rowe*, 593 S.W.2d 303, 306 (Tex. 1979). The court and the jury should assume that parties to a contract are in the best position to know what they intended by the language used. *Harris*, 593 S.W.2d at 306. One factor to be considered in determining the construction the parties placed on a contract is their conduct. *Consolidated Engineering Co. v. Southern Steel Co.*, 699 S.W.2d 188, 192–93 (Tex. 1985).

Patent and latent ambiguities. An ambiguity in a contract may be either "patent" or "latent." *URI, Inc.*, 543 S.W.3d at 765; *National Union Fire Insurance Co. of*

Pittsburgh v. CBI Industries, Inc., 907 S.W.2d 517, 520 (Tex. 1995). A patent ambiguity is evident on the face of the contract, while a latent ambiguity arises when a contract, unambiguous on its face, is applied to subject matter with which it deals, and an ambiguity appears by reason of some collateral matter. *URI, Inc.*, 543 S.W.3d at 765; *National Union Fire Insurance Co. of Pittsburgh*, 907 S.W.2d at 520.

PJC 305.20   Question and Instruction on Reformation as an Affirmative Cause of Action

QUESTION 1

Prior to the time the [*instrument*] was reduced to writing, did *Paul Payne* and *Don Davis* agree that [*insert all disputed terms*]?

Answer "Yes" or "No."

Answer: _____

If you answered "Yes" to Question 1, then answer Question 2. Otherwise, do not answer Question 2.

QUESTION 2

Did the failure of the [*instrument*] to set out the [*disputed terms*] result from a mutual mistake?

"Mutual mistake" occurs when the parties have previously reached an agreement, but because of a mistake common to both parties the [*instrument*] as written does not reflect the prior agreement.

Unilateral mistake by one party, and knowledge of that mistake by the other party, is equivalent to mutual mistake.

Answer "Yes" or "No."

Answer: _____

COMMENT

When to use.   PJC 305.20 is appropriate for use when a party claims that a mutual mistake in reducing the agreement to writing failed to accurately reflect the prior agreement and that the instrument should be "reformed" by the court to correctly state the prior agreement.

Source of question.   PJC 305.20 is derived from *Davis v. Grammer*, 750 S.W.2d 766, 768 (Tex. 1988), and *Sun Oil Co. v. Bennett*, 84 S.W.2d 447, 451 (Tex. 1935). The broad form of this question is adapted from the Texas Supreme Court's analysis in *Cherokee Water Co. v. Forderhause*, 741 S.W.2d 377, 380 (Tex. 1987). Although the court disapproved of the jury questions actually submitted in that case, it held that the charge would have been correct had the jury been instructed to find (1) the terms of an agreement that was made prior to reducing the relevant instruments to writing and (2) that a mutual mistake was made in presenting those terms within the documents.

Broad-form submission.   PJC 305.20 is a broad-form question designed to be accompanied by one or more appropriate instructions. Tex. R. Civ. P. 277 requires that "the court shall, whenever feasible, submit the cause upon broad-form questions." Tex. R. Civ. P. 277; *see Thota v. Young*, 366 S.W.3d 678, 689 (Tex. 2012) (rule 277's use of "whenever feasible" mandates broad-form submission in any or every instance in which it is capable of being accomplished).

Requirements for reformation.   "[R]eformation requires two elements: (1) an original agreement and (2) a mutual mistake, made *after* the original agreement, in reducing the original agreement to writing." *Cherokee Water Co.*, 741 S.W.2d at 379 (emphasis added). An exception to the requirement that the mistake be mutual is the unilateral mistake by one party "accompanied by fraud or other inequitable conduct of the remaining party." *Cambridge Companies, Inc. v. Williams*, 602 S.W.2d 306, 308 (Tex. App.—Texarkana 1980), *aff'd on other grounds*, 615 S.W.2d 172 (Tex. 1981). *See Liu v. Yang*, 69 S.W.3d 225, 228 (Tex. App.—Corpus Christi–Edinburg 2001, no pet.). "Unilateral mistake by one party, and knowledge of that mistake by the other party, is equivalent to mutual mistake." *Davis*, 750 S.W.2d at 768 (citing *Cambridge Companies, Inc.*, 602 S.W.2d at 308).

See PJC 312.9 for an instruction on the defense of mutual mistake due to a scrivener's error.

Disputed terms.   The disputed terms inserted in the question should reflect the contention of the party bearing the burden of proof.

Burden of proof.   Reformation requires clear, exact, and satisfactory evidence of mutual mistake. *Sun Oil Co.*, 84 S.W.2d at 452; *Estes v. Republic National Bank of Dallas*, 462 S.W.2d 273, 275 (Tex. 1970). The general rule, however, is that the burden of proof in civil cases is by a preponderance of the evidence. *See, e.g., Ellis County State Bank v. Keever*, 888 S.W.2d 790 (Tex. 1994); *State v. Turner*, 556 S.W.2d 563, 565 (Tex. 1977). *But cf. Hardy v. Bennefield*, 368 S.W.3d 643, 648 (Tex. App.—Tyler 2012, no pet.) (citing *Estes* and noting "burden at trial is proof by clear and convincing evidence" for reformation).

PJC 305.21   Question on Main Purpose Doctrine

QUESTION _____

Did *Don Davis* promise to be primarily responsible for paying the debt of [*name of third party*], and was *Don Davis*'s main purpose for the promise, if any, to gain a benefit for *himself*?

Answer "Yes" or "No."

Answer: _____

COMMENT

When to use.   The "main purpose" doctrine is an exception to the statute of frauds requirement that an obligation to pay the debt of another be in writing. See PJC 312.14. The doctrine requires that (1) the promisor intended to create primary responsibility in itself to pay the debt of another; (2) there was consideration for the promise; and (3) the consideration was primarily for the promisor's own use and benefit—that is, the benefit it received was the promisor's main purpose for making the promise.

Source of question.   PJC 305.21 is derived from *Cruz v. Andrews Restoration, Inc.*, 364 S.W.3d 817, 828 (Tex. 2012).

Broad-form submission.   PJC 305.21 is a broad-form question designed to be accompanied by one or more appropriate instructions. Tex. R. Civ. P. 277 requires that "the court shall, whenever feasible, submit the cause upon broad-form questions." Tex. R. Civ. P. 277; *see Thota v. Young*, 366 S.W.3d 678, 689 (Tex. 2012) (rule 277's use of "whenever feasible" mandates broad-form submission in any or every instance in which it is capable of being accomplished).

Consideration essential.   The promise to become liable for the debt of another must be supported by consideration. *See Gulf Liquid Fertilizer Co. v. Titus*, 354 S.W.2d 378, 387 (Tex. 1962). To take the promise out of the statute of frauds, the consideration must be primarily for the promisor's own use and benefit. *Gulf Liquid Fertilizer Co.*, 354 S.W.2d at 386–87. Whether a particular matter constitutes adequate legal consideration is a question of law for the court. *Williams v. Hill*, 396 S.W.2d 911, 913 (Tex. App.—Dallas 1965, no writ). The court's determination, however, may be based on facts found by the jury. *See, e.g., Houston Medical Testing Services v. Mintzer*, 417 S.W.3d 691, 695–96 (Tex. App.—Houston [14th Dist.] 2013, no pet.).

Burden of proof.   The party pleading the statute of frauds bears the initial burden of establishing its applicability. Tex. R. Civ. P. 94; *Dynegy, Inc. v. Yates*, 422 S.W.3d 638 (Tex. 2013). Once that party meets its initial burden, the burden shifts to the opposing party to establish an exception that would take the verbal contract out of the statute of frauds. *Dynegy, Inc.*, 422 S.W.3d at 641. A party relying on the main purpose doctrine therefore must plead and establish facts to take a verbal contract out of the statute of frauds. *Dynegy, Inc.*, 422 S.W.3d at 641.

PJC 305.22   Third-Party Beneficiaries (Comment)

Third-party beneficiaries. A third party may enforce an agreement as a beneficiary to that agreement if the contracting parties (1) "intended to secure a benefit to th[e] third party" and (2) "entered into the contract directly for the third party's benefit." *First Bank v. Brumitt*, 519 S.W.3d 95, 102 (Tex. 2017). *See also Basic Capital Management, Inc. v. Dynex Commercial, Inc.*, 348 S.W.3d 894, 900 (Tex. 2011) (quoting *MCI Telecommunications Corp. v. Texas Utilities Electric Co.*, 995 S.W.2d 647, 651 (Tex. 1999)); *City of Houston v. Williams*, 353 S.W.3d 128, 145 (Tex. 2011). The "intention to contract or confer a direct benefit to a third party must be clearly and fully spelled out or enforcement by the third party must be denied." *Basic Capital Management, Inc.*, 348 S.W.3d at 900 (quoting *MCI Telecommunications Corp.*, 995 S.W.2d at 651).

It is presumed that parties contract solely for themselves, "only a clear expression of the intent to create a third-party beneficiary can overcome that presumption," and doubts regarding the parties' intent "must be resolved against conferring third-party beneficiary status." *First Bank*, 519 S.W.3d at 103; *Sharyland Water Supply Corp. v. City of Alton*, 354 S.W.3d 407, 420 (Tex. 2011). A court will not create a third-party-beneficiary contract by implication. *Basic Capital Management, Inc.*, 348 S.W.3d at 900.

It is not enough that the third party would benefit—whether directly or indirectly— from the parties' performance, or that the parties knew that the third party would benefit. *First Bank*, 519 S.W.3d at 102; *Sharyland Water Supply Corp.*, 354 S.W.3d at 421. Nor does it matter that the third party intended or expected to benefit from the contract, for only the "intention of the contracting parties in this respect is of controlling importance." *First Bank*, 519 S.W.3d at 102 (quoting *Banker v. Breaux*, 128 S.W.2d 23, 24 (Tex. 1939)).

Form of question. Ordinarily, construction of an unambiguous written instrument to determine third-party-beneficiary status is a question of law for the court. *See First Bank*, 519 S.W.3d at 105–06 (court should determine whether agreement is ambiguous and whether it "clearly, fully, and unequivocally express[es] the parties' mutual intent" to confer third-party-beneficiary status); *Basic Capital Management, Inc.*, 348 S.W.3d at 900. When deciding whether the parties to an unambiguous contract intended to create a third-party beneficiary, the court must look solely to the contract's language construed as a whole. *First Bank*, 519 S.W.3d at 106.

If the court determines the agreement is ambiguous such that there is a fact issue regarding whether the contracting parties intended to confer third-party-beneficiary status on a nonparty, the Committee recommends that the following question be submitted to the jury:

QUESTION _____

Did *Paul Payne* and *Don Davis* enter into the agreement with the intent to confer some direct benefit on *Third-Party Tom*?

[Insert instructions and definitions, if appropriate.]

Answer "Yes" or "No."

Answer: _____

See First Bank, 519 S.W.3d at 102–04; *Basic Capital Management, Inc.*, 348 S.W.3d at 899–900; *MCI Telecommunications Corp.*, 995 S.W.2d at 651. For more detailed discussion regarding what may constitute a "direct benefit," see *Sharyland Water Supply Corp.*, 354 S.W.3d at 421; *City of Houston*, 353 S.W.3d at 145; and *Basic Capital Management, Inc.*, 348 S.W.3d at 900.

Upon an affirmative answer to this question, the third-party beneficiary may submit PJC 305.3 to determine compliance of the party allegedly in breach.

PJC 305.23   Question on Promissory Estoppel

QUESTION _____

Did *Paul Payne* substantially rely to *his* detriment on *Don Davis*'s promise, if any, and was this reliance foreseeable by *Don Davis*?

Answer "Yes" or "No."

Answer: _____

COMMENT

When to use.   The doctrine of promissory estoppel may be invoked as a cause of action. It is appropriate if a promisee has acted to his detriment in reasonable reliance on an otherwise unenforceable promise. The theory supplies a remedy enabling an injured party to be compensated for "foreseeable, definite and substantial reliance." *Wheeler v. White*, 398 S.W.2d 93, 96–97 (Tex. 1965). See PJC 313.20 for a question on promissory estoppel—reliance damages.

Source of question.   PJC 305.23 is derived from *Wheeler*, 398 S.W.2d at 96–97; *see also English v. Fischer*, 660 S.W.2d 521, 524 (Tex. 1983) (requisites of promissory estoppel are "(1) a promise, (2) foreseeability of reliance thereon by the promisor, and (3) substantial reliance by the promisee to his detriment"); *Restatement (Second) of Contracts* § 90 (1981).

Broad-form submission.   PJC 305.23 is a broad-form question designed to be accompanied by one or more appropriate instructions. Tex. R. Civ. P. 277 requires that "the court shall, whenever feasible, submit the cause upon broad-form questions." Tex. R. Civ. P. 277; *see Thota v. Young*, 366 S.W.3d 678, 689 (Tex. 2012) (rule 277's use of "whenever feasible" mandates broad-form submission in any or every instance in which it is capable of being accomplished). For further discussion, see PJC 314.2 regarding broad-form and the *Casteel* doctrine.

Exception to statute of frauds.   This doctrine also can be used as a plea in avoidance of a statute-of-frauds defense when the promise at issue is a promise to sign a written agreement which itself complies with the statute of frauds. *"Moore" Burger, Inc. v. Phillips Petroleum Co.*, 492 S.W.2d 934, 937–40 (Tex. 1972).

PJC 305.24   Question and Instruction on Quantum Meruit

QUESTION _____

Did *Paul Payne* perform compensable work for *Don Davis* for which *he* was not compensated?

Paul Payne performed compensable work if *he* rendered valuable services or furnished valuable materials to *Don Davis*; *Don Davis* accepted, used, and benefited from the services or materials; and, under the circumstances, *Don Davis* was reasonably notified that *Paul Payne* expected to be compensated for the services or materials.

Answer "Yes" or "No."

Answer: _____

COMMENT

When to use.   If one party receives a benefit by accepting the services of another, the accepting party is obligated by principles of equity to pay the reasonable value of those services. *Hill v. Shamoun & Norman, LLP*, 544 S.W.3d 724, 732 (Tex. 2018); *In re Kellogg Brown & Root, Inc.*, 166 S.W.3d 732, 740 (Tex. 2005); *Colbert v. Dallas Joint Stock Land Bank*, 150 S.W.2d 771, 773 (Tex. 1941). The elements of a quantum meruit claim are set out in *Vortt Exploration Co. v. Chevron U.S.A.*, 787 S.W.2d 942 (Tex. 1990) (citing *Bashara v. Baptist Memorial Hospital System*, 685 S.W.2d 307, 310 (Tex. 1985)).

If a valid express contract covering the services rendered or materials furnished exists, recovery on quantum meruit generally is not allowed under Texas law. *Hill*, 544 S.W.3d at 733, 737; *In re Kellogg Brown & Root, Inc.*, 166 S.W.3d at 740; *Truly v. Austin*, 744 S.W.2d 934, 936 (Tex. 1988); *see also Woodard v. Southwest States, Inc.*, 384 S.W.2d 674, 675 (Tex. 1964). When the existence of or the terms of a contract are in doubt, the party disputing recovery in quantum meruit has the burden of proving that an express contract exists covering the subject matter of the dispute. *Freeman v. Carroll*, 499 S.W.2d 668 (Tex. App.—Tyler 1973, writ ref'd n.r.e.), *cited with approval in Fortune Production Co. v. Conoco, Inc.*, 52 S.W.3d 671, 684 (Tex. 2000); *see Truly*, 744 S.W.2d at 936 (discussing the general rule that one may recover in quantum meruit only when there is no express contract).

The existence of an express contract does not, however, preclude recovery in quantum meruit for the reasonable value of work performed and accepted but not covered by the contract. *Hill*, 544 S.W.3d at 737; *Black Lake Pipe Line Co. v. Union Construc-*

tion Co., 538 S.W.2d 80, 86 (Tex. 1976), *overruled on other grounds by Sterner v. Marathon Oil Co.*, 767 S.W.2d 686 (Tex. 1989). When "the evidence shows that no contract covers the service at issue, *then* the question of whether a party may recover in quantum meruit is for the trier of fact." *Gulf Liquids New River Project, LLC v. Gulsby Engineering, Inc.*, 356 S.W.3d 54, 70 (Tex. App.—Houston [1st Dist.] 2011, no pet.). The right to recover in quantum meruit is based on a promise "implied by law to pay for beneficial services rendered and knowingly accepted." *Hill*, 544 S.W.3d at 732; *In re Kellogg Brown & Root, Inc.*, 166 S.W.3d at 740; *Davidson v. Clearman*, 391 S.W.2d 48, 50 (Tex. 1965).

Recovery in quantum meruit is allowed for partial performance of an express contract if (1) the defendant's breach prevents the plaintiff's completion or (2) the contract is unilateral and requires no performance by the plaintiff. *Truly*, 744 S.W.2d at 936–37.

Texas cases involving building or construction contracts have permitted a *breaching plaintiff* to recover in quantum meruit. *Murray v. Crest Construction, Inc.*, 900 S.W.2d 342, 345 (Tex. 1995) (construction contracts are an exception to the general rule that a party may not recover under quantum meruit when there is an express contract covering the services or materials furnished); *Truly*, 744 S.W.2d at 937. *See also Dobbins v. Redden*, 785 S.W.2d 377, 378 (Tex. 1990); *Beeman v. Worrell*, 612 S.W.2d 953, 956 (Tex. App.—Dallas 1981, no writ). For further discussion of construction contracts, see the current edition of State Bar of Texas, *Texas Pattern Jury Charges— Business, Consumer, Insurance & Employment* PJC 101.46–.49.

Quantum meruit may also permit a recovery in equity when a contract is unenforceable because it is barred by the statute of frauds. *See Quigley v. Bennett*, 227 S.W.3d 51, 55 (Tex. 2007) (holding that alleged oral agreement to receive royalty interest was barred by the statute of frauds but remanding for consideration of quantum meruit claim).

See PJC 313.21 for a question on quantum meruit recovery.

Broad-form submission. PJC 305.24 is a broad-form question designed to be accompanied by one or more appropriate instructions. Tex. R. Civ. P. 277 requires that "the court shall, whenever feasible, submit the cause upon broad-form questions." Tex. R. Civ. P. 277; *see Thota v. Young*, 366 S.W.3d 678, 689 (Tex. 2012) (rule 277's use of "whenever feasible" mandates broad-form submission in any or every instance in which it is capable of being accomplished). For further discussion, see PJC 314.2 regarding broad-form and the *Casteel* doctrine.

Modification of instruction. The above instruction may be modified to delete references to either materials or services if one is not at issue in the case.

PJC 305.25 Money Had and Received (Comment)

Texas has long recognized a claim for money had and received if a defendant holds money that "in equity and good conscience" belongs to the plaintiff. *See Plains Exploration & Production Co. v. Torch Energy Advisors Inc.*, 473 S.W.3d 296, 302 n.4 (Tex. 2015); *Merryfield v. Willson*, 14 Tex. 224, 225 (1855). But the boundaries of the claim are not always clear, as it is "less restricted and fettered by technical rules and formalities than any other form of action." *Staats v. Miller*, 243 S.W.2d 686, 687–88 (Tex. 1951) (quoting *United States v. Jefferson Electric Manufacturing Co.*, 291 U.S. 386, 402–03 (1934)).

For example, the textbook money-had-and-received claim involves a mistaken overpayment to a defendant, *see Pickett v. Republic National Bank of Dallas*, 619 S.W.2d 399, 400 (Tex. 1981), or payment to the wrong party, *see Amoco Production Co. v. Smith*, 946 S.W.2d 162, 165 (Tex. App.—El Paso 1997, no writ). But recovery for money had and received may not be available in either case, depending on the circumstances. *Samson Exploration, LLC v. T.S. Reed Properties, Inc.*, 521 S.W.3d 766, 780 (Tex. 2017) (denying recovery of overpayment deemed voluntary); *Holden Business Forms Co. v. Columbia Medical Center of Arlington Subsidiary, L.P.*, 83 S.W.3d 274, 278 (Tex. App.—Fort Worth 2002, no pet.) (denying recovery of insurer's mistaken payment to hospital); *see also Best Buy Co. v. Barrera*, 248 S.W.3d 160, 162 (Tex. 2007) (presuming without deciding that claim applied to restocking fee charged for returned items). Circumstances that may permit or limit the claim are discussed below.

Prerequisite findings. Money had and received "is not premised on wrongdoing." *Plains Exploration & Production Co.*, 473 S.W.3d at 302 n.4. Thus, a bank that puts too much money in a customer's account can recover it even if the customer did nothing wrong. *See Pickett*, 619 S.W.2d at 400. But "equity follows the law," so equitable doctrines like money had and received generally must conform to legal rules. *Fortis Benefits v. Cantu*, 234 S.W.3d 642, 648 (Tex. 2007). For example, when a valid contract addresses a matter, recovery under equity cannot rewrite the parties' contract. *Fortune Production Co. v. Conoco, Inc.*, 52 S.W.3d 671, 685 (Tex. 2000). Thus, if a plaintiff's claim to money held by another depends on a contract, statute, will, or other legal claim, failure to establish the prerequisite claim may defeat the money-had-and-received claim too. *Southwestern Electric Power Co. v. Burlington Northern Railroad Co.*, 966 S.W.2d 467, 471 (Tex. 1998). This is true whether the contract is written or oral. *Tex Star Motors, Inc. v. Regal Finance Co.*, 401 S.W.3d 190, 202 (Tex. App.—Houston [14th Dist.] 2012, no pet.).

While a claim for money had and received cannot seek more than a contract specifies, it can seek a refund of amounts overpaid according to the contract's own terms. *Southwestern Electric Power Co.*, 966 S.W.2d at 469. Recovery for money had and received may also be available if a contract "is unenforceable, impossible, not fully performed, thwarted by mutual mistake, or void for other legal reasons." *City of Harker Heights v. Sun Meadows Land, Ltd.*, 830 S.W.2d 313, 319 (Tex. App.—Austin 1992, no writ); *see also McCullough v. Scarbrough, Medlin & Associates, Inc.*, 435 S.W.3d 871, 891 (Tex. App.—Dallas 2014, pet. denied). The Texas Supreme Court has noted only that equity "might" allow recovery of money when a contract is voidable. *Gotham Insurance Co. v. Warren E&P, Inc.*, 455 S.W.3d 558, 563 n.11 (Tex. 2014); *cf. Neese v. Lyon*, 479 S.W.3d 368, 391 (Tex. App.—Dallas 2015, no pet.) ("If the instrument is voidable rather than void, the party must sue for rescission and cannot sue for money had and received."). One court has allowed recovery for money had and received despite no damages under the related contract. *See Norhill Energy LLC v. McDaniel*, 517 S.W.3d 910, 917 (Tex. App.—Fort Worth 2017, pet. filed).

Money received.   Money had and received requires that the defendant actually received the money. Receipt of goods is not enough. *Hurst v. Mellinger*, 11 S.W. 184, 185 (Tex. 1889). Nor is a claim that the defendant will receive money in the future. *Mary E. Bivins Foundation v. Highland Capital Management L.P.*, 451 S.W.3d 104, 112 (Tex. App.—Dallas 2014, no pet.). The claim does not include other damages measures like benefit of the bargain or cost of replacement. *Everett v. TK-Taito, L.L.C.*, 178 S.W.3d 844, 860 (Tex. App.—Fort Worth 2005, no pet.). It is no defense that the defendant no longer has the same money on hand. *Pickett*, 619 S.W.2d at 399. But it is a defense that the defendant materially changed its position in reliance on a mistaken payment. *Bryan v. Citizens National Bank in Abilene*, 628 S.W.2d 761, 763 (Tex. 1982).

Equity and good conscience.   "A claim for money had and received is equitable in nature." *Plains Exploration & Production Co.*, 473 S.W.3d at 302 n.4. Texas courts have traditionally submitted such claims to a jury. *See Staats*, 243 S.W.2d at 688 ("[T]he trial court erred in refusing to submit to the jury the petitioners' case on the theory of money had and received."). "As a general rule, the trial court, not the jury, determines the 'expediency, necessity, or propriety of equitable relief.'" *Hill v. Shamoun & Norman, LLP*, 544 S.W.3d 724, 741 (Tex. 2018) (quoting *State v. Texas Pet Foods, Inc.*, 591 S.W.2d 800, 803 (Tex. 1979)). But "when contested fact issues must be resolved before equitable relief can be determined, a party is entitled to have that resolution made by a jury." *Hill*, 544 S.W.3d at 741 (quoting *Burrow v. Arce*, 997 S.W.2d 229, 245 (Tex. 1999)). "Once any such necessary factual disputes have been resolved, the weighing of all equitable considerations . . . and the ultimate decision of how much, if any, equitable relief should be awarded, must be determined by the trial court." *Hill*, 544 S.W.3d at 741 (citation omitted).

But "equity and good conscience" is a term of art unfamiliar to most jurors. Many factors might bear on what "equity and good conscience" require, so it is not possible to comprehensively list all the instructions jurors should receive in such cases. *See, e.g., Stonebridge Life Insurance Co. v. Pitts*, 236 S.W.3d 201, 206 (Tex. 2007) (listing factors like knowledge of and consent to credit card charges and desire for product regardless of the charges); *Edwards v. Mid-Continent Office Distributors, L.P.*, 252 S.W.3d 833, 841 (Tex. App.—Dallas 2008, pet. denied) (listing factors like the parties' business practices, communications, reliance, and the *status quo ante*). Some relevant factors may be legal questions beyond the competence of jurors. *See Restatement (Third) of Restitution and Unjust Enrichment* § 32 cmt. c (2011) (noting that availability of restitution when a contract is illegal or unenforceable "involves a complex assessment of interrelated factors" including "the nature of the illegality; the strength of the prohibition; the extent of the claimant's culpability; whether illegal conduct was central or merely tangential to the performance in question; the deterrent effect, if any, of a decision one way or the other; the cost and difficulty of the adjudications necessitated by alternative legal rules; and the extent to which a remedy in restitution would tend to carry out (or, conversely, to frustrate) a transaction that the law has in some way sought to suppress").

Adequate legal remedy. Equitable claims are sometimes supplanted if an adequate legal remedy exists. *Best Buy Co.*, 248 S.W.3d at 161 n.1. For example, a claim for money had and received may not be available if a statutory remedy supplants it. *See Bryan*, 628 S.W.2d at 763 (supplanted by Tex. Bus. & Com. Code § 4.403); *Vista Medical Center Hospital v. Texas Mutual Insurance Co.*, 416 S.W.3d 11, 40 (Tex. App.—Austin 2013, no pet.) (supplanted by workers' compensation administrative procedures). The Texas Supreme Court has noted but not decided the issue of whether a claim for money had and received requires proof that no adequate legal remedy exists in other contexts. *See Best Buy Co.*, 248 S.W.3d at 161 n.1; *Stonebridge Life Insurance Co.*, 236 S.W.3d at 203 n.1.

But equity may require a plaintiff to pursue legal remedies against a wrongdoer rather than an equitable claim for money had and received against an innocent bystander. Thus, an insured's claim that policy proceeds were wrongly paid to a third party must pursue a contract claim against the insurer, not a money-had-and-received claim against the third party who received the proceeds. *Evans v. Opperman*, 13 S.W. 312, 313 (Tex. 1890). Similarly, if *A* fraudulently causes *B* to pay a debt *A* owes to *C*, *B* must sue *A* for fraud rather than suing *C* for receiving money it was rightfully due. *Edwards*, 252 S.W.3d at 841.

Defenses. The defendant may "raise any defenses that would deny the claimant's right or show that the claimant should not recover." *Best Buy Co.*, 248 S.W.3d at 162. Since "equity and good conscience" may depend on the validity of those defenses, the supreme court has indicated they may relate to the plaintiff's case-in-chief and do not present independent affirmative defenses as traditionally defined. *Best Buy Co.*, 248 S.W.3d at 163.

Voluntary payment. Voluntary payment may be an additional defense to claims for money had and received. A party cannot recover for voluntary payments made on a claim of right, with full knowledge of all the facts and in the absence of fraud, deception, duress, or compulsion, even if the party was mistaken about the law. *Samson Exploration, LLC*, 521 S.W.3d at 779.

"Voluntary payment" is a term of art that may turn on the facts in each case, so it is not possible to comprehensively list all the instructions jurors should receive. *See BMG Direct Marketing, Inc. v. Peake*, 178 S.W.3d 763, 771 (Tex. 2005) ("[A]lthough the voluntary-payment rule may have been widely used by parties and some Texas courts at one time, its scope has diminished as the rule's equitable policy concerns have been addressed through statutory or other legal remedies.").

PJC 305.26   Unjust Enrichment (Comment)

The doctrine of unjust enrichment is appropriate "when one person has obtained a benefit from another by fraud, duress, or the taking of an undue advantage." *Southwestern Bell Telephone Co. v. Marketing on Hold Inc.*, 308 S.W.3d 909, 921 (Tex. 2010) (quoting *Heldenfels Bros. v. City of Corpus Christi*, 832 S.W.2d 39, 41 (Tex. 1992)). Because unjust enrichment is quasi-contractual, it may not be submitted to the jury "when a valid, express contract covers the subject matter of the parties' dispute." *Fortune Production Co. v. Conoco, Inc.*, 52 S.W.3d 671, 684 (Tex. 2000) (citing *TransAmerican Natural Gas Corp. v. Finkelstein*, 933 S.W.2d 591, 600 (Tex. App.— San Antonio 1996, writ denied) (no recovery for unjust enrichment if the same subject is covered by an express contract)). But overpayments under a contract can be recovered under unjust enrichment. *Southwestern Electric Power Co. v. Burlington Northern Railroad Co.*, 966 S.W.2d 467, 469–70 (Tex. 1998).

The Committee has not identified any authority specifically defining "undue advantage" in this context. But the Dallas, San Antonio, and Corpus Christi–Edinburg courts of appeals have explained that unjust enrichment occurs when someone "has wrongfully secured a benefit or has passively received one which it would be unconscionable to retain." *Texas Integrated Conveyor Systems, Inc. v. Innovative Conveyor Concepts, Inc.*, 300 S.W.3d 348, 367 (Tex. App.—Dallas 2009, pet. denied) (citing *Villarreal v. Grant Geophysical, Inc.*, 136 S.W.3d 265, 270 (Tex. App.—San Antonio 2004, pet. denied) (quoting *City of Corpus Christi v. S.S. Smith & Sons Masonry, Inc.*, 736 S.W.2d 247, 250 (Tex. App.—Corpus Christi–Edinburg 1987, writ denied))).

The Texas Supreme Court has referred to unjust enrichment as an independent "cause of action" (*HECI Exploration Co. v. Neel*, 982 S.W.2d 881, 891 (Tex. 1998)), "claim" (*Elledge v. Friberg-Cooper Water Supply Corp.*, 240 S.W.3d 869, 870 (Tex. 2007) (per curiam)), and "theory" of recovery (*Marketing on Hold, Inc.*, 308 S.W.3d at 921). Some courts of appeals have questioned whether unjust enrichment is an independent cause of action as opposed to a remedy for fraud or other improper conduct. *See, e.g., Casstevens v. Smith*, 269 S.W.3d 222, 229 (Tex. App.—Texarkana 2008, pet. denied) (is not an independent cause of action); *R.M. Dudley Construction Co. v. Dawson*, 258 S.W.3d 694, 703 (Tex. App.—Waco 2008, pet. denied) (same); *Argyle Independent School District v. Wolf*, 234 S.W.3d 229, 246 (Tex. App.—Fort Worth 2007, no pet.) (same); *Mowbray v. Avery*, 76 S.W.3d 663, 679 (Tex. App.—Corpus Christi–Edinburg 2002, pet. denied) (same); *Walker v. Cotter Properties*, 181 S.W.3d 895, 900 (Tex. App.—Dallas 2006, no pet.) (same); *but see, e.g., Pepi Corp. v. Galliford*, 254 S.W.3d 457, 460 (Tex. App.—Houston [1st Dist.] 2007, pet. denied) (is an independent cause of action); *Elledge*, 240 S.W.3d at 870 (determining that "unjust enrichment claims are governed by the two-year statute of limitations"); *Clark v. Dillard's, Inc.*, 460 S.W.3d 714, 720–21 (Tex. App.—Dallas 2015, no pet.) (same).

PJC 305.27   **Basic Question and Instructions on Breach of Joint Operating Agreement—Compliance**

Did *Don Davis* fail to comply with the joint operating agreement [*set forth provisions or conduct at issue, if appropriate*]?

[*You are instructed that the joint operating agreement requires the operator to conduct operations* [*insert appropriate standard of care as set forth in the JOA*]*.*]

[*Insert additional instructions, if appropriate.*]

Answer "Yes" or "No."

Answer: _____

COMMENT

When to use.   PJC 305.27 is appropriate to address contract compliance in the case of an alleged breach of a joint operating agreement (JOA). See also PJC 305.3, which generally addresses the question of contract compliance in the case of an alleged breach of contract. The operator's standard of care and liability are determined by the specific language of the operating agreement at issue.

Liability for breach within the scope of exculpatory provisions.   If the alleged breach falls within the scope of the JOA's exculpatory provision, an additional finding of either gross negligence or willful misconduct may be necessary to impose liability. See PJC 305.28.

PJC 305.28   Questions and Instructions on Breach by Operator under Joint Operating Agreement Exculpatory Provision

If you answered "Yes" to Question _____ [*305.27*], then answer the following questions. Otherwise, do not answer the following questions.

QUESTION 1

Did *Don Davis*'s failure to comply result from willful misconduct?

Answer "Yes" or "No."

Answer: _____

QUESTION 2

Did *Don Davis*'s failure to comply result from gross negligence?

"Gross negligence" means [*insert appropriate definition, e.g., more than momentary thoughtlessness, inadvertence, or error of judgment. It means such an entire want of care as to establish that the act or omission in question was the result of actual conscious indifference to the rights, welfare, or safety of the persons affected by it.*].

Answer "Yes" or "No."

Answer: _____

COMMENT

When to use.   PJC 305.28 should be used when the court has determined that an exculpatory provision of the joint operating agreement applies to the breach alleged. It should be predicated on a "Yes" answer to PJC 305.27. A "Yes" answer to either Question 1 or Question 2 will trigger liability. Either one or both questions should be submitted when appropriate under the language at issue or when supported by the evidence. As to whether the exculpatory clause applies to particular conduct, compare *Reeder v. Wood County Energy, L.L.C.*, 395 S.W.3d 789, 792–93 (Tex. 2012), and *Abraxas Petroleum Corp. v. Hornburg*, 20 S.W.3d 741, 759 (Tex. App.—El Paso 2000, no pet.), with *Stine v. Marathon Oil Co.*, 976 F.2d 254, 260–61 (5th Cir. 1992).

Source of question.   PJC 305.28 is derived from *Reeder*, 395 S.W.3d at 792–93; *Abraxas*, 20 S.W.3d at 759; and *Stine*, 976 F.2d at 260–61.

Submission of exculpatory clause question.   Although Question 1 and Question 2 are included as separate questions, in *Reeder*, the court decided the jury was properly instructed when the breach question included instructions on gross negligence and willful misconduct. *See Reeder*, 395 S.W.3d 789.

Instruction on gross negligence.　The appropriate definition of gross negligence is dependent on the definition that existed at the time the contract was executed. *See* Tex. Civ. Prac. & Rem. Code § 41.001(11); *Reeder*, 395 S.W.3d at 795–96; *Burk Royalty Co. v. Walls*, 616 S.W.2d 911, 920 (Tex. 1981). The statutory definitions of terms in a contract are deemed to be incorporated into the contract at the time of execution if the parties did not otherwise define the terms. *Amarillo Oil Co. v. Energy-Agri Products, Inc.*, 794 S.W.2d 20, 22 (Tex. 1990); *Smith v. Elliott & Deats*, 39 Tex. 201, 212 (1873) (laws that subsist at the time and place of the making of a contract enter into and form a part of it, as if they were expressly referred to or incorporated in its terms).

Willful misconduct.　At least one Texas court has determined that willful misconduct is a term of ordinary meaning and readily understood by the average person and, therefore, does not need to be defined. *Green Tree Acceptance, Inc. v. Combs*, 745 S.W.2d 87, 90 (Tex. App.—San Antonio 1988, writ denied); *but see IP Petroleum Co. v. Wevanco Energy, L.L.C.*, 116 S.W.3d 888, 898 (Tex. App.—Houston [1st Dist.] 2003, pet. denied) (willful misconduct has been defined in a manner akin to gross negligence).

[Chapters 306–311 are reserved for expansion.]

PJC 312.1 Defenses—Basic Question

If you answered "Yes" to Question _____ [*305.2*], then answer the following question. Otherwise, do not answer the following question.

QUESTION _____

Was *Don Davis*'s failure to comply excused?

[Insert instructions; see PJC 312.2–312.13.]

Answer "Yes" or "No."

Answer: _____

COMMENT

When to use. PJC 312.1 poses the controlling question for cases where a defendant asserts one or more defenses to a contract suit.

Broad-form submission. PJC 312.1 is a broad-form question designed to be accompanied by one or more appropriate instructions. Tex. R. Civ. P. 277 requires that "the court shall, whenever feasible, submit the cause upon broad-form questions." Tex. R. Civ. P. 277; *see Thota v. Young*, 366 S.W.3d 678, 689 (Tex. 2012) (rule 277's use of "whenever feasible" mandates broad-form submission in any or every instance in which it is capable of being accomplished).

Instructions on grounds of defense required. In the absence of one or more independent grounds of defense, the jury is not permitted to excuse the defendant from complying with the agreement. Standing alone, PJC 312.1 does not encompass any grounds of defense, so it is mandatory that grounds raised by the pleadings and evidence be submitted by including instructions such as PJC 312.2–312.13. *See, e.g., Traeger v. Lorenz*, 749 S.W.2d 249 (Tex. App.—San Antonio 1988, no writ) (separate grounds of waiver and abandonment should have been submitted in deed restriction case).

PJC 312.2   Defenses—Instruction on Plaintiff's Material Breach (Failure of Consideration)

Failure to comply by *Don Davis* is excused by *Paul Payne*'s previous failure to comply with a material obligation of the same agreement.

COMMENT

When to use. PJC 312.2 may accompany PJC 312.1 if the defendant raises the affirmative defense of the plaintiff's material breach of the agreement. Generally, when one party to a contract commits a material breach of that contract, the other party is discharged or excused from future performance. *Bartush-Schnitzius Foods Co. v. Cimco Refrigeration, Inc.*, 518 S.W.3d 432, 436 (Tex. 2017); *see also Mustang Pipeline Co. v. Driver Pipeline Co.*, 134 S.W.3d 195, 196 (Tex. 2004). A material breach does not discharge a claim for damages that have already arisen. *Bartush-Schnitzius Foods Co.*, 518 S.W.3d at 437.

Form of instruction. The instruction is suggested by *Huff v. Speer*, 554 S.W.2d 259, 262 (Tex. App.—Houston [1st Dist.] 1977, writ ref'd n.r.e.), and *King Title Co. v. Croft*, 562 S.W.2d 536, 537 (Tex. App.—El Paso 1978, no writ).

If the plaintiff's alleged failure to comply involves the timeliness of the plaintiff's performance and if no date for completion is specified in the agreement, this instruction may be modified to incorporate applicable language from PJC 305.11.

Material breach vs. failure of consideration. Although designated here as plaintiff's material breach, the issue is commonly referred to as failure or partial failure of consideration. The Committee considers the latter designation inappropriate and confusing, however, because it suggests issues relating to contract formation. See PJC 305.4; see also PJC 305.15. The facts involved usually pertain instead to the affirmative defense that the party seeking to recover on a contract has breached it in a manner sufficient to excuse the defendant's noncompliance. *See National Bank of Commerce v. Williams*, 84 S.W.2d 691, 692 (Tex. 1935); *Austin Lake Estates, Inc. v. Meyer*, 557 S.W.2d 380, 384 (Tex. App.—Austin 1977, no writ).

Whether a breach is so material as to support this defense is a question of fact for the jury. *Bartush-Schnitzius Foods Co.*, 518 S.W.3d at 436. In determining the materiality of a breach, courts will consider, among other things, "the extent to which the nonbreaching party will be deprived of the benefit that it could have reasonably anticipated from full performance." *Lennar Corp. v. Markel American Insurance Co.*, 413 S.W.3d 750, 755 (Tex. 2013); *see also Restatement (Second) of Contracts* § 241(a) (1981).

If the parties dispute whether the alleged breach is a material one, the court should insert any or all of the following instructions regarding materiality, as appropriate:

A failure to comply must be material. The circumstances to consider in determining whether a failure to comply is material include:

1.   the extent to which the injured party will be deprived of the benefit which he reasonably expected;

2.   the extent to which the injured party can be adequately compensated for the part of that benefit of which he will be deprived;

3.   the extent to which the party failing to perform or to offer to perform will suffer forfeiture;

4.   the likelihood that the party failing to perform or to offer to perform will cure his failure, taking into account the circumstances including any reasonable assurances;

5.   the extent to which the behavior of the party failing to perform or to offer to perform comports with standards of good faith and fair dealing.

See Mustang Pipeline Co., 134 S.W.3d at 199 (adopting *Restatement (Second) of Contracts* § 241 (1981)).

PJC 312.3   Defenses—Instruction on Anticipatory Repudiation

Failure to comply by *Don Davis* is excused by *Paul Payne*'s prior repudiation of the same agreement.

A party repudiates an agreement when he indicates, by his words or actions, that he is not going to perform his obligations under the agreement in the future, showing a fixed intention to abandon, renounce, and refuse to perform the agreement. The repudiation must be absolute and unconditional.

COMMENT

When to use.   PJC 312.3 submits the doctrine of anticipatory repudiation as a defensive measure. It may also be appropriate, in slightly different form, as an element of the plaintiff's cause of action. Upon a party's repudiation of a contract, the nonrepudiating party may treat the repudiation as a breach or may continue to perform under the contract and await the time of the agreed-upon performance. *Ingersoll-Rand Co. v. Valero Energy Corp.*, 997 S.W.2d 203, 211 (Tex. 1999); *Pagosa Oil & Gas, L.L.C. v. Marrs & Smith Partnership*, 323 S.W.3d 203, 216 (Tex. App.—El Paso 2010, pet. denied).

Source of instruction.   The elements in the instruction are adapted from the discussion of the doctrine in *Universal Life & Accident Insurance Co. v. Sanders*, 102 S.W.2d 405, 406–07 (Tex. 1937); *Moore v. Jenkins*, 211 S.W. 975, 976 (Tex. 1919); *Pollack v. Pollack*, 39 S.W.2d 853, 856–57 (Tex. Comm'n App. 1931, holding approved); and *Group Life & Health Insurance Co. v. Turner*, 620 S.W.2d 670, 672–73 (Tex. App.—Dallas 1981, no writ).

"Without just excuse."   To excuse a failure to comply, the repudiation must have been "without just excuse." *Group Life & Health Insurance Co.*, 620 S.W.2d at 673 (quoting *Sanders*, 102 S.W.2d at 407); *Parkway Dental Associates, P.A. v. Ho & Huang Properties, L.P.*, 391 S.W.3d 596, 606 (Tex. App.—Houston [14th Dist.] 2012, no pet.); *see Pollack*, 39 S.W.2d at 855.

UCC cases.   In cases involving the sale of goods, the instruction defining anticipatory repudiation may need to be revised. *See* Tex. Bus. & Com. Code § 2.610 (Tex. UCC).

PJC 312.4   Defenses—Instruction on Waiver

Failure to comply by *Don Davis* is excused if compliance is waived by *Paul Payne*.

Waiver is an intentional surrender of a known right or intentional conduct inconsistent with claiming the right.

COMMENT

When to use. PJC 312.4 is appropriate to submit the affirmative defense of waiver. It may also be appropriate, in slightly different form, as an element of the plaintiff's cause of action, because waiver is an independent ground of recovery. *See Middle States Petroleum Corp. v. Messenger*, 368 S.W.2d 645, 654 (Tex. App.—Dallas 1963, writ ref'd n.r.e.). The Committee believes that an instruction on waiver should be submitted if the issue is raised by the evidence. *But see Island Recreational Development Corp. v. Republic of Texas Savings Ass'n*, 710 S.W.2d 551 (Tex. 1986) (affirming judgment notwithstanding lack of submission of waiver).

Source of definition. The definition is adapted from *Chalker Energy Partners III, LLC v. Le Norman Operating LLC*, 595 S.W.3d 668, 676 (Tex. 2020); *see also Gage v. Langford*, 582 S.W.2d 203, 207 (Tex. App.—Eastland 1979, writ ref'd n.r.e.) (definition of waiver incorrectly omitted "intentionally" from phrase "giving up, relinquishment, or surrender of some known right"). Silence or inaction for a long period of time can show an intent to yield a known right and constitute waiver. *Tenneco Inc. v. Enterprise Products Co.*, 925 S.W.2d 640, 643 (Tex. 1996).

Distinguished from estoppel. The supreme court has emphasized the unilateral character of waiver and distinguished it from estoppel:

> [W]aiver is essentially unilateral in its character; it results as a legal consequence from some act or conduct of the party against whom it operates; no act of the party in whose favor it is made is necessary to complete it. It need not be founded upon a new agreement or be supported by consideration, nor is it essential that it be based upon an estoppel.

Massachusetts Bonding & Insurance Co. v. Orkin Exterminating Co., 416 S.W.2d 396, 401 (Tex. 1967).

UCC article 2 cases. A waiver affecting an executory portion of the agreement may be retracted on reasonable notification that strict performance will be required. Tex. Bus. & Com. Code § 2.209(e) (Tex. UCC).

PJC 312.5   Defenses—Instruction on Equitable Estoppel

Failure to comply by *Don Davis* is excused if the following circumstances occurred:

1. *Paul Payne*

   a.   by words or conduct made a false representation or concealed material facts, and

   b.   with knowledge of the facts or with knowledge or information that would lead a reasonable person to discover the facts, and

   c.   with the intention that *Don Davis* would rely on the false representation or concealment in acting or deciding not to act; and

2. *Don Davis*

   a.   did not know and had no means of knowing the real facts and

   b.   relied to *his* detriment on the false representation or concealment of material facts.

COMMENT

When to use.   PJC 312.5 submits the affirmative defense of equitable estoppel.

Source of definition.   The elements of estoppel are adapted from *Schroeder v. Texas Iron Works, Inc.*, 813 S.W.2d 483, 489 (Tex. 1991); *Gulbenkian v. Penn*, 252 S.W.2d 929, 932 (Tex. 1952). For a general discussion of equitable estoppel, see *Barfield v. Howard M. Smith Co. of Amarillo*, 426 S.W.2d 834 (Tex. 1968).

Equitable estoppel distinguished from other types of estoppel.   Equitable estoppel differs from other types of estoppel because it requires some deception practiced on a party who was misled to his injury. *Bocanegra v. Aetna Life Insurance Co.*, 605 S.W.2d 848, 851 (Tex. 1980). That party, however, must show his reliance on the representation. *Shields Limited Partnership v. Bradberry*, 526 S.W.3d 471, 486 (Tex. 2017).

Estoppel based on silence.   Estoppel may also be based on silence or inaction, rather than on affirmative misrepresentations, if one under a duty to speak or act has by his silence or inaction misled the opposing party to his detriment. *Smith v. National Resort Communities, Inc.*, 585 S.W.2d 655, 658 (Tex. 1979); *Scott v. Vandor*, 671 S.W.2d 79, 87 (Tex. App.—Houston [1st Dist.] 1984, writ ref'd n.r.e.). If estoppel is based on something other than affirmative misrepresentations, a different instruction should be substituted for PJC 312.5.

PJC 312.6   Defenses—Instruction on Duress

Failure to comply by *Don Davis* is excused if the agreement was made under duress caused by *Paul Payne*.

Duress is the mental, physical, or economic coercion of another, causing that party to act contrary to his free will and interest.

COMMENT

When to use.   PJC 312.6 is appropriate if one party claims the agreement is voidable because it was made under duress. It may also be used in slightly different language to submit an affirmative claim for rescission. As a general rule, a party seeking cancellation or rescission must do equity by restoring the other party to his original status. *Texas Co. v. State*, 281 S.W.2d 83, 91 (Tex. 1955); *Freyer v. Michels*, 360 S.W.2d 559, 562 (Tex. App.—Dallas 1962, writ dism'd). It is not clear whether this rule applies if the doctrine is asserted as a defense.

Source of definition.   The definition is derived from *Black Lake Pipe Line Co. v. Union Construction Co.*, 538 S.W.2d 80, 85 n.2 (Tex. 1976), *overruled on other grounds by Sterner v. Marathon Oil Co.*, 767 S.W.2d 686 (Tex. 1989); *Brooks v. Taylor*, 359 S.W.2d 539, 542 (Tex. App.—Amarillo 1962, writ ref'd n.r.e.); and *Housing Authority of City of Dallas v. Hubbell*, 325 S.W.2d 880, 905 (Tex. App.—Dallas 1959, writ ref'd n.r.e.).

Caveat.   Unless the alleged coercion can legally constitute duress, PJC 312.6 should not be submitted. It is never duress to threaten to do that which a party has a legal right to do. *In re First Merit Bank, N.A.*, 52 S.W.3d 749, 758 (Tex. 2001). Filing or threatening to file a civil suit cannot, as a matter of law, constitute duress. *Continental Casualty Co. v. Huizar*, 740 S.W.2d 429, 430 (Tex. 1987). The vice arises only if extortive measures are employed or if improper demands are made in bad faith. *Matthews v. Matthews*, 725 S.W.2d 275, 279 (Tex. App.—Houston [1st Dist.] 1986, writ ref'd n.r.e.); *Sanders v. Republic National Bank*, 389 S.W.2d 551, 555 (Tex. App.—Tyler 1965, no writ); *see also Mitchell v. C.C. Sanitation Co.*, 430 S.W.2d 933 (Tex. App.—Houston [14th Dist.] 1968, writ ref'd n.r.e.). *State National Bank v. Farah Manufacturing Co.*, 678 S.W.2d 661 (Tex. App.—El Paso 1984, judgm't dism'd by agr.), gives a general overview of this topic. A threat to file criminal prosecution may constitute duress even if the threatened party is guilty of the crime. *Pierce v. Estate of Haverlah*, 428 S.W.2d 422, 425 (Tex. App.—Tyler 1968, writ ref'd n.r.e.).

Economic duress.   If economic duress is alleged, this instruction should be submitted only if the party against whom duress is charged was responsible for the other party's financial distress. *Simpson v. MBank Dallas, N.A.*, 724 S.W.2d 102, 109 (Tex.

App.—Dallas 1987, writ ref'd n.r.e.); *Griffith v. Geffen & Jacobsen, P.C.*, 693 S.W.2d 724, 728 (Tex. App.—Dallas 1985, no writ).

Imminence of harm.   The threat of harm must be imminent, and the threatened party must have no present means of protection. It must cause the threatened person to do what there was no legal obligation to do. *Dale v. Simon*, 267 S.W. 467, 470 (Tex. Comm'n App. 1924, judgm't adopted); *Creative Manufacturing, Inc. v. Unik, Inc.*, 726 S.W.2d 207, 211 (Tex. App.—Fort Worth 1987, writ ref'd n.r.e.).

PJC 312.7   Defenses—Instruction on Undue Influence

Failure to comply by *Don Davis* is excused if the agreement was made as the result of undue influence by *Paul Payne*.

"Undue influence" means that there was such dominion and control exercised over the mind of the person executing the agreement, under the facts and circumstances then existing, as to overcome his free will. In effect, the will of the party exerting undue influence was substituted for that of the party entering the agreement, preventing him from exercising his own discretion and causing him to do what he would not have done but for such dominion and control.

COMMENT

When to use.   PJC 312.7 is appropriate when one party disputes the existence of the agreement because it was made under undue influence. As a general rule, a party seeking cancellation or rescission must do equity by restoring the other party to his original status. *Texas Co. v. State*, 281 S.W.2d 83, 91 (Tex. 1955); *Freyer v. Michels*, 360 S.W.2d 559, 562 (Tex. App.—Dallas 1962, writ dism'd). It is not clear whether this rule applies if the doctrine is asserted as a defense.

Source of definition.   The definition is adapted from *Rothermel v. Duncan*, 369 S.W.2d 917, 922 (Tex. 1963). Although that case concerns a will contest, the definition for undue influence used in *Rothermel* is often used in cases involving disputes over agreements. *See Decker v. Decker*, 192 S.W.3d 648, 651 (Tex. App.—Fort Worth 2006, no pet.) (dispute over agreement to transfer deed); *Seymour v. American Engine & Grinding Co.*, 956 S.W.2d 49, 59 (Tex. App.—Houston [14th Dist.] 1996, pet. denied) (dispute involving stock purchase agreement).

"Undue influence."   Not every influence exerted on the will of another is undue. *Rothermel*, 369 S.W.2d at 922. The exertion of undue influence is usually a subtle thing involving an extended course of dealings and circumstances, and it may be proved by circumstantial as well as direct evidence. *Rothermel*, 369 S.W.2d at 922. Influence is not undue merely because it is persuasive and effective, and the law does not condemn all persuasion, entreaty, importunity, or intercession. *B.A.L. v. Edna Gladney Home*, 677 S.W.2d 826, 830 (Tex. App.—Fort Worth 1984, writ ref'd n.r.e.); *In re C.E.*, No. 02-14-0054-CV, 2014 WL 3866159, at *6 (Tex. App.—Fort Worth Aug. 7, 2014, no pet.).

PJC 312.8   Defenses—Instruction on Mutual Mistake of Fact

Failure to comply is excused if the agreement was made as the result of a mutual mistake.

A mutual mistake results from a mistake of fact common to both parties if both parties had the same misconception concerning the fact in question. A mistake by one party but not the other is not a mutual mistake.

COMMENT

When to use.   PJC 312.8 is appropriate when a party disputes terms of the agreement on the basis that they were established by mutual mistake of fact. See PJC 312.9 for an instruction on mutual mistake due to a scrivener's error.

Mistake must relate to same subject matter.   To prove a mutual mistake, evidence must show that both parties had the same misunderstanding of the same material fact. *A.L.G. Enterprises v. Huffman*, 660 S.W.2d 603, 606 (Tex. App.—Corpus Christi–Edinburg 1983), *aff'd & remanded for mutual mistake issue only*, 672 S.W.2d 230 (Tex. 1984).

Excuses failure to perform.   Mutual mistake is an equitable defense that, if proved, excuses a party's failure to perform a contract. *A.L.G. Enterprises*, 660 S.W.2d at 606; *but see Geodyne Energy Income Production Partnership I-E v. Newton Corp.*, 161 S.W.3d 482, 491 (Tex. 2005) (holding that "[a] person who intentionally assumes the risk of unknown facts cannot escape a bargain by alleging mistake or misunderstanding" (footnote omitted)). The question of mutual mistake is for the jury. *See, e.g., Davis v. Grammer*, 750 S.W.2d 766, 767 (Tex. 1988) (illustrating that mutual mistake is submitted to the jury); *see also James T. Taylor & Son, Inc. v. Arlington Independent School District*, 335 S.W.2d 371, 376 (Tex. 1960). This instruction may also be used, in slightly different language, to submit an affirmative claim for rescission.

Caveat: unilateral mistake.   Case law has drawn a distinction between unilateral and mutual mistake. Evidence may give rise to a defense based on unilateral mistake but fail to raise a defense based on mutual mistake. *See Durham v. Uvalde Rock Asphalt Co.*, 599 S.W.2d 866, 870 (Tex. App.—San Antonio 1980, no writ). For a discussion of issues involved in cases of unilateral mistake, see *Monarch Marking System Co. v. Reed's Photo Mart, Inc.*, 485 S.W.2d 905 (Tex. 1972).

PJC 312.9   **Defenses—Instruction on Mutual Mistake—Scrivener's Error**

Failure to comply is excused if [*the breached term*] resulted from a mutual mistake.

A mutual mistake arises when the parties have previously reached an agreement but, because of a mistake common to both parties, the [*instrument*] as written does not reflect the prior agreement.

Unilateral mistake by one party, and knowledge of that mistake by the other party, is equivalent to mutual mistake.

COMMENT

When to use.   PJC 312.9 is appropriate if a party seeks to avoid the enforcement of a disputed term of the agreement because it resulted from a mutual mistake in reducing the agreement to writing. For an instruction on mutual mistake of fact, see PJC 312.8; for a question and instruction on reformation as an affirmative cause of action resulting from mutual mistake due to a scrivener's error, see PJC 305.20.

Source of instruction.   When addressing the elements of mutual mistake as a defense, Texas courts incorporate the elements of reformation. *See Samson Exploration, LLC v. T.S. Reed Properties, Inc.*, 521 S.W.3d 766 (Tex. 2017); *CenterPoint Energy Houston Electric, L.L.P. v. Old TJC Co.*, 177 S.W.3d 425, 430 n.3 (Tex. App.—Houston [1st Dist.] 2005, pet. denied) (mutual mistake is an affirmative defense); *Gail v. Berry*, 343 S.W.3d 520, 524 (Tex. App.—Eastland 2011, pet. denied) (recognizing that a scrivener's error is a type of mutual mistake); *Wright v. Gernandt*, 559 S.W.2d 864, 868 (Tex. App.—Corpus Christi–Edinburg 1977, no writ) (analyzing elements of reformation for affirmative defense of mutual mistake based on scrivener's error).

"[R]eformation requires two elements: (1) an original agreement and (2) a mutual mistake, made *after* the original agreement, in reducing the original agreement to writing." *Cherokee Water Co. v. Forderhause*, 741 S.W.2d 377, 379 (Tex. 1987) (emphasis added). An exception to the requirement that the mistake be mutual is the unilateral mistake by one party "accompanied by fraud or other inequitable conduct of the remaining party." *Cambridge Companies, Inc. v. Williams*, 602 S.W.2d 306, 308 (Tex. App.—Texarkana 1980), *aff'd on other grounds*, 615 S.W.2d 172 (Tex. 1981). "Unilateral mistake by one party, and knowledge of that mistake by the other party, is equivalent to mutual mistake." *Davis v. Grammer*, 750 S.W.2d 766, 768 (Tex. 1988) (citing *Cambridge Companies, Inc.*, 602 S.W.2d at 308).

PJC 312.10   Defenses—Instruction on Novation

Failure to comply with one agreement is excused if the parties agreed that a new agreement would take its place.

COMMENT

When to use.   PJC 312.10 may be used to submit the affirmative defense of novation. Novation occurs when the rights of the parties are determined by a new agreement that extinguishes the previous one. *See Flanagan v. Martin*, 880 S.W.2d 863, 867 (Tex. App.—Waco 1994, writ dism'd w.o.j.); *DoAll Dallas Co. v. Trinity National Bank*, 498 S.W.2d 396, 400–401 (Tex. App.—Texarkana 1973, writ ref'd n.r.e.). A novation may also be the substitution of new for old parties to an agreement. *See Russell v. Northeast Bank*, 527 S.W.2d 783, 786 (Tex. App.—Houston [1st Dist.] 1975, writ ref'd n.r.e.).

If reasonable minds differ on the evidence of a new express agreement, novation is a question of law for the court. Absent an express agreement, novation is a question of fact. *Chastain v. Cooper & Reed*, 257 S.W.2d 422, 424 (Tex. 1953).

Accord and satisfaction distinguished from novation.   The defense of accord and satisfaction "rests upon a new contract, express or implied, in which the parties agree to the discharge of an existing obligation in a manner otherwise than originally agreed." *Harris v. Rowe*, 593 S.W.2d 303, 306 (Tex. 1979).

"An accord and satisfaction may or may not be also a novation, but where the new promise itself is accepted as satisfaction the transaction is more properly termed a novation." *DoAll Dallas Co.*, 498 S.W.2d at 400.

PJC 312.11   Defenses—Instruction on Modification

Failure to comply with a term in an agreement is excused if the parties agreed that a new term would take its place.

COMMENT

When to use. PJC 312.11 is appropriate if the defendant claims he was excused from complying with a term of the agreement because the parties had agreed to modify the agreement by substituting a new term for an old term. *See Hathaway v. General Mills, Inc.*, 711 S.W.2d 227, 228 (Tex. 1986) (parties have power to modify their contracts); *Mandril v. Kasishke*, 620 S.W.2d 238, 244 (Tex. App.—Amarillo 1981, writ ref'd n.r.e.) (parties have power to make and modify contracts). A modification must satisfy the elements of a contract: a meeting of the minds supported by consideration. *Hathaway*, 711 S.W.2d at 228. The question of whether a modification has taken place is one of fact and depends on the intent of the parties. *Hathaway*, 711 S.W.2d at 228–29.

Burden of proof. The burden of proving modification rests on the party asserting the modification. *Hathaway*, 711 S.W.2d at 229.

UCC article 2 cases. An agreement modifying a sales contract needs no consideration to be binding, but any modification must meet the test of good faith imposed by the Code. Tex. Bus. & Com. Code § 2.209(a) & cmt. 2 (Tex. UCC). *See El Paso Natural Gas Co. v. Minco Oil & Gas, Inc.*, 8 S.W.3d 309, 314 (Tex. 1999).

Accord and satisfaction and novation. For instructions on accord and satisfaction and novation, see PJC 312.12 and 312.10.

PJC 312.12   Defenses—Instruction on Accord and Satisfaction

Failure to comply with an agreement is excused if a different performance was accepted as full satisfaction of performance of the original obligations of the agreement.

COMMENT

When to use.   PJC 312.12 is appropriate to submit the affirmative defense of accord and satisfaction. This defense is raised by pleading and evidence that the plaintiff agreed to and accepted performance different from that of the original agreement, in full satisfaction of the original obligation. *Jenkins v. Henry C. Beck Co.*, 449 S.W.2d 454, 455 (Tex. 1969); *see also Pileco, Inc. v. HCI, Inc.*, 735 S.W.2d 561 (Tex. App.— Houston [1st Dist.] 1987, writ ref'd n.r.e.). If the plaintiff refuses to accept the defendant's performance of an executory accord, the defendant may seek to enforce the terms of the accord and satisfaction by specific performance but is not absolved of its obligation to perform under the accord and satisfaction. *See Alexander v. Handley*, 146 S.W.2d 740, 743 (Tex. Comm'n App. 1941, holding approved) (nonbreaching party to executory accord can choose to enforce the original agreement or seek enforcement of the agreement in accord and satisfaction); *BACM 2001-1 San Felipe Road Ltd. Partnership v. Trafalgar Holdings I, Ltd.*, 218 S.W.3d 137, 146 (Tex. App.—Houston [14th Dist.] 2007, pet. denied) (when debtor failed to perform under an executory accord, creditor could sue to recover under the original cause of action or the accord).

If existence of accord is disputed.   If existence of the accord is disputed, the above instruction should be accompanied by an instruction on the elements of agreement, mutual assent, and, if appropriate, other elements of contract formation as suggested in PJC 305.4–305.9.

PJC 312.13 Defenses—Instruction on Mental Capacity

Failure to comply is excused if *Don Davis* lacked sufficient mind and memory to understand the nature and consequences of *his* acts and the business *he* was transacting.

COMMENT

When to use. PJC 312.13 is appropriate if a party defends on the basis of lack of mental capacity. It may also be used, in slightly different language, to submit an affirmative claim for rescission.

Source of instruction. The instruction is derived from *Mandell & Wright v. Thomas*, 441 S.W.2d 841, 845 (Tex. 1969); *see also Kinsel v. Lindsey*, 526 S.W.3d 411, 419 (Tex. 2017).

Burden of proof. The burden of proof falls on the party seeking to show lack of mental capacity. *Walker v. Eason*, 643 S.W.2d 390, 391 (Tex. 1982).

PJC 312.14   Defenses—Statute of Frauds (Comment)

Agreements that must be in writing.   It is a defense to the enforcement of certain contracts that the promise or agreement was not made or reflected in a writing signed by the party against whom enforcement is sought. *See* Tex. Bus. & Com. Code § 26.01(a)(1), (a)(2) ("A promise or agreement [described in this statute] is not enforceable unless the promise or agreement, or a memorandum of it, is in writing; and signed by the person to be charged with the promise or agreement or by someone lawfully authorized to sign for him.").

Contracts that require a writing include but are not limited to a promise by an executor or administrator to answer for a debt due from the estate; a promise to answer for the debt of another; an agreement made on consideration of marriage; a contract for the sale of real estate; a lease of real estate for a term longer than one year; an agreement that is not to be performed within one year of the date of making the agreement; a promise to pay a commission for an oil or gas lease, royalty, or mineral interest; and a promise of cure relating to medical care by a health-care provider. *See, e.g.,* Tex. Bus. & Com. Code § 26.01(b). In oil and gas cases this defense most often arises in connection with challenges to the sufficiency of the description of land included in a conveyance.

Description of land.   A contract to convey real property or a contract affecting real property, such as an area of mutual interest agreement, an oil and gas lease, an exploration agreement, a participation agreement, or a joint operating agreement, falls within the statute of frauds. *See* Tex. Bus. & Com. Code § 26.01; *see also Westland Oil Development Corp. v. Gulf Oil Corp.*, 637 S.W.2d 903, 908–09 (Tex. 1982). To satisfy the requirements of the statute of frauds, a contract "must furnish within itself, or by reference to some other existing writing, the means or data by which the [property] to be conveyed may be identified with reasonable certainty." *Long Trusts v. Griffin*, 222 S.W.3d 412, 416 (Tex. 2006) (per curiam) (quoting *Morrow v. Shotwell*, 477 S.W.2d 538, 539 (Tex. 1972)). If there is no written description of the property covered by the agreement, a map or other pictorial representation must be capable of identifying the property with reasonable certainty. *Guenther v. Amer-Tex Construction Co.*, 534 S.W.2d 396, 397 (Tex. App.—Austin 1976, no writ). The issue of the sufficiency of the land description is a question of law. *Haines v. McLean*, 276 S.W.2d 777, 781–82 (Tex. 1955); *Dixon v. Amoco Production Co.*, 150 S.W.3d 191, 194 (Tex. App.—Tyler 2004, pet. denied).

Legal question.   Whether a contract falls within the statute of frauds is a legal question. *Bratcher v. C.K. Dozier*, 346 S.W.2d 795, 796 (Tex. 1961) (holding that duration of a contract is a legal question and not an issue for the jury to decide). *But see Metromarketing Services, Inc. v. HTT Headwear, Ltd.*, 15 S.W.3d 190, 196 (Tex. App.—Houston [14th Dist.] 2000, no pet.) (stating that if extrinsic evidence is disputed about whether an agreement can be completed within one year and thus does not fall within statute of frauds, what constitutes reasonable time for completion is question of fact).

The defense must be raised, or it is waived; a contract subject to the statute of frauds is voidable, not void. *See* Tex. R. Civ. P. 94 (requiring parties to plead statute of frauds as an affirmative defense); *Crill, Inc. v. Bond*, 76 S.W.3d 411, 420 (Tex. App.—Dallas 2001, no writ) (holding that agreement subject to statute of frauds could not be challenged by third party, as it was voidable and not void).

Exceptions to writing requirement.   Equitable remedies exist for enforcing an oral promise or unsigned agreement that is otherwise unenforceable because of the statute of frauds, where application of the statute of frauds would be unfair due to partial or full performance of the oral agreement or detrimental reliance. These exceptions can involve questions of fact. *Adams v. Petrade International, Inc.*, 754 S.W.2d 696, 705 (Tex. App.—Houston [1st Dist.] 1988, writ denied). Examples include the main purpose doctrine (see PJC 305.21); promissory estoppel (see PJC 305.23); and quantum meruit (see PJC 305.24). In addition, although the statute of frauds forecloses a fraudulent inducement claim, a limited fraud claim for out-of-pocket damages is not similarly barred. *See Haase v. Glazner*, 62 S.W.3d 795, 799 (Tex. 2001).

Burden of proof.   The party pleading the statute of frauds bears the initial burden of establishing its applicability. Tex. R. Civ. P. 94; *Dynegy, Inc. v. Yates*, 422 S.W.3d 638 (Tex. 2013). Once that party meets its initial burden, the burden shifts to the opposing party to establish an exception that would take the verbal contract out of the statute of frauds. *Dynegy, Inc.*, 422 S.W.3d at 641.

Electronic satisfaction.   Regarding the electronic satisfaction of the requirement for a writing, see the Texas Uniform Electronic Transactions Act, chapter 322 of the Texas Business and Commerce Code. Tex. Bus. & Com. Code §§ 322.001–.021.

Contracts for international sale of goods.   The statute of frauds does not apply to contracts subject to the 1980 United Nations Convention on Contracts for the International Sale of Goods. United Nations Convention on Contracts for the International Sale of Goods, Apr. 11, 1980, 1489 U.N.T.S. 3 ("A contract of sale need not be concluded in or evidenced by a writing and is not subject to any other requirement as to form. It may be proved by any means, including witnesses.").

PJC 312.15 Question on Statute of Limitations—Discovery Rule

QUESTION _____

By what date should *Paul Payne*, in the exercise of reasonable diligence, have discovered the [*event(s) giving rise to the plaintiff's claim*]?

Answer with a date in the blank below.

Answer: _____

COMMENT

When to use. PJC 312.15 should be used when the discovery rule is submitted to the jury as a plea in confession and avoidance to a statute-of-limitations defense. The events that give rise to the plaintiff's claim may be either the conduct or the injury. *See Exxon Corp. v. Emerald Oil & Gas Co.*, 348 S.W.3d 194, 207 (Tex. 2011). If the discovery rule is submitted in terms of the plaintiff's discovery of a wrongfully caused injury, it may be necessary to define "injury" and "wrongful acts"; otherwise, the jury might be impermissibly allowed to speculate on the meanings of those terms.

Source of question. PJC 312.15 is derived from *Willis v. Maverick*, 760 S.W.2d 642, 647 (Tex. 1988), and *Cosgrove v. Cade*, 468 S.W.3d 32 (Tex. 2015). See also the current edition of State Bar of Texas, *Texas Pattern Jury Charges—Business, Consumer, Insurance & Employment* PJC 102.23, 105.5.

Application of the discovery rule. "The discovery rule applies 'only when the nature of the plaintiff's injury is both inherently undiscoverable and objectively verifiable.'" *Shell Oil Co. v. Ross*, 356 S.W.3d 924, 930 (Tex. 2011) (quoting *Wagner & Brown, Ltd. v. Horwood*, 58 S.W.3d 732, 734 (Tex. 2001)); *see also HECI Exploration Co. v. Neel*, 982 S.W.2d 881, 886 (Tex. 1998). "An injury is inherently undiscoverable if by its nature, it is 'unlikely to be discovered within the prescribed limitations period despite due diligence.'" *Ross*, 356 S.W.3d at 930 (quoting *S.V. v. R.V.*, 933 S.W.2d 1, 7 (Tex. 1996)). "The legal question of whether an injury is inherently undiscoverable is determined on a categorical basis." *Ross*, 356 S.W.3d at 930. *See also Cosgrove*, 468 S.W.3d at 36. For a question and instruction on reformation as an affirmative cause of action, see PJC 305.20.

Distinct damages claims. If the plaintiff has multiple claims involving distinctly different conduct and the limitations defense is raised, the Committee recommends that separate liability, damages, and limitations questions be submitted.

PJC 312.16   Question and Instruction on Repudiation of Title

If you answered "Yes" to Question _____ [*applicable liability question*], then answer the following question. Otherwise, do not answer the following question.

QUESTION _____

Was *Larry Lessee*'s failure to comply with the oil and gas lease excused?

A lessee's failure to comply with the terms of an oil and gas lease is excused by the lessor's repudiation of the lease. A lessor repudiates an oil and gas lease when a lessor gives the lessee unqualified notice asserting the lessee's interest has terminated or been forfeited.

Answer "Yes" or "No."

Answer: _____

COMMENT

When to use.   PJC 312.16 is appropriate to use when repudiation is asserted as a defense to either breach of lease or a lease termination claim and should be predicated on an appropriate finding in such a case.

Source of question and instruction.   PJC 312.16 is derived from *Coastal Oil & Gas Corp. v. Garza Energy Trust*, 268 S.W.3d 1, 20 (Tex. 2008); *Ridge Oil Co. v. Guinn Investments, Inc.*, 148 S.W.3d 143, 157 (Tex. 2004); *Kothmann v. Boley*, 308 S.W.2d 1, 4 (Tex. 1958); and *Cheyenne Resources, Inc. v. Criswell*, 714 S.W.2d 103, 105 (Tex. App.—Eastland 1986, no writ).

Reliance.   Some Texas appellate courts have recognized that a lessee's suspension of operations in reliance on, or as a result of, the lessor's alleged repudiation, while seemingly implicit in the doctrine of repudiation of a lease, has also been stated to be part of the showing that the lessee must make to establish the lessor's repudiation. *Rippy Interests, LLC v. Nash*, 475 S.W.3d 353, 363 (Tex. App.—Waco 2014, pet. denied) (reversing lessor's no-reliance summary judgment on lessee's repudiation claims because lessee had raised a fact issue on reliance); *Atlantic Richfield Co. v. Hilton*, 437 S.W.2d 347, 355 (Tex. App.—Tyler 1969, writ ref'd n.r.e.) (holding that to establish "repudiation" creating an estoppel, lessee had the affirmative burden of establishing that it had actual notice of the repudiation and that, in reliance thereon, operations were suspended). In instances in which reliance is in dispute, the above question may be modified accordingly.

PJC 312.17   Question and Instruction on Statutory Defense to Withholding of Payments and Prejudgment Interest

QUESTION _____

Was [*Don Davis/Polly Payor*]'s withholding of payment [*and/or*] prejudgment interest excused?

[*Don Davis/Polly Payor*] is excused if on [*date payment due*] there was—

1.   a title dispute that would affect distribution of payment[*s*]; or

2.   a reasonable doubt that [*Paul Payne/Perry Payee*]—

   a.   sold or authorized sale of [*Paul Payne/Perry Payee*]'s share to [*purchaser*], or

   b.   had clear title to the interest of the proceeds of production; or

3.   a title opinion that places at issue title, identity, or whereabouts of [*Paul Payne/Perry Payee*], and [*Don Davis/Polly Payor*] made a reasonable request for curative information that has not been satisfied by [*Paul Payne/ Perry Payee*].

Answer "Yes" or "No."

Answer: _____

COMMENT

When to use.   PJC 312.17 is appropriate for use in payment disputes under Texas Natural Resources Code sections 91.401–.408. If there is a dispute regarding whether payment was late, see PJC 303.5 on untimely payment of royalty under the Texas Natural Resources Code.

Source of question and instruction.   PJC 312.17 is derived from Tex. Nat. Res. Code §§ 91.401(1)–(2), 91.402(b), 91.403(b); *Concord Oil Co. v. Pennzoil Exploration & Production Co.*, 966 S.W.2d 451, 461 (Tex. 1998); and *Headington Oil Co., L.P. v. White*, 287 S.W.3d 204, 209–10 (Tex. App.—Houston [14th Dist.] 2009, no pet.).

PJC 312.18   **Question and Instruction on Bona Fide Purchaser Defense**

QUESTION _____

Is *Don Davis* a bona fide purchaser of the real property?

A "bona fide purchaser" is one who purchases real property in good faith for valuable consideration without notice of a third-party claim to the property.

[Insert additional instructions regarding notice, if appropriate.]

Answer "Yes" or "No."

Answer: _____

COMMENT

When to use.   PJC 312.18 is appropriate to use when the defendant asserts the defense of bona fide purchaser.

Source of question and instruction.   PJC 312.18 is derived from *Madison v. Gordon*, 39 S.W.3d 604, 606 (Tex. 2001) (per curiam); *Westland Oil Development Corp. v. Gulf Oil Corp.*, 637 S.W.2d 903, 908 (Tex. 1982); *NRG Exploration, Inc. v. Rauch*, 671 S.W.2d 649, 653 (Tex. App.—Austin 1984, writ ref'd n.r.e.); *Pierson v. McClintock*, 78 S.W. 706, 707–08 (Tex. App.—Galveston 1904, no writ); and Tex. Prop. Code § 13.001.

Notice.   Notice of a third party's claim may be actual or constructive:

> "Actual notice" literally means express or positive personal information or knowledge directly communicated to the person to be affected. In a more comprehensive sense, the term also embraces knowledge of all those facts which reasonable inquiry would have disclosed, the duty of inquiry extending only to matters that are fairly suggested by the facts really known. In other words, whatever fairly puts a person upon inquiry is actual notice of the facts which would have been discovered by reasonable use of the means at hand.

Flack v. First National Bank, 226 S.W.2d 628, 631–32 (Tex. 1950). *See also Nguyen v. Chapa*, 305 S.W.3d 316, 323 (Tex. App.—Houston [14th Dist.] 2009, pet. denied) (citing *Madison*, 39 S.W.3d at 606). Generally, the question of whether a party has notice is a question of fact; it becomes a question of law only when there is no room for ordinary minds to differ about the proper conclusion to be drawn from the evidence.

O'Ferral v. Coolidge, 228 S.W.2d 146, 148 (Tex. 1950); *Morris v. Reaves*, 580 S.W.2d 891, 893 (Tex. App.—Houston [14th Dist.] 1979, no writ).

PJC 313.1   Predicate—Instruction Conditioning Damages Questions on Liability

If you answered "Yes" to Question _____ [*insert number of appropriate liability question*], then answer the following question. Otherwise, do not answer the following question.

COMMENT

When to use.   PJC 313.1 is used to condition answers to damages questions. The damages questions in this chapter assume liability in the question, so this predicate should always precede those questions. The Comments following damages questions in this chapter refer to corresponding liability questions in other chapters.

PJC 313.2   **Instruction on Whether Compensatory Damages Are Subject to Income Taxes (Actions Filed on or after September 1, 2003)**

You are instructed that any monetary recovery for [*list each element of economic or noneconomic damages that is subject to taxation*] is subject to [*federal or state*] income taxes. Any recovery for [*list each element of economic or noneconomic damages that is not subject to taxation*] is not subject to [*federal or state*] income taxes.

COMMENT

When to use. PJC 313.2 should be submitted with the damages question in any action filed on or after September 1, 2003, in which a claimant seeks recovery for loss of earnings, loss of earning capacity, loss of contributions of a pecuniary value, or loss of inheritance. Whether an element of damages is taxable depends on the substantive tax law pertaining to each cause of action.

Source of instruction. Section 18.091 of the Texas Civil Practice and Remedies Code, entitled "Proof of Certain Losses; Jury Instruction," provides:

(a) Notwithstanding any other law, if any claimant seeks recovery for loss of earnings, loss of earning capacity, loss of contributions of a pecuniary value, or loss of inheritance, evidence to prove the loss must be presented in the form of a net loss after reduction for income tax payments or unpaid tax liability pursuant to any federal income tax law.

(b) If any claimant seeks recovery for loss of earnings, loss of earning capacity, loss of contributions of a pecuniary value, or loss of inheritance, the court shall instruct the jury as to whether any recovery for compensatory damages sought by the claimant is subject to federal or state income taxes.

Tex. Civ. Prac. & Rem. Code § 18.091.

PJC 313.3   **Question and Instruction on Damages for Trespass Resulting in Production of Minerals**

[Insert predicate, PJC 313.1.]

QUESTION _____

What sum of money, if any, if paid now in cash, would fairly and reasonably compensate *Paul Payne* for *his* damages, if any, resulting from [*insert description of act or omission for which liability was determined*]?

Consider only the fair market value of minerals produced from *Paul Payne*'s land after the date the trespass began.

"Market value" is the price a willing seller not obligated to sell can obtain from a willing buyer not obligated to buy.

Do not include interest on any amount of damages you find.

Answer in dollars and cents, if any.

Answer: _____

COMMENT

When to use.   PJC 313.3 should be used when the plaintiff alleges that a damage caused by the trespass included the defendant producing minerals belonging to the plaintiff. This question should be predicated on a "Yes" answer to PJC 302.4. See PJC 302.5 and 313.4 for questions regarding the affirmative defense of "good-faith" trespass and damages applicable after an affirmative finding of good faith.

Source of question and instruction.   The question and instructions are derived from *Cage Brothers v. Whiteman*, 163 S.W.2d 638, 642 (Tex. Comm'n App. 1942), and *Mayfield v. Benavides*, 693 S.W.2d 500, 506 (Tex. App.—San Antonio 1985, writ ref'd n.r.e.).

PJC 313.4   **Question on Reduction of Damages Resulting from Good-Faith Trespass**

If you answered "Yes" to Question _____ [*302.5*], then answer the following question. Otherwise, do not answer the following question.

QUESTION _____

What reasonable drilling and operating costs, if any, did [*Don Davis*] incur in producing minerals from [*Paul Payne*]'s land after the date the trespass began?

Answer in dollars and cents, if any.

Answer: _____

COMMENT

When to use.   PJC 313.4 should be conditioned on an affirmative finding of good faith in answer to PJC 302.5.

Damages when trespass not in good faith.   If the trespasser is not found to have acted in good faith, damages are measured by the market value of the minerals produced, without any deductions. *Cage Brothers v. Whiteman*, 163 S.W.2d 638, 642 (Tex. Comm'n App. 1942); *Mayfield v. Benavides*, 693 S.W.2d 500, 506 (Tex. App.—San Antonio 1985, writ ref'd n.r.e.). The question for this measure of damages is at PJC 302.5.

Liability of good-faith trespasser.   A good-faith trespasser who produces oil or gas is liable to the owner only for the value of the minerals removed, after deducting reasonable drilling and operating costs. *Right of Way Oil Co. v. Gladys City Oil, Gas & Manufacturing Co.*, 157 S.W. 737, 740 (Tex. 1913); *Bender v. Brooks*, 127 S.W. 168, 170–71 (Tex. 1910); *Hunt v. HNG Oil Co.*, 791 S.W.2d 191, 193, 194 (Tex. App.—Corpus Christi–Edinburg 1990, writ denied); *Benavides*, 693 S.W.2d at 506. In *Hunt*, deductions were permitted for completion costs, production taxes, transportation charges, operating expenses, and royalties paid to the landowner.

Initial costs of drilling the well were not an allowable deduction in *Hunt* because they were incurred while the lease was in effect (and thus not during the trespass). Initial drilling costs incurred while the lease is in effect may be recoverable in equity, however. *See Wagner & Brown, Ltd. v. Sheppard*, 282 S.W.3d 419, 428–29 (Tex. 2008).

Regarding other deductions from market value that may be allowable for a good-faith trespasser, the Texas Supreme Court has analogized to cotenancy accounting rules, which permit the producing cotenant to deduct "necessary and reasonable costs of production and marketing." *Sheppard*, 282 S.W.3d at 426 (citing *Byrom v. Pendley*, 717 S.W.2d 602 (Tex. 1986)); *see also White v. Smyth*, 214 S.W.2d 967 (Tex. 1948) (upholding operating cotenant's right to deduct "payrolls, salaries, depreciation, repairs, insurance, commissions" as well as reasonable compensation for operator's personal services).

PJC 313.5   Monetary Damages Recoverable for Claims Involving
                 Physical Injury to Real Property (Other Than by
                 Production of Minerals) (Comment)

When real property has been damaged, monetary damages may be recoverable, regardless of the cause of action asserted. *Gilbert Wheeler, Inc. v. Enbridge Pipelines (E. Tex.), L.P.*, 449 S.W.3d 474, 479 (Tex. 2014) (application of the temporary-versus-permanent distinction in cases involving injury to real property is not limited to causes of action that sound in tort rather than contract).

Whether damages are available for future or only past injuries is determined by whether the injury is permanent or temporary. *Schneider National Carriers, Inc. v. Bates*, 147 S.W.3d 264, 275–76 (Tex. 2004). The general rule provides that the concepts of permanent and temporary injuries are mutually exclusive, and damages for both may not be recovered in the same action. *Schneider National Carriers, Inc.*, 147 S.W.3d at 275–76; *Gilbert Wheeler, Inc.*, 449 S.W.3d at 481. For an exception to the general rule that damages for permanent and temporary injuries may not be recovered in the same action, see *Parkway Co. v. Woodruff*, 901 S.W.2d 434, 441 (Tex. 1995), and *Ludt v. McCullum*, 762 S.W.2d 575, 576 (Tex. 1988) (per curiam).

The Texas Supreme Court has held that an injury to real property is considered permanent if (1) it cannot be repaired, fixed, or restored *or* (2) even though the injury can be repaired, fixed, or restored, it is substantially certain that the injury will repeatedly, continually, and regularly recur, such that future injury can be reasonably evaluated. *Gilbert Wheeler, Inc.*, 449 S.W.3d at 480. Loss of fair market value is the proper measure of damages in a case involving permanent injury. *Crosstex North Texas Pipeline, L.P. v. Gardiner*, 505 S.W.3d 580, 611 (Tex. 2016); *Gilbert Wheeler, Inc.*, 449 S.W.3d at 481. The recovery is measured as the "lost market value," which "should be ascertained at the date of trial, and it should be the market value of the property for any use to which it might be appropriated." *Crosstex North Texas Pipeline, L.P.*, 505 S.W.3d at 611 (quoting *Sherman Gas & Electric Co. v. Belden*, 123 S.W. 119, 121 (Tex. 1909)).

An injury to real property is considered temporary if (1) it can be repaired, fixed, or restored *and* (2) any anticipated recurrence would be only occasional, irregular, intermittent, and not reasonably predictable, such that future injury could not be estimated with reasonable certainty. *Gilbert Wheeler, Inc.*, 449 S.W.3d at 480. Generally, the proper measure of damages in cases involving temporary injuries is the cost of restoration (or replacement) plus loss of use; however, there appears to be some conflict in the cases regarding the relevant time period for which loss of use is awarded and how to measure loss of use. *See Crosstex North Texas Pipeline, L.P.*, 505 S.W.3d at 610 (loss of use up to the time of trial); *Coastal Transport Co. v. Crown Central Petroleum Corp.*, 136 S.W.3d 227, 235 (Tex. 2004) (permitting loss of use incurred while repairs were ongoing, which presumably could continue after trial was begun); *Gilbert Wheeler, Inc.*, 449 S.W.3d at 481 (noting recovery for loss of use while building is repaired permitted during interim); *J&D Towing, LLC v. American Alternative Insurance Corp.*, 478 S.W.3d 649, 677 (permitting loss of use damages so long as "reasonably needed").

Whether a physical injury to real property is permanent or temporary is a question of law to be decided by the court. *Gilbert Wheeler, Inc.*, 449 S.W.3d at 481. However, questions regarding the facts that underlie the court's legal determination, including the frequency, extent, and duration of the injury and the resulting amount of damages, must be resolved by the jury on proper request. *Gilbert Wheeler, Inc.*, 449 S.W.3d at 481.

The general rules discussed above, however, have exceptions. *See Gilbert Wheeler, Inc.*, 449 S.W.3d at 481 (noting that "general rule" should be applied with "some flexibility" and that there are "a number of exceptions"); *see also Parkway Co.*, 901 S.W.2d at 441; *Ludt*, 762 S.W.2d at 576. Exceptions to the general rule include permitting recovery of damages for "intrinsic value" (*Gilbert Wheeler, Inc.*, 449 S.W.3d at 481–82) and for limiting recovery because of the "economic feasibility" exception (*ExxonMobil Corp. v. Lazy R Ranch*, 511 S.W.3d 538, 540 (Tex. 2017)). The economic feasibility exception requires a temporary injury to be deemed a permanent one if the cost of repair "disproportionately" exceeds the diminution in the property's market value; if so the temporary injury is deemed permanent as a matter of law, and damages are awarded only for loss in fair market value. *Gilbert Wheeler, Inc.*, 449 S.W.3d at 481; *see also Houston Unlimited, Inc. v. Mel Acres Ranch*, 443 S.W.3d 820 (Tex. 2014) (discussing "stigma" damages but denying them based on a failure of evidence).

In addition to compensation for permanent or temporary injury to the real property, and in addition to the value of minerals produced in connection with a trespass (see PJC 302.4, 313.3, and 313.6–313.8), a plaintiff asserting physical injury to real property may also be entitled to recover for personal injuries and harm to personal property. The Texas Supreme Court has noted that "considerable authority" exists for the proposition that a nuisance that impairs the comfortable enjoyment of real property may give rise to damages for "annoyance and discomfiture." *Crosstex North Texas Pipeline, L.P.*, 505 S.W.3d at 610 n.21. However, because no such damages were sought in *Crosstex*, the court did not decide the scope of these damages or determine for what causes of action they are recoverable. *See also Schneider National Carriers, Inc.*, 147 S.W.3d at 276 n.53; *Vestal v. Gulf Oil Corp.*, 235 S.W.2d 440, 441–42 (Tex. 1951); *Vann v. Bowie Sewerage Co.*, 90 S.W.2d 561, 563 (Tex. Comm'n App. 1936); *City of Uvalde v. Crow*, 713 S.W.2d 154, 158–59 (Tex. App.—Texarkana 1986, writ ref'd n.r.e.). Because emotional distress, mental anguish, and punitive damages are not recoverable if based solely on a claim of negligent damage to property, a separate question on whether the property damage at issue was caused intentionally or maliciously may be needed. *Coinmach Corp. v. Aspenwood Apartment Corp.*, 417 S.W.3d 909, 922 (Tex. 2013); *Tyler v. Likes*, 962 S.W.2d 489, 497 (Tex. 1997). For damages questions on injuries to the person or personal property, which should be modified to fit the case facts, see the current edition of State Bar of Texas, *Texas Pattern Jury Charges—General Negligence, Intentional Personal Torts & Workers' Compensation* ch. 28 (personal injuries), ch. 31 (personal property).

PJC 313.6   **Question on Frequency and Duration of Injury**

[Insert predicate, PJC 313.1.]

QUESTION _____

Was the injury to the property—

1. capable of being repaired, fixed, or restored, and

2. of such a type that any anticipated recurrence would be only occasional, irregular, intermittent, and not reasonably predictable, such that future injury could not be estimated with reasonable certainty?

Answer "Yes" or "No."

Answer: _____

COMMENT

When to use. PJC 313.6 is appropriate when injury to real property has been established and the frequency, extent, or duration of the injury is disputed and must be resolved before the court may classify the injury as either temporary or permanent as a matter of law, which then determines which measure of damages is appropriate. *See Gilbert Wheeler, Inc. v. Enbridge Pipelines (E. Tex.), L.P.*, 449 S.W.3d 474, 478 (Tex. 2014) (quoting *Schneider National Carriers, Inc. v. Bates*, 147 S.W.3d 264 (Tex. 2004)). This question should be predicated on a "Yes" answer to PJC 302.2 or 302.4. The question presumes the plaintiff is seeking a finding by the court of temporary damages.

Source of question. PJC 313.6 is derived from *Gilbert Wheeler, Inc.*, 449 S.W.3d at 479–81; *see also Schneider National Carriers, Inc.*, 147 S.W.3d at 272, 276–77.

PJC 313.7   **Question and Instruction on Cost to Repair, Fix, or Restore Temporary Injury**

[Insert predicate, PJC 313.1.]

QUESTION _____

What sum of money, if any, if paid now in cash, would fairly and reasonably compensate *Paul Payne* for the injury resulting from *[insert description of act or omission for which liability was determined]*?

Consider the elements of damages listed below and none other. Consider each element separately. Do not award any sum of money on any element if you have otherwise, under some other element, awarded a sum of money for the same loss. That is, do not compensate twice for the same loss, if any. Do not include interest on any amount of damages you find.

Answer separately in dollars and cents for damages, if any.

[Insert as applicable.]

1.   The amount necessary to repair, fix, or restore *Paul Payne*'s property to the condition immediately preceding the injury.

Answer: _____

2.   The amount necessary to compensate *Paul Payne* for *his* loss of use of the property that was sustained in the past.

Answer: _____

3.   The amount that, in reasonable probability, will be sustained in the future for *Paul Payne*'s loss of the use of the property until the property can be repaired, fixed, or restored.

Answer: _____

COMMENT

When to use.   PJC 313.7 submits the measure of damages recoverable for temporary injury. *Gilbert Wheeler, Inc. v. Enbridge Pipelines (E. Tex.), L.P.*, 449 S.W.3d 474, 481 (Tex. 2014); *Schneider National Carriers, Inc. v. Bates*, 147 S.W.3d 264, 276 (Tex. 2004); *but cf. Crosstex North Texas Pipeline, L.P. v. Gardiner*, 505 S.W.3d 580, 610 (Tex. 2016) (loss of use recoverable only up to trial of the action). This question should be conditioned on a finding of liability for unreasonable use, trespass, or nuisance.

Source of question and instruction. PJC 313.7 is derived from *Crosstex North Texas Pipeline, L.P.*, 505 S.W.3d at 610; *Coinmach Corp. v. Aspenwood Apartment Corp.*, 417 S.W.3d 909 (Tex. 2013); *Schneider National Carriers, Inc.*, 147 S.W.3d at 276; *Coastal Transport Co. v. Crown Central Petroleum Corp.*, 136 S.W.3d 227, 235 (Tex. 2004); *Vestal v. Gulf Oil Corp.*, 235 S.W.2d 440, 442 (Tex. 1951); and *Mieth v. Ranchquest, Inc.*, 177 S.W.3d 296, 306 (Tex. App.—Houston [1st Dist.] 2005, no pet.). *Cf. Kraft v. Langford*, 565 S.W.2d 223, 227 (Tex. 1978), *disapproved on other grounds by Schneider National Carriers, Inc.*, 147 S.W.3d at 281 n.78 ("[T]he proper measure of damages for a temporary injury to real property is the amount necessary to place the owner of the property in the same position he occupied prior to the injury."); *C.C. Carlton Industries v. Blanchard*, 311 S.W.3d 654, 663 (Tex. App.—Austin 2010, no pet.) (quoting *Kraft*).

Economic feasibility exception. If the cost to restore the property exceeds the diminution in the property's market value to such a disproportionately high degree that the repairs are no longer economically feasible, the injury may be deemed permanent as a matter of law. *Gilbert Wheeler, Inc.*, 449 S.W.3d at 481. Therefore, the Committee recommends that questions concerning both market value *and* cost to restore be submitted to the jury. See PJC 313.8. It is unclear whether disproportionality between cost to restore and diminution in value is always a matter of law or whether, in some circumstances, it may be a fact question. In any event, upon the court's determination of the nature of the injury, only the appropriate calculation of damages (i.e., repair costs or diminution in value) should be considered. *See Gilbert Wheeler, Inc.*, 449 S.W.3d at 481. *But see Ludt v. McCullum*, 762 S.W.2d 575, 576 (Tex. 1988) (per curiam) (in DTPA case, plaintiff should be permitted to recover repairs and permanent reduction in postrepair value to real property).

Stigma damages. For a discussion of whether stigma damages are available in cases involving temporary injury to real property, i.e., damages representing the market's perception of a decrease in a property's value that may continue to exist after an injury to real property has been fully repaired or remediated, see *Houston Unlimited, Inc. v. Mel Acres Ranch*, 443 S.W.3d 820, 824 (Tex. 2014) (describing this effect as "damage to the reputation of the realty" from a prior injury).

Prejudgment interest. Instructing the jury not to add interest is suggested because prejudgment interest, if recoverable, will be calculated by the court at the time of judgment. If interest paid on an obligation is claimed as an element of damages, it may be necessary to modify the instruction on interest.

PJC 313.8   **Question and Instruction on Diminution in Market Value**

[Insert predicate, PJC 313.1.]

QUESTION _____

What sum of money, if any, if paid now in cash, would fairly and reasonably compensate *Paul Payne* for the injury resulting from [*insert description of act or omission for which liability was determined*]?

Consider only the difference in market value of *Paul Payne*'s land resulting from [*insert description of act or omission for which liability was determined*].

"Market value" is the price a willing seller not obligated to sell can obtain from a willing buyer not obligated to buy.

The difference in market value is the decrease in market value in the time immediately before and after the act or omission occurred.

Do not include interest on any amount of damages you find.

Answer in dollars and cents for damages, if any.

Answer: _____

COMMENT

When to use.   PJC 313.8 submits the measure of damages recoverable for permanent injury to real property and should be conditioned on a finding of liability. *Schneider National Carriers, Inc. v. Bates*, 147 S.W.3d 264, 276 (Tex. 2004); *General Crude Oil Co. v. Aiken*, 344 S.W.2d 668, 672–73 (Tex. 1961); *Vestal v. Gulf Oil Corp.*, 235 S.W.2d 440, 442 (Tex. 1951); *Lone Star Gas Co. v. Hutton*, 58 S.W.2d 19, 20 (Tex. Comm'n App. 1933); *Mieth v. Ranchquest, Inc.*, 177 S.W.3d 296, 303–04 (Tex. App.—Houston [1st Dist.] 2005, no pet.).

Source of question and instruction.   PJC 313.8 is derived from *Gilbert Wheeler, Inc. v. Enbridge Pipelines (E. Tex.), L.P.*, 449 S.W.3d 474 (Tex. 2014); *Schneider National Carriers, Inc.*, 147 S.W.3d at 276; *General Crude Oil Co.*, 344 S.W.2d at 672–73; *Vestal*, 235 S.W.2d at 442; *Lone Star Gas Co.*, 58 S.W.2d at 20; and *Mieth*, 177 S.W.3d at 303–04.

Intrinsic value of trees damages.   If the reduction in market value caused by a permanent injury is "essentially nominal," the plaintiff may be able to recover the damaged property's "intrinsic value." *Gilbert Wheeler, Inc.*, 449 S.W.3d at 482–83 (discussing the "intrinsic value of trees" exception and extending *Porras v. Craig*, 675

S.W.2d 503, 506 (Tex. 1984)). In such a circumstance, the following question may be used:

QUESTION _____

What sum of money, if any, if paid now in cash, would fairly and reasonably compensate *Paul Payne* for the injury resulting from [*insert description*]?

Consider only the damaged property's intrinsic worth based upon such factors as cost, depreciation, present usefulness, past return on investment, and the ornamental and utilitarian value of the property to *Paul Payne*.

Answer in dollars and cents for damages, if any.

Answer: _____

Prejudgment interest. Instructing the jury not to add interest is suggested because prejudgment interest, if recoverable, will be calculated by the court at the time of judgment. If interest paid on an obligation is claimed as an element of damages, it may be necessary to modify the instruction on interest.

PJC 313.9   **Question and Instruction on Damages for Breach of Express Pooling Provisions and Implied Duty to Pool in Good Faith**

[Insert predicate, PJC 313.1.]

QUESTION _____

What sum of money, if any, if paid now in cash, would fairly and reasonably compensate *Paul Payne* for *his* damages, if any, that resulted from *Larry Lessee*'s failure to pool *Paul Payne*'s lease in [*good faith/in accordance with the express pooling provision*]?

[Include the following if the well is a vertical well.]

Paul Payne's damages, if any, are measured by the difference in royalty *Paul Payne* would have received had the unit not been formed, less royalties already received from the unit, if any.

[Include the following if the well is a horizontal well.]

Paul Payne's damages, if any, are measured by the royalty *Paul Payne* would have received on the production attributable with reasonable probability to *Paul Payne*'s lease as if the pooled unit had not been formed, less royalties already received from the pooled unit, if any.

Do not add any amount for interest on damages, if any.

Answer in dollars and cents for damages, if any.

Answer: _____

COMMENT

When to use. PJC 313.9 should be used when the plaintiff's lease is a drillsite tract in the unit and should be predicated on a "Yes" answer to PJC 303.2 or 303.3. The applicable instruction regarding either a vertical well or a horizontal well should be included depending on the facts of the case.

Source of question and instruction. The question and instruction are derived from *Browning Oil Co. v. Luecke*, 38 S.W.3d 625, 645, 647 (Tex. App.—Austin 2000, pet. denied), and *Circle Dot Ranch, Inc. v. Sidwell Oil & Gas, Inc.*, 891 S.W.2d 342, 346 (Tex. App.—Amarillo 1995, writ denied).

Vertical vs. horizontal wells.   Oil and gas wells may be drilled "vertically," generally meaning the surface location of the well is at or near the bottom hole location of the well, or "horizontally," where the wellbore traverses a long distance horizontally with multiple drain holes along its horizontal axis. A pooling dispute may involve a pooled unit formed for either a vertical or horizontal well, and the measure of damages is different depending on which type of well is at issue. *See Browning Oil Co.*, 38 S.W.3d at 642–47 (measure of damages when lessee lacked pooling authority). Usually, in a pooling case involving a vertical well, the lessor owns the royalty under the drillsite lease where the well is located. Thus, if that lessor prevails, the pooled unit is void and "held for naught," and under the rule of capture, a drillsite lessor is entitled to the amount of additional royalty that would have been paid had there been no pooled unit, less that already received for pooled unit production. In that event, because the pooled unit is void, royalties thereafter also are paid on a lease basis, and this takes care of the lessor as to future damages. However, if the plaintiff is not a drillsite owner, presumably that plaintiff would be required to prove past and future damages on a different basis or ask for other remedies depending on the factual circumstances of each case.

If a horizontal well is involved, the damages instruction should be based on the legal principles set out in *Browning Oil Co.*, 38 S.W.3d 625. The *Browning* court gave consideration to the effect of horizontal drilling on traditional concepts of oil and gas ownership and held that a pooled unit formed without authority was invalid with respect to the drillsite lease but that the drillsite lessor's damages were limited to the royalty value of production from the land covered by the lease. *Browning Oil Co.*, 38 S.W.3d 625. The traditional rule of capture did not apply, because in a horizontal drain hole situation, each tract through which the drain hole traverses is in essence a "drillsite" tract even though production may not come to the surface at that location.

Submission of separate answers.   If there are multiple plaintiffs or lessees, it will normally be necessary to require an answer for each. It may also be necessary to require an answer for each well and each month in issue in the dispute if the plaintiff is seeking to recover prejudgment interest from multiple wells or sales or if the statute of limitations is in issue. Tex. Nat. Res. Code §§ 91.401–.406; Tex. Fin. Code §§ 304.101–.107.

Prejudgment interest.   Instructing the jury not to add interest is suggested because prejudgment interest, if recoverable, will be calculated by the court at the time of judgment. If interest paid on an obligation is claimed as an element of damages, it may be necessary to modify the instruction on interest.

PJC 313.10   **Question and Instruction on Damages for Breach of Express Royalty Provision**

[Insert predicate, PJC 313.1.]

QUESTION _____

What sum of money, if any, if paid now in cash, would fairly and reasonably compensate *Paul Payne* for *his* damages, if any, that resulted from *Larry Lessee*'s failure to pay royalties according to the lease?

Consider only the difference, if any, between the royalty *Paul Payne* would have received if *Larry Lessee* had paid royalties according to the lease, and the royalty *Paul Payne* actually received.

Do not add any amount for interest on damages, if any.

Answer in dollars and cents for damages, if any.

Answer: _____

COMMENT

When to use.   PJC 313.10 should be used to determine damages for breach of the express royalty provision and should be predicated on a "Yes" answer to PJC 303.4.

Causation.   To recover damages for breach of contract, a plaintiff must establish damages sustained as a result of the breach. *Southern Electrical Services, Inc. v. City of Houston*, 355 S.W.3d 319, 324 (Tex. App.—Houston [1st Dist.] 2011, pet. denied).

Damages for failure to pay proceeds under Texas Natural Resources Code.   A "payee" can recover damages for nonpayment of oil or gas proceeds or interest on those proceeds as required by Texas Natural Resources Code sections 91.402 and 91.403. Tex. Nat. Res. Code § 91.404(b). A successful action thereunder shall further entitle the plaintiff to attorney's fees. Tex. Nat. Res. Code § 91.406. For a question on untimely payment of proceeds of production under Tex. Nat. Res. Code §§ 91.401–.408, see PJC 303.5.

Submission of separate answers.   If there are multiple plaintiffs or lessees, it will normally be necessary to require an answer for each. It may also be necessary to require an answer for each well and each month in issue in the royalty dispute if the plaintiff is seeking to recover prejudgment interest from multiple wells or sales or if the statute of limitations is in issue. Tex. Nat. Res. Code §§ 91.401–.406; Tex. Fin. Code §§ 304.101–.107.

Prejudgment interest. Instructing the jury not to add interest is suggested because prejudgment interest, if recoverable, will be calculated by the court at the time of judgment. If interest paid on an obligation is claimed as an element of damages, it may be necessary to modify the instruction on interest.

PJC 313.11   Question and Instruction on Damages for Breach of Implied Duty to Reasonably Market Production

[Insert predicate, PJC 313.1.]

QUESTION _____

What sum of money, if any, if paid now in cash, would fairly and reasonably compensate *Paul Payne* for *his* damages, if any, that resulted from *Larry Lessee*'s failure to reasonably market the [*oil/gas*]?

Consider only the difference, if any, between the royalty *Paul Payne* would have received if *Larry Lessee* had acted as a reasonably prudent operator would under the same or similar circumstances, taking into account the interests of both *Larry Lessee* and *Paul Payne* in marketing the [*oil/gas*] produced from the lease, and the royalty *Paul Payne* actually received.

Do not add any amount for interest on damages, if any.

Answer in dollars and cents for damages, if any.

Answer: _____

COMMENT

When to use.   PJC 313.11 should be used when seeking damages for breach of the duty to reasonably market and should be predicated on a "Yes" answer to PJC 303.7.

Causation.   To recover damages for breach of contract, a plaintiff must establish damages sustained as a result of the breach. *Southern Electrical Services, Inc. v. City of Houston*, 355 S.W.3d 319, 324 (Tex. App.—Houston [1st Dist.] 2011, pet. denied).

Submission of separate answers.   If there are multiple plaintiffs or lessees, it will normally be necessary to require an answer for each. It may also be necessary to require an answer for each well and each month in issue in the dispute if the plaintiff is seeking to recover prejudgment interest from multiple wells or sales or if the statute of limitations is in issue. Tex. Nat. Res. Code §§ 91.401–.406; Tex. Fin. Code §§ 304.101–.107.

Prejudgment interest.   Instructing the jury not to add interest is suggested because prejudgment interest, if recoverable, will be calculated by the court at the time of judgment. If interest paid on an obligation is claimed as an element of damages, it may be necessary to modify the instruction on interest.

PJC 313.12   Question and Instruction on Damages for Breach of Express Market Value Royalty Provision

[Insert predicate, PJC 313.1.]

QUESTION _____

What sum of money, if any, if paid now in cash, would fairly and reasonably compensate *Paul Payne* for *his* damages, if any, that resulted from *Larry Lessee*'s failure to pay royalty based on the market value of the *[gas/other product]* at the well?

Consider only the difference, if any, between the market value at the well of *Paul Payne*'s royalty share of *[gas/other product]* produced from the subject well*[s]* and the amount of royalty that *Paul Payne* was actually paid on *[gas/other product]* produced from such well*[s]*.

Do not add any amount for interest on damages, if any.

Answer in dollars and cents for damages, if any.

Answer: _____

COMMENT

When to use.   PJC 313.12 should be used to determine damages for breach of the express market value royalty provision and should be predicated on a "Yes" answer to PJC 303.8.

Causation.   To recover damages for breach of contract, a plaintiff must establish damages sustained as a result of the breach. *Southern Electrical Services, Inc. v. City of Houston*, 355 S.W.3d 319, 324 (Tex. App.—Houston [1st Dist.] 2011, pet. denied).

Submission of separate answers.   If there are multiple plaintiffs or lessees, it will normally be necessary to require an answer for each. It may also be necessary to require an answer for each well and each month in issue in the royalty dispute if the plaintiff is seeking to recover prejudgment interest from multiple wells or sales or if the statute of limitations is in issue. Tex. Nat. Res. Code §§ 91.401–.406; Tex. Fin. Code §§ 304.101–.107.

Prejudgment interest.   Instructing the jury not to add interest is suggested because prejudgment interest, if recoverable, will be calculated by the court at the time of judgment. If interest paid on an obligation is claimed as an element of damages, it may be necessary to modify the instruction on interest.

Modification depending on lease terms. If the lease provision requires valuation at some place other than at the well (e.g., at the point of sale or point of transfer to a nonaffiliated third party) or if it provides for a different method of valuation (e.g., highest index price), then the question and instruction should be altered to be consistent with the lease terms.

**PJC 313.13   Question and Instruction on Damages for Unreasonable
                 Deductions**

[Insert predicate, PJC 313.1.]

QUESTION _____

What sum of money, if any, if paid now in cash, would fairly and reasonably
compensate *Paul Payne* for *his* damages, if any, that resulted from *Larry Lessee*'s unreasonable deductions from royalty payments?

Consider the difference, if any, between the royalty *Paul Payne* would have
received had no unreasonable deductions been taken and the amount *Paul
Payne* actually received.

Do not add any amount for interest on damages, if any.

Answer in dollars and cents for damages, if any.

Answer: _____

COMMENT

When to use.   PJC 313.13 should be used to determine damages for unreasonable
deductions and should be predicated on a "Yes" answer to PJC 303.9.

Causation.   To recover damages for breach of contract, a plaintiff must establish
damages sustained as a result of the breach. *Southern Electrical Services, Inc. v. City
of Houston*, 355 S.W.3d 319, 324 (Tex. App.—Houston [1st Dist.] 2011, pet. denied).

Submission of separate answers.   If there are multiple plaintiffs or lessees, it will
normally be necessary to require an answer for each. It may also be necessary to
require an answer for each well and each month in issue in the royalty dispute if the
plaintiff is seeking to recover prejudgment interest from multiple wells or sales or if
the statute of limitations is in issue. Tex. Nat. Res. Code §§ 91.401–.406; Tex. Fin.
Code §§ 304.101–.107.

Prejudgment interest.   Instructing the jury not to add interest is suggested
because prejudgment interest, if recoverable, will be calculated by the court at the time
of judgment. If interest paid on an obligation is claimed as an element of damages, it
may be necessary to modify the instruction on interest.

PJC 313.14   Question and Instruction on Drainage Damages

[Insert predicate, PJC 313.1.]

QUESTION _____

What sum of money, if any, if paid now in cash, would fairly and reasonably compensate *Paul Payne* for the lost royalties, if any, that resulted from *Larry Lessee*'s failure to act as a reasonably prudent operator in preventing substantial drainage from the lease?

The measure of damages for *Larry Lessee*'s failure to prevent substantial drainage is the amount of royalties that *Paul Payne* would have received had *Larry Lessee* acted as a reasonably prudent operator.

Do not add any amount for interest on damages, if any.

Answer in dollars and cents for damages, if any.

1.   Damages sustained in the past.

Answer: _____

2.   Damages that, in reasonable probability, will be sustained in the future.

Answer: _____

COMMENT

When to use.   PJC 313.14 should be used to determine damages for failure to prevent substantial drainage and should be predicated on a "Yes" answer to PJC 303.11.

Source of question and instruction.   PJC 313.14 is derived from *Texas Pacific Coal & Oil Co. v. Barker*, 6 S.W.2d 1031, 1036–37 (Tex. 1928).

Causation.   To recover damages for breach of contract, a plaintiff must establish damages sustained as a result of the breach. *Southern Electrical Services, Inc. v. City of Houston*, 355 S.W.3d 319, 324 (Tex. App.—Houston [1st Dist.] 2011, pet. denied).

Damages.   The measure of damages for breach of the drainage covenant is the royalty lost on past and future production by the lessee's failure to prevent drainage. *Mandell v. Hamman Oil & Refining Co.*, 822 S.W.2d 153, 164 (Tex. App.—Houston [1st Dist.] 1991, writ denied); *Wes-Tex Land Co. v. Simmons*, 566 S.W.2d 719, 721 (Tex. App.—Eastland 1978, writ ref'd n.r.e.). In most cases, the alleged failure to protect against drainage will be a failure of the lessee to drill or timely drill an offset well to prevent the drainage. Accordingly, the damages are calculated on what the lessor or royalty owner would have received as a royalty from such a well if it had been drilled or timely drilled. This involves a component of both past and future damages; the future production component of such a well (whether hypothetical or actual) must be discounted back to a present value and is often the subject of contested expert testimony. The Texas Supreme Court has noted that the basis for damages is not the amount of oil or gas actually drained, although that amount may affect actual damages. *See Coastal Oil & Gas Corp. v. Garza Energy Trust*, 268 S.W.3d 1 (Tex. 2008) (royalty owner sought drainage damages occurring because of alleged trespass). The court found there was no competent evidence to support the drainage claim. The supreme court in *Garza* comments on drainage damages in two paragraphs at 18, in what may be dicta. *See Garza Energy Trust*, 268 S.W.3d at 18. The Committee expresses no opinion on what is meant by these comments or whether the supreme court intended to change the standard for damages in drainage cases accepted since *Barker*.

Prejudgment interest.   Instructing the jury not to add interest is suggested because prejudgment interest, if recoverable, will be calculated by the court at the time of judgment. If interest paid on an obligation is claimed as an element of damages, it may be necessary to modify the instruction on interest.

PJC 313.15   **Question and Instruction on Damages for Breach of Implied Covenant to Develop**

[Insert predicate, PJC 313.1.]

QUESTION _____

What sum of money, if any, if paid now in cash, would fairly and reasonably compensate *Paul Payne* for the lost royalties, if any, that resulted from *Larry Lessee*'s failure to drill additional wells on the lease that a reasonably prudent operator would have drilled?

The measure of damages for *Larry Lessee*'s failure to reasonably develop is the amount of royalties that *Paul Payne* would have received from the drilling of additional wells on the lease.

Do not add any amount for interest on damages, if any.

Answer in dollars and cents for damages, if any.

> 1.   Damages sustained in the past.
>
> Answer: _____
>
> 2.   Damages that, in reasonable probability, will be sustained in the future.
>
> Answer: _____

COMMENT

When to use.   PJC 313.15 should be used to determine damages for breach of the implied covenant to develop and should be predicated on a "Yes" answer to PJC 303.12.

Source of question and instruction.   PJC 313.15 is derived from *Texas Pacific Coal & Oil Co. v. Barker*, 6 S.W.2d 1031, 1036–37 (Tex. 1928).

Causation.   To recover damages for breach of contract, a plaintiff must establish damages sustained as a result of the breach. *Southern Electrical Services, Inc. v. City of Houston*, 355 S.W.3d 319, 324 (Tex. App.—Houston [1st Dist.] 2011, pet. denied).

Damages.   The measure of damages for breach of the development covenant is the royalty lost on past and future production by the lessee's failure to prevent drainage. *Kerr-McGee Corp. v. Helton*, 133 S.W.3d 245, 253 (Tex. 2004) (quoting *Texas Pacific Coal & Oil Co.*, 6 S.W.2d at 1036–37).

Remedies.   If the lessor is seeking monetary damages, this issue should be conditionally submitted after the breach issue. In a case alleging a breach of the implied covenant to develop in an oil and gas lease, the lessor is generally required to seek monetary damages and cannot obtain cancellation, except in extraordinary circumstances where the lessor has no adequate remedy at law. *W.T. Waggoner Estate v. Sigler Oil Co.*, 19 S.W.2d 27, 29–31 (Tex. 1929). *See also Sun Exploration & Production Co. v. Jackson*, 783 S.W.2d 202 (Tex. 1989); *Christie, Mitchell & Mitchell Co. v. Howell*, 359 S.W.2d 658 (Tex. App.—Fort Worth 1962, writ ref'd n.r.e.). Texas generally follows the view that conditional cancellation is the preferred remedy when cancellation is sought. *See W.T. Waggoner Estate*, 19 S.W.2d at 32; *see also Perkins v. Mitchell*, 268 S.W.2d 907, 908 (Tex. 1954).

Prejudgment interest.   Instructing the jury not to add interest is suggested because prejudgment interest, if recoverable, will be calculated by the court at the time of judgment. If interest paid on an obligation is claimed as an element of damages, it may be necessary to modify the instruction on interest.

PJC 313.16   **Question and Instruction on Actual Damages for Breach of Executive Rights Duty**

[Insert predicate, PJC 313.1.]

QUESTION _____

What sum of money, if any, if paid now in cash, would fairly and reasonably compensate *Paul Payne* for *his* damages, if any, that were proximately caused by *Don Davis*'s failure to comply with such executive duty?

[Insert definition of proximate cause, PJC 300.13.]

Consider the following elements of damages, if any, and none other.

[Insert appropriate instructions, e.g., Lost royalties.*]*

Do not add any amount for interest on damages, if any.

Answer in dollars and cents for damages, if any.

    1.   *[Element A]* sustained in the past.

    Answer: _____

    2.   *[Element A]* that, in reasonable probability, will be sustained in the future.

    Answer: _____

    3.   *[Element B]* sustained in the past.

    Answer: _____

    4.   *[Element B]* that, in reasonable probability, will be sustained in the future.

    Answer: _____

COMMENT

When to use.   PJC 313.16 should be predicated on a "Yes" answer to PJC 304.2 and is appropriate when the non-executive rights holder seeks actual damages.

Elements of damages submitted separately.   The Committee generally recommends that multiple elements of damages be separately submitted to the jury. *Harris*

County v. Smith, 96 S.W.3d 230, 233–34 (Tex. 2002) (broad-form submission of multiple elements of damages may lead to harmful error if there is a proper objection raising insufficiency of the evidence to support one or more of the elements submitted); *see also* Tex. Civ. Prac. & Rem. Code § 41.008(a) ("In an action in which a claimant seeks recovery of damages, the trier of fact shall determine the amount of economic damages separately from the amount of other compensatory damages."). Separating economic from noneconomic damages is required to allow the court to apply the limits on recovery of exemplary damages based on economic and noneconomic damages as required by Tex. Civ. Prac. & Rem. Code § 41.008(b).

Further, "[p]rejudgment interest may not be assessed or recovered on an award of future damages." Tex. Fin. Code § 304.1045 (wrongful death, personal injury, or property damage cases). Therefore, separation of past and future damages is required.

Elements considered separately. *Golden Eagle Archery, Inc. v. Jackson*, 116 S.W.3d 757, 770 (Tex. 2002), provides an instruction for cases involving undefined or potentially overlapping categories of damages. In those cases, the following language should be substituted for the instruction to consider each element separately:

> Consider the following elements of damages, if any, and none other. You shall not award any sum of money on any element if you have otherwise, under some other element, awarded a sum of money for the same loss. That is, do not compensate twice for the same loss, if any.

Prejudgment interest. Instructing the jury not to add interest is suggested because prejudgment interest, if recoverable, will be calculated by the court at the time of judgment. If interest paid on an obligation is claimed as an element of damages, it may be necessary to modify the instruction on interest.

Exemplary damages. The non-executive may recover exemplary damages from the executive rights holder. *Manges v. Guerra*, 673 S.W.2d 180, 184 (Tex. 1984); *Luecke v. Wallace*, 951 S.W.2d 267, 276 (Tex. App.—Austin 1997, no writ); *Dearing, Inc. v. Spiller*, 824 S.W.2d 728, 734 (Tex. App.—Fort Worth 1992, writ denied); *Mims v. Beall*, 810 S.W.2d 876, 881 (Tex. App.—Texarkana 1991, no writ). Chapter 41 of the Texas Civil Practice and Remedies Code has supplanted the common law and now controls the evidentiary standard for an award of exemplary damages. For discussion of appropriate questions and instructions for exemplary damages, see the current edition of State Bar of Texas, *Texas Pattern Jury Charges—Business, Consumer, Insurance & Employment* PJC 115.37.

Equitable remedies. Equitable remedies for breach of the executive duty are awardable by the trial court. *See, e.g., Manges*, 673 S.W.2d at 184 (affirmed trial court judgment canceling oil and gas lease and deed of trust); *Lesley v. Veterans Land*

Board, 352 S.W.3d 479, 491 (Tex. 2011) ("pre-approving" remedy of cancellation of restrictive covenants upon remand to trial court).

Other remedies. For a discussion of other remedies that may be available in cases involving breach of the executive duty, including rescission, constructive trust, and injunction, see the current edition of State Bar of Texas, *Texas Pattern Jury Charges—Business, Consumer, Insurance & Employment* PJC 115.15.

PJC 313.17   Question on Contract Damages

[Insert predicate, PJC 313.1.]

QUESTION _____

What sum of money, if any, if paid now in cash, would fairly and reasonably compensate *Paul Payne* for *his* damages, if any, that resulted from such failure to comply?

Consider the following elements of damages, if any, and none other.

*[Insert appropriate instructions. See samples in PJC 313.18
and instructions in PJC 313.19.]*

Do not add any amount for interest on damages, if any.

Answer separately in dollars and cents for damages, if any.

1.   *[Element A]* sustained in the past.

Answer: _____

2.   *[Element A]* that, in reasonable probability, will be sustained in the future.

Answer: _____

3.   *[Element B]* sustained in the past.

Answer: _____

4.   *[Element B]* that, in reasonable probability, will be sustained in the future.

Answer: _____

COMMENT

When to use.   PJC 313.17 should be predicated on a "Yes" answer to PJC 305.3 and may be adapted for use in most breach-of-contract cases by the addition of appropriate instructions setting out legally available measures of damages. See PJC 313.18 and 313.19. If only one measure of damages is supported by the pleadings and proof, the measure may be incorporated into the question.

Instruction required. PJC 313.17 *should not* be submitted without an instruction on the appropriate measures of damages. *See Jackson v. Fontaine's Clinics, Inc.*, 499 S.W.2d 87, 90 (Tex. 1973). See PJC 313.18 and 313.19 for sample instructions.

Causation. To recover damages for breach of contract, a plaintiff must establish damages sustained as a result of the breach. *Southern Electrical Services, Inc. v. City of Houston*, 355 S.W.3d 319, 324 (Tex. App.—Houston [1st Dist.] 2011, pet. denied).

Parallel theories. If the breach-of-contract cause of action is only one of several theories of recovery submitted in the charge and any theory has a different legal measure of damages to be applied to a factually similar claim for damages, a separate damages question for each theory may be submitted and the following additional instruction may be included earlier in the charge:

> In answering questions about damages, answer each question separately. Do not increase or reduce the amount in one answer because of your answer to any other question about damages. Do not speculate about what any party's ultimate recovery may or may not be. Any recovery will be determined by the court when it applies the law to your answers at the time of judgment.

Elements of damages submitted separately. The Committee generally recommends that multiple elements of damages be separately submitted to the jury. *Harris County v. Smith*, 96 S.W.3d 230, 233–34 (Tex. 2002) (broad-form submission of valid and invalid elements of damages may lead to harmful error if there is a proper objection raising insufficiency of the evidence to support one or more of the elements submitted); *see also* Tex. Civ. Prac. & Rem. Code § 41.008(a) ("In an action in which a claimant seeks recovery of damages, the trier of fact shall determine the amount of economic damages separately from the amount of other compensatory damages."). Separating economic from noneconomic damages is required to allow the court to apply the limits on recovery of exemplary damages based on economic and noneconomic damages as required by Tex. Civ. Prac. & Rem. Code § 41.008(b).

Further, "[p]rejudgment interest may not be assessed or recovered on an award of future damages." Tex. Fin. Code § 304.1045 (wrongful death, personal injury, or property damage cases). Therefore, separation of past and future damages is required.

Elements considered separately. *Golden Eagle Archery, Inc. v. Jackson*, 116 S.W.3d 757, 770 (Tex. 2003), provides an instruction for cases involving undefined or potentially overlapping categories of damages. In those cases, the following language should be substituted for the instruction to consider each element separately:

> Consider the following elements of damages, if any, and none other. You shall not award any sum of money on any element if you have otherwise, under some other element, awarded a sum of money

for the same loss. That is, do not compensate twice for the same loss, if any.

Prejudgment interest.   Instructing the jury not to add interest is suggested because prejudgment interest, if recoverable, will be calculated by the court at the time of judgment. If interest paid on an obligation is claimed as an element of damages, it may be necessary to modify the instruction on interest.

PJC 313.18   Sample Instructions on Direct and Incidental Damages—
Contracts

Explanatory note: Damages instructions in contract actions are often necessarily fact-specific. Unlike most other form instructions in this volume, therefore, the following sample instructions are illustrative only, using a hypothetical situation to give a few examples of how instructions may be worded to submit various legal measures of damages for use in connection with the contract damages question, PJC 313.17.

Sample A—Loss of the benefit of the bargain

The difference, if any, between the value of the paint job agreed to by the parties and the value of the paint job performed by *Don Davis*. The difference in value, if any, shall be determined at the time and place the paint job was performed.

Sample B—Remedial damages

The reasonable and necessary cost to repaint *Paul Payne*'s truck.

Sample C—Loss of contractual profit

The difference between the agreed price and the cost *Paul Payne* would have incurred in painting the truck.

Sample D—Loss of contractual profit plus expenses incurred before breach

The amount *Don Davis* agreed to pay *Paul Payne* less the expenses *Paul Payne* saved by not completing the paint job.

Sample E—Damages after mitigation

The difference between the amount paid by *Paul Payne* to *John Jones* for painting the truck and the amount *Paul Payne* had agreed to pay *Don Davis* for that work.

Sample F—Mitigation expenses

Reasonable and necessary expenses incurred in attempting to have the truck repainted.

Sample G—Incidental damages

Reasonable and necessary costs to store *Paul Payne*'s tools while the truck was being repainted.

COMMENT

When to use.   See explanatory note above. Because damages instructions in contract suits are necessarily fact-specific, no true "pattern" instructions are given—only samples of some measures of general damages available in contract actions. This list is not exhaustive. The samples are illustrative only, adapted to a hypothetical fact situation, and must be rewritten to fit the particular damages raised by the pleadings and proof and recoverable under a legally accepted theory. The instructions should be drafted in an attempt to make the plaintiff factually whole but not to put the plaintiff in a better position than he would have been in had the defendant fully performed the contract. *See Osoba v. Bassichis*, 679 S.W.2d 119, 122 (Tex. App.—Houston [14th Dist.] 1984, writ ref'd n.r.e.). For a comprehensive discussion of the theories of contract damages, see *Restatement (Second) of Contracts* §§ 346–356 (1981).

Measures generally alternative.   The measures outlined here are generally alternatives, although some, particularly incidental damages, may be available in addition to one of the other measures, as may consequential damages (see PJC 313.19).

Direct damages.   Since *Hadley v. Baxendale*, 9 Exch. 341, 156 Eng. Rep. 145 (1854), contract damages have been divided into two categories: direct and consequential. *See Arthur Andersen & Co. v. Perry Equipment Corp.*, 945 S.W.2d 812, 816 (Tex. 1997). Direct damages "are the necessary and usual result of the defendant's wrongful act; they flow naturally and necessarily from the wrong." *El Paso Marketing, L.P. v. Wolf Hollow I, L.P.*, 383 S.W.3d 138, 144 (Tex. 2012). Direct damages "compensate a plaintiff for a loss that is conclusively presumed to have been foreseen by the defendant as a usual and necessary consequence of the defendant's act." *DaimlerChrysler Motors Co. v. Manuel*, 362 S.W.3d 160, 179 (Tex. App.—Fort Worth 2012, no pet.). The general or direct nature of a type of damages is a determination of law to be made by the court. No question should be submitted concerning the foreseeability of direct damages; even if the evidence shows that such damages were not factually foreseeable to the parties, recovery is permitted if the damages are properly characterized by the court as direct rather than consequential. *American Bank v. Thompson*, 660 S.W.2d 831, 834 (Tex. App.—Waco 1983, writ ref'd n.r.e.).

Even damages usually not considered recoverable may be deemed direct damages if they stem as a matter of law from the breach of the contract in question. *See Cactus Utility Co. v. Larson*, 709 S.W.2d 709, 716 (Tex. App.—Corpus Christi–Edinburg 1986), *rev'd in part on other grounds*, 730 S.W.2d 640 (Tex. 1987) (expert witness fee, for accountant, recoverable as direct damages for breach of agreement to provide accounting services).

Benefit of the bargain and remedial damages.   Whether difference in value or cost of repair is the proper measure of damages depends on the particular facts and circumstances in each case. *Fidelity & Deposit Co. of Maryland v. Stool*, 607 S.W.2d 17, 21 (Tex. App.—Tyler 1980, no writ).

Loss of contractual profit. Lost profits from collateral contracts are generally classified as consequential damages. Profits lost from the actual contract in question, however, are direct damages for the seller. *Continental Holdings, Ltd. v. Leahy*, 132 S.W.3d 471, 475 (Tex. App.—Eastland 2003, no pet.).

Lost profit plus capital expenditures. If the plaintiff has incurred expenses in preparation or performance and reasonably expected to recoup that investment as well as make a profit, this lost profit plus capital expenditures may be an appropriate measure of damages. *Houston Chronicle Publishing Co. v. McNair Trucklease, Inc.*, 519 S.W.2d 924, 929–31 (Tex. App.—Houston [1st Dist.] 1975, writ ref'd n.r.e.).

Reliance damages. The plaintiff may elect to recover expenditures made in preparation or performance instead of claiming lost benefit of the bargain or profit damages. If the plaintiff makes this election because he would have lost money had the contract been completed and the defendant proves the amount of loss avoided as a result of the breach, the jury should also be instructed to deduct those prospective losses from the reliance damages. *Mistletoe Express Service v. Locke*, 762 S.W.2d 637, 638–39 (Tex. App.—Texarkana 1988, no writ).

Mitigation damages. Although normally raised defensively, the reasonable expenses of mitigating an economic loss are recoverable as actual damages for breach of contract. *Hycel, Inc. v. Wittstruck*, 690 S.W.2d 914, 924 (Tex. App.—Waco 1985, writ dism'd).

Incidental damages. A variety of expenditures and other incidental damages may be recoverable as direct damages, depending on the particular facts and circumstances of each case. *See, e.g., LaChance v. Hollenbeck*, 695 S.W.2d 618, 621–22 (Tex. App.—Austin 1985, writ ref'd n.r.e.) (improvements to real property); *Anderson Development Corp. v. Coastal States Crude Gathering Co.*, 543 S.W.2d 402, 405 (Tex. App.—Houston [14th Dist.] 1976, writ ref'd n.r.e.) (additional salaries and expenses for equipment, maintenance, and supervision). Whether any particular incidental damages are characterized as direct or consequential is, as discussed above, a question for the court. If a claimed expense is deemed consequential, it should be submitted as such, using the form in PJC 313.19.

UCC cases. If the contract is for the sale of goods, the damages instructions should be drafted to incorporate the appropriate damages provisions in Tex. Bus. & Com. Code §§ 2.701–.724 (Tex. UCC). The following examples are illustrative only, using only a few damages provisions in the Uniform Commercial Code.

Sample A—(§ 2.708) Seller's damages for nonacceptance

The difference between the market price of the goods at the time and place *Paul Payne* was to tender them to *Don Davis* and the unpaid contract price.

Sample B—(§ 2.710) Seller's incidental damages

Commercially reasonable charges, expenses, or commissions *Paul Payne* incurred in stopping delivery of goods.

Commercially reasonable charges *Paul Payne* incurred for transportation, care, and custody of goods in connection with their return or resale.

Sample C—(§ 2.713) Buyer's damages for nondelivery

The difference between the market price at the time *Paul Payne* learned of *Don Davis*'s failure to comply and the contract price.

PJC 313.19   Instructions on Consequential Damages—Contracts

Lost profits that were a natural, probable, and foreseeable consequence of *Don Davis*'s failure to comply.

Damage to credit reputation that was a natural, probable, and foreseeable consequence of *Don Davis*'s failure to comply.

COMMENT

When to use.   PJC 313.19, with its added element of foreseeability, should be used for recoverable elements of consequential damages that do not, as a matter of law, directly flow from the defendant's breach. *See Basic Capital Management, Inc. v. Dynex Commercial, Inc.*, 348 S.W.3d 894, 901–02 (Tex. 2011); *Stuart v. Bayless*, 964 S.W.2d 920, 921 (Tex. 1998). See PJC 313.18 Comment.

Foreseeability.   "Foreseeability is a fundamental prerequisite to the recovery of consequential damages for breach of contract." *Basic Capital Management, Inc.*, 348 S.W.3d at 901. Consequential damages may be recovered only if proved to be the "natural, probable, and foreseeable consequence" of the defendant's breach. *Basic Capital Management, Inc.*, 348 S.W.3d at 901–02.

Caveat.   Damages usually characterized as consequential may be deemed direct if they are so directly related to the contract that they stem as a matter of law from the breach. Conversely, not all factually foreseeable damages are legally recoverable. *See Myrtle Springs Reverted Independent School District v. Hogan*, 705 S.W.2d 707, 710 (Tex. App.—Texarkana 1985, writ ref'd n.r.e.) (loss of earning capacity and mental anguish not recoverable for breach of teaching contract).

Lost profits.   If lost profits are not proved with reasonable certainty but are merely speculative, no recovery is allowed as a matter of law, and this instruction should not be included in the damages question. *Texas Instruments, Inc. v. Teletron Energy Management, Inc.*, 877 S.W.2d 276, 278–81 (Tex. 1994); *see Southwestern Energy Production Co. v. Berry-Helfand*, 491 S.W.3d 699, 711 (Tex. 2016). If, however, there is legally sufficient evidence of lost profits, a fact question is raised. *Southwest Battery Corp. v. Owen*, 115 S.W.2d 1097, 1099 (Tex. 1938).

UCC cases.   For transactions covered by article 2 of the Uniform Commercial Code, see Tex. Bus. & Com. Code § 2.715(b)(1) (Tex. UCC) (buyer's consequential damages).

PJC 313.20   Question on Promissory Estoppel—Reliance Damages

[Insert predicate, PJC 313.1.]

QUESTION _____

What sum of money, if any, if paid now in cash, would fairly and reasonably compensate *Paul Payne* for *his* damages, if any, that resulted from *his* reliance on *Don Davis*'s promise?

Consider the following elements of damages, if any, and none other.

[Insert appropriate instructions.]

Do not add any amount for interest on damages, if any.

Answer separately in dollars and cents for damages, if any.

1.   *[Element A]* sustained in the past.

Answer: _____

2.   *[Element A]* that, in reasonable probability, will be sustained in the future.

Answer: _____

3.   *[Element B]* sustained in the past.

Answer: _____

4.   *[Element B]* that, in reasonable probability, will be sustained in the future.

Answer: _____

COMMENT

When to use.   PJC 313.20 and appropriate instructions tailored to the specific reliance damages alleged by the plaintiff should be submitted following the liability question for promissory estoppel. See PJC 305.23.

Reliance damages only.   In a claim based on promissory estoppel, the plaintiff is not entitled to recover expectancy damages or to receive the full benefit of the bargain. Only reliance damages are allowed. *Fretz Construction Co. v. Southern National Bank*, 626 S.W.2d 478, 483 (Tex. 1981).

Elements of damages submitted separately.   The Committee generally recommends that multiple elements of damages be separately submitted to the jury. *Harris County v. Smith*, 96 S.W.3d 230, 233–34 (Tex. 2002) (broad-form submission of valid and invalid elements of damages may lead to harmful error if there is a proper objection raising insufficiency of the evidence to support one or more of the elements submitted); *see also* Tex. Civ. Prac. & Rem. Code § 41.008(a) ("In an action in which a claimant seeks recovery of damages, the trier of fact shall determine the amount of economic damages separately from the amount of other compensatory damages."). Separating economic from noneconomic damages is required to allow the court to apply the limits on recovery of exemplary damages based on economic and noneconomic damages as required by Tex. Civ. Prac. & Rem. Code § 41.008(b).

Further, "[p]rejudgment interest may not be assessed or recovered on an award of future damages." Tex. Fin. Code § 304.1045 (wrongful death, personal injury, or property damage cases). Therefore, separation of past and future damages is required.

Elements considered separately.   *Golden Eagle Archery, Inc. v. Jackson*, 116 S.W.3d 757, 770 (Tex. 2003), provides an instruction for cases involving undefined or potentially overlapping categories of damages. In those cases, the following language should be substituted for the instruction to consider each element separately:

> Consider the following elements of damages, if any, and none other. You shall not award any sum of money on any element if you have otherwise, under some other element, awarded a sum of money for the same loss. That is, do not compensate twice for the same loss, if any.

Prejudgment interest.   Instructing the jury not to add interest is suggested because prejudgment interest, if recoverable, will be calculated by the court at the time of judgment. If interest paid on an obligation is claimed as an element of damages, it may be necessary to modify the instruction on interest.

PJC 313.21   Question on Quantum Meruit Recovery

[Insert predicate, PJC 313.1.]

QUESTION _____

What is the reasonable value of such compensable work at the time and place it was performed?

Answer in dollars and cents, if any.

Answer: _____

COMMENT

When to use.   PJC 313.21 submits the measure of recovery for quantum meruit. *Hill v. Shamoun & Norman, LLP*, 544 S.W.3d 724, 733 (Tex. 2018) ("The measure of damages for recovery under a quantum-meruit theory is the reasonable value of the work performed and the materials furnished."). *See, e.g., Heldenfels Bros. v. City of Corpus Christi*, 832 S.W.2d 39, 41 (Tex. 1992) (allowing for recovery under quantum meruit for services and materials); *Texas Delta Upsilon Foundation v. Fehr*, 307 S.W.2d 124, 127 (Tex. App.—Austin 1957, writ ref'd n.r.e.). The question must be predicated on an affirmative finding that the work is compensable under this theory. See PJC 305.24.

PJC 313.22   Defensive Instruction on Mitigation—Contract Damages

Do not include in your answer any amount that you find *Paul Payne* could have avoided by the exercise of reasonable care.

COMMENT

When to use.   If the evidence raises a question about the plaintiff's failure to mitigate damages after the defendant's actionable conduct, an instruction on mitigation should be included with the damages question. *Alexander & Alexander of Texas, Inc. v. Bacchus Industries, Inc.*, 754 S.W.2d 252, 253 (Tex. App.—El Paso 1988, writ denied).

Defendant's burden of proof.   Failure to mitigate is an affirmative defense, and the burden of proof is on the party asserting such a failure. The supreme court has approved the submission of affirmative defenses by instruction, "provided that the burden of proof is properly placed." *Cropper v. Caterpillar Tractor Co.*, 754 S.W.2d 646, 651 (Tex. 1988). Where appropriate, the trial court may specifically state the burden of proof by supplementing the above instruction or the general instructions (see PJC 300.3), or the trial court may submit a question on the defense. The defendant must offer evidence showing not just the plaintiff's lack of care but also the amount by which the damages were increased by such failure to mitigate. *Cocke v. White*, 697 S.W.2d 739, 744 (Tex. App.—Corpus Christi–Edinburg 1985, writ ref'd n.r.e.); *R.A. Corbett Transport, Inc. v. Oden*, 678 S.W.2d 172, 176 (Tex. App.—Tyler 1984, no writ); *Copenhaver v. Berryman*, 602 S.W.2d 540, 544 (Tex. App.—Corpus Christi–Edinburg 1980, writ ref'd n.r.e.).

Settlement offers and expense to plaintiff of mitigation.   The supreme court has held that a mere refusal to accept a settlement offer cannot support submission of a mitigation-of-damages instruction and that the long-standing law of this state requires a claimant to mitigate damages only if it can do so with "trifling expense or with reasonable exertions." *Gunn Infiniti, Inc. v. O'Byrne*, 996 S.W.2d 854, 857 (Tex. 1999).

DTPA and Insurance Code.   Several appellate opinions have cited the duty to mitigate as grounds for allowing DTPA consumers to recover mitigation expenses as actual damages. *See, e.g., Hycel, Inc. v. Wittstruck*, 690 S.W.2d 914, 924 (Tex. App.—Waco 1985, writ dism'd); *Orkin Exterminating Co. v. LeSassier*, 688 S.W.2d 651, 653 (Tex. App.—Beaumont 1985, no writ). The duty to mitigate has been used defensively in DTPA and Insurance Code suits. *See, e.g., Pinson v. Red Arrow Freight Lines, Inc.*, 801 S.W.2d 14, 15 (Tex. App.—Austin 1990, no writ) (DTPA); *Alexander & Alexan- der of Texas, Inc.*, 754 S.W.2d at 253 (Insurance Code article 21.21).

Mitigation damages.   Mitigation may also be the basis for an affirmative recovery of damages for the plaintiff. See PJC 313.18.

UCC cases.   A buyer's recovery of consequential damages is limited to those "which could not reasonably be prevented by cover or otherwise." Tex. Bus. & Com. Code § 2.715(b)(1) (Tex. UCC).

[PJC 313.23–313.32 are reserved for expansion.]

PJC 313.33　　　Question on Attorney's Fees

[Insert predicate, PJC 313.1.]

QUESTION _____

What is a reasonable fee for the necessary legal services of *Paul Payne*'s attorney for the [*breach of contract claim*]?

A reasonable fee is the reasonable hours worked, and to be worked, multiplied by a reasonable hourly rate for that work.

Do not include fees that relate solely to any other claim.

Answer with an amount in dollars and cents for each of the following:

　　1.　For representation in the trial court.

　　Answer: _____

　　2.　For representation in the court of appeals.

　　Answer: _____

　　3.　For representation at the petition for review stage in the Supreme Court of Texas.

　　Answer: _____

　　4.　For representation at the merits briefing stage in the Supreme Court of Texas.

　　Answer: _____

　　5.　For representation through oral argument and the completion of proceedings in the Supreme Court of Texas.

　　Answer: _____

COMMENT

When to use.　To secure an award of attorney's fees from an opponent, the prevailing party "must prove that: (1) recovery of attorney's fees is legally authorized, and (2) the requested attorney's fees are reasonable and necessary for the legal representation, so that such an award will compensate the prevailing party generally for its losses resulting from the litigation process." *Rohrmoos Venture v. UTSW DVA Healthcare, LLP*, 578 S.W.3d 469, 487 (Tex. 2019).

As to the first element, the legal authorization may be found in a contract or a statute. *Rohrmoos Venture*, 578 S.W.3d at 487. There may also be common law grounds for the recovery of attorney's fees, as in the case of innocent stakeholders in interpleader actions who may be able to recover attorney's fees from the interpleaded funds. *See, e.g., Fort Worth Transportation Authority v. Rodriguez*, 547 S.W.3d 830, 850 (Tex. 2018).

Some other guiding considerations. "When a claimant wishes to obtain attorney's fees from the opposing party, the claimant must prove that the requested fees are both reasonable and necessary." *Rohrmoos Venture*, 578 S.W.3d at 489. Both of these "elements are questions of fact to be determined by the fact finder and act as limits on the amount of fees that a prevailing party can shift to the non-prevailing party." *Rohrmoos Venture*, 578 S.W.3d at 489.

The lodestar analysis applies to any situation in which an objective calculation of reasonable hours worked times a reasonable rate can be employed. The "fact finder's starting point for calculating an attorney's fee award is determining the reasonable hours worked multiplied by a reasonable hourly rate, and the fee claimant bears the burden of providing sufficient evidence on both counts." *Rohrmoos Venture*, 578 S.W.3d at 498. The process applies to both jury trials and bench trials. *See Rohrmoos Venture*, 578 S.W.3d at 494. This applies even in cases where the fee agreement is one for an arrangement other than hourly billing, as well as in the sanctions context. *Rohrmoos Venture*, 578 S.W.3d at 499 n.10; *Nath v. Texas Children's Hospital*, 576 S.W.3d 707, 710 (Tex. 2019) (per curiam).

Factors to consider. In an appropriate case, additional considerations may be taken into account in determining a reasonable and necessary attorney's fee. *See Rohrmoos Venture*, 578 S.W.3d at 500–01.

In such a case, the following instruction should be used. However, the additional consideration cannot be a consideration already subsumed in the reasonable fee. *Rohrmoos Venture*, 578 S.W.3d at 500–02.

> A reasonable fee is presumed to be the reasonable hours worked, and to be worked, multiplied by a reasonable hourly rate for that work. But other considerations may justify an enhancement or reduction to that amount. You must determine whether evidence of those considerations overcomes the presumption and necessitates an adjustment to a reasonable fee.

Additional predicate findings may be required. Under certain statutes, a party may only recover attorney's fees after satisfying other legal requirements such as recovering actual damages. *See Ortiz v. State Farm Lloyds*, 589 S.W.3d 127, 134 (Tex.

2019) (recovery of attorney's fees under Tex. Ins. Code ch. 541 "premised on an award of underlying 'actual damages'"). In those circumstances, the following modified predicate question may be used:

> If you have answered "Yes" to Question _____ [*breach of contract claim*] and awarded an amount other than zero in Question _____ [*damages for breach of contract claim*], then answer the following question. Otherwise, do not answer the following question.

Do not use "if any" if the law requires the award of some fees. The phrase "if any" should not be added in jury questions for fees where the legal authorization for fees requires the award of some amount of trial and appellate fees, such as Texas Civil Practice and Remedies Code chapter 38 or the Texas Theft Liability Act if supported by some evidence. *See Ventling v. Johnson*, 466 S.W.3d 143, 154 (Tex. 2015). In those instances, the jury determines the amount of reasonable and necessary fees, not whether fees should be recovered.

Zero fees. Unless evidence was admitted that no fee was needed to assert or defend a claim, a zero-fee award may be reversible error. *See Smith v. Patrick W.Y. Tam Trust*, 296 S.W.3d 545, 548 (Tex. 2009). The trial court can correct the error by directing jurors before they are discharged to return to the jury room and reform their answer. *See* Tex. R. Civ. P. 295; *Smith*, 296 S.W.3d at 548. In such cases, the following instruction may be used:

> The evidence in this case indicates that some amount of attorney's fees is reasonable, making the finding of zero inappropriate. It is up to the court to fashion a judgment from the answers to the jury questions. Therefore, I am instructing you to return to your deliberations to make a decision on the question[*s*] for attorney's fees that is consistent with the evidence and other instructions given by the court to the jury.

Submit additional fact questions to the jury. In cases where additional elements must be proven and a fact question exists, those must be submitted to the jury. *See Svoboda v. Thai*, No. 01-17-00584-CV, 2019 WL 1442434, at *7 (Tex. App.—Houston [1st Dist.] Apr. 2, 2019, no pet.) (reversible error not to submit presentment question to the jury where presentment was a contested fact issue).

Segregation of fees. If any attorney's fees relate solely to a claim for which such fees are unrecoverable, a claimant must segregate recoverable from unrecoverable fees. Intertwined facts do not make unrecoverable fees recoverable; it is only when discrete legal services advance both a recoverable and unrecoverable claim that they are so intertwined that they need not be segregated. *Tony Gullo Motors I, L.P. v. Chapa*, 212 S.W.3d 299, 313–14 (Tex. 2006); *see also Kinsel v. Lindsey*, 526 S.W.3d 411, 427 (Tex. 2017). A party, however, may recover attorney's fees incurred in overcoming defenses or counterclaims to a claim for which attorney's fees are recoverable. *Varner v. Cardenas*, 218 S.W.3d 68, 69 (Tex. 2007). Segregation of fees may be required on a claim-by-claim basis. *See Horizon Health Corp. v. Acadia Healthcare Co.*, 520 S.W.3d 848, 884 (Tex. 2017) (no evidence to support breach of contract claim, but evidence supported Texas Theft Liability Act claim so remand for testimony segregating on a claim-by-claim basis); *Chapa*, 212 S.W.3d at 313–14.

Any error in failing to segregate attorney's fees is waived by a failure to object to the lack of apportionment. *Green International, Inc. v. Solis*, 951 S.W.2d 384, 389 (Tex. 1997). Accordingly, the question to be submitted may vary from the pattern above in cases involving multiple claims where fees are not recoverable under one or more of the claims or where there are multiple defendants who may not be charged with fee shifting.

CHAPTER 314   PRESERVATION OF CHARGE ERROR

PJC 314.1   Preservation of Charge Error (Comment)

The purpose of this Comment is to make practitioners aware of the need to preserve their complaints about the jury charge for appellate review and to inform them of general considerations when attempting to perfect those complaints. It is not intended as an in-depth analysis of the topic.

Basic rules for preserving charge error.

Objections and requests.   Errors in the charge consist of (1) defective questions, instructions, and definitions actually submitted (that is, definitions, instructions, and questions that, while included in the charge, are nevertheless incorrectly submitted); and (2) questions, instructions, and definitions that are omitted entirely. Objections are required to preserve error as to any defect in the charge. In addition, a written request for a substantially correct question, instruction, or definition is required to preserve error for certain omissions.

- Defective question, definition, or instruction: *Objection*

  Affirmative errors in the jury charge must be preserved by objection, regardless of which party has the burden of proof for the submission. Tex. R. Civ. P. 274. Therefore, if the jury charge contains a *defective* question, definition, or instruction, an objection pointing out the error will preserve error for review.

- Omitted definition or instruction: *Objection and request*

  If the omission concerns a definition or an instruction, error must be preserved by an objection and a request for a substantially correct definition or instruction. Tex. R. Civ. P. 274, 278. For this type of omission, it does not matter which party has the burden of proof. Therefore, a request must be tendered even if the erroneously omitted definition or instruction is in the opponent's claim or defense.

- Omitted question, Party's burden: *Objection and request*;
  Opponent's burden: *Objection*

  If the omission concerns a question relied on by the party complaining of the judgment, error must be preserved by an objection and a request for a substantially correct question. Tex. R. Civ. P. 274, 278. If the omission concerns a question relied on by the opponent, an objection alone will preserve error for review. Tex. R. Civ. P. 278. To determine whether error preservation is required for an opponent's omission, consider that, if no element of an independent ground of recovery or defense is submitted in the charge or is requested, the ground is waived. Tex. R. Civ. P. 279.

- Uncertainty about whether the error constitutes an omission or a defect: *Objection and request*

  If there is uncertainty whether an error in the charge constitutes an affirmative error or an omission, the practitioner should both request and object to ensure the error is preserved. *See State Department of Highways & Public Transportation v. Payne*, 838 S.W.2d 235, 239–40 (Tex. 1992).

Timing and form of objections and requests.

- Objections, requests, and rulings must be made—

  1. before the reading of the charge to the jury, Tex. R. Civ. P. 272; or

  2. by an earlier deadline set by the trial court, *King Fisher Marine Service, L.P. v. Tamez*, 443 S.W.3d 838, 843 (Tex. 2014) (providing that such a deadline must "afford[] the parties a 'reasonable time' to inspect and object to the charge").

- Objections must—

  1. be made in writing or dictated to the court reporter in the presence of the court and opposing counsel, Tex. R. Civ. P. 272; and

  2. specifically point out the error and the grounds of complaint, Tex. R. Civ. P. 274.

- Requests must—

  1. be made separate and apart from any objections to the charge, Tex. R. Civ. P. 273;

  2. be in writing and tendered to the court, Tex. R. Civ. P. 278; and

  3. be in substantially correct wording, Tex. R. Civ. P. 278, which does not mean that the request be absolutely correct, nor does it mean that the request be merely sufficient to call the matter to the attention of the court, but instead means that the request is substantively correct and not affirmatively incorrect. *Placencio v. Allied Industrial International, Inc.*, 724 S.W.2d 20, 21 (Tex. 1987).

Rulings on objections and requests.

- Rulings on objections may be oral or in writing. Tex. R. Civ. P. 272.

- Rulings on requests must be in writing and must indicate whether the court refused, granted, or granted but modified the request. Tex. R. Civ. P. 276.

Submitting wrong theory. "[Where] the wrong theory of recovery was submitted and the correct theory of recovery was omitted entirely, the defendant has no obligation to object." *United Scaffolding, Inc. v. Levine*, 537 S.W.3d 463, 481 (Tex.

2017). The court held that error had been preserved by raising the argument in the trial court in a motion for judgment notwithstanding the verdict. *Levine*, 537 S.W.3d at 482; *see also* Tex. R. Civ. P. 279.

Common mistakes that may result in waiver of charge error.

- Failing to submit requests in writing (oral or dictated requests will not preserve error).

- Failing to make requests separately from objections to the charge (generally it is safe to present a party's requests at the beginning of the formal charge conference, but separate from a party's objections).

- Offering requests "en masse," that is, tendering a complete charge or obscuring a proper request among unfounded or meritless requests (submit each question, definition, or instruction separately, and submit only those important to the outcome of the trial).

- Failing to file with the clerk all requests that the court has marked "refused" (a prudent practice is to also keep a copy for one's own file).

- Failing to make objections to the court's charge on the record.

- Failing to make objections to the court's charge before the reading of the charge to the jury or by an earlier deadline set by the trial court.

- Making objections on the record while the jury is deliberating even if by agreement and with court approval.

- Adopting by reference objections to other portions of the court's charge.

- Dictating objections to the court reporter in the judge's absence (the judge and opposing counsel should be present).

- Relying on or adopting another party's objections to the court's charge without obtaining court approval to do so beforehand (as a general rule, each party must make its own objections).

- Relying on a pretrial ruling. *See Wackenhut Corp. v. Gutierrez*, 453 S.W.3d 917, 919–20, 920 n.3 (Tex. 2015) (per curiam).

- Failing to assert at trial the same grounds for charge error urged on appeal (grounds not distinctly pointed out to the trial court cannot be raised for the first time on appeal).

- Failing to obtain a ruling on an objection or request.

Principle of error preservation.   In *State Department of Highways & Public Transportation v. Payne*, the supreme court stated:

There should be but one test for determining if a party has preserved error in the jury charge, and that is whether the party made the trial court aware of the complaint, timely and plainly, and obtained a ruling. The more specific requirements of the rules should be applied, while they remain, to serve rather than defeat this principle.

Payne, 838 S.W.2d at 241. The goal is to apply the charge rules "in a common sense manner to serve the purposes of the rules, rather than in a technical manner which defeats them." *Alaniz v. Jones & Neuse, Inc.*, 907 S.W.2d 450, 452 (Tex. 1995) (per curiam). The keys to error preservation are (1) when in doubt about how to preserve, both object and request; and (2) in either case, clarity is essential: make your arguments timely and plainly enough that the trial court is aware of the claimed error, and get a ruling on the record. *See, e.g., Wackenhut*, 453 S.W.3d at 919–20.

PJC 314.2   Broad-Form Issues and the *Casteel* Doctrine (Comment)

In *Crown Life Insurance Co. v. Casteel*, 22 S.W.3d 378 (Tex. 2000), the supreme court held that inclusion of a legally invalid theory in a broad-form liability question taints the question and requires a new trial. *Casteel*, 22 S.W.3d at 388–89. The court has since extended this rule to legal sufficiency challenges to an element of a broad-form damages question, *see Harris County v. Smith*, 96 S.W.3d 230, 235–36 (Tex. 2002), and to complaints about inclusion of an invalid liability theory in a comparative responsibility finding, *see Romero v. KPH Consolidation, Inc.*, 166 S.W.3d 212, 226–28 (Tex. 2005).

The supreme court has recently clarified that harmful error must be presumed, as in *Casteel*, when an appellate court cannot determine whether the jury found liability on an improper basis because a necessary limiting instruction was not submitted despite a timely request or objection. *Benge v. Williams*, 548 S.W.3d 466, 475–76 (Tex. 2018) (reiterating this proposition and stating that "we have twice held that when the question allows a finding of liability based on evidence that cannot support recovery, the same presumption-of-harm rule [from *Casteel*] must be applied"); *see Texas Commission on Human Rights v. Morrison*, 381 S.W.3d 533, 535 (Tex. 2012) (per curiam); *Columbia Rio Grande Healthcare, L.P. v. Hawley*, 284 S.W.3d 851, 863 (Tex. 2009).

When a broad-form submission is infeasible under the *Casteel* doctrine and a granulated submission would cure the alleged charge defect, a specific objection to the broad-form nature of the charge question is necessary to preserve error. *Thota v. Young*, 366 S.W.3d 678, 690–91 (Tex. 2012) (citing *In re A.V.*, 113 S.W.3d 355, 363 (Tex. 2003); *In re B.L.D.*, 113 S.W.3d 340, 349–50 (Tex. 2003)). But when a broad-form submission is infeasible under the *Casteel* doctrine and a granulated submission would still be erroneous because there is no evidence to support the submission of a separate question, a specific and timely objection "to the lack of evidence to support submission of a jury question," to "the form of the submission," or both is necessary. *Burbage v. Burbage*, 447 S.W.3d 249, 256 (Tex. 2014) ("[W]hether or not an objection to *both* [the lack of evidence to support submission of a jury question *and* the form of the submission] is required, *some* timely and specific objection must raise the issue in the trial court."). However, "in situations where a party does not raise a *Casteel*-type objection, that party surely cannot raise a *Casteel* issue when it failed to preserve a claim of an invalid theory of liability that forms the basis of a *Casteel*-type error." *Burbage*, 447 S.W.3d at 256.

APPENDIX

Following are the tables of contents of the other volumes in the *Texas Pattern Jury Charges* series. These tables represent the 2020 editions of these volumes, which were the current editions when this book was published. Other topics may be added in future editions.

The practitioner may also be interested in the *Texas Criminal Pattern Jury Charges* series. Please visit **https://www.texasbarpractice.com/texas-bar-books/** for more information.

Contents of
TEXAS PATTERN JURY CHARGES—GENERAL NEGLIGENCE, INTENTIONAL PERSONAL TORTS & WORKERS' COMPENSATION (2020 Ed.)

Contents of
TEXAS PATTERN JURY CHARGES—MALPRACTICE,
***PREMISES & PRODUCTS* (2020 Ed.)**

[Chapters 62–64 are reserved for expansion.]

Contents of
TEXAS PATTERN JURY CHARGES—BUSINESS, CONSUMER, INSURANCE & EMPLOYMENT (2020 Ed.)

[PJC 101.52–101.55 are reserved for expansion.]

Contents of
TEXAS PATTERN JURY CHARGES—FAMILY & PROBATE (2020 Ed.)

[Chapters 208–214 are reserved for expansion.]

STATUTES AND RULES CITED

[Decimal references are to PJC numbers.]

Texas Business & Commerce Code

Texas Civil Practice & Remedies Code

Texas Finance Code

Texas Insurance Code

Texas Natural Resources Code

Texas Property Code

Texas Tax Code

Texas Rules of Civil Procedure

Texas Rules of Evidence

United Nations

CASES CITED

[Decimal references are to PJC numbers.]

A

Abraxas Petroleum Corp. v. Hornburg, 305.28

Adams v. Petrade International, Inc., 312.14

Adams v. Valley Federal Credit Union, 300.8

Advantage Physical Therapy, Inc. v. Cruz, 305.12

Alexander v. Handley, 312.12

Alexander & Alexander of Texas, Inc. v. Bacchus Industries, Inc., 313.22

A.L.G. Enterprises v. Huffman, 312.8

Altman v. Blake, 304.1

Amarillo Oil Co. v. Energy-Agri Products, Inc., 305.28

American Bank v. Thompson, 313.18

America's Favorite Chicken Co. v. Samaras, 305.2

Amoco v. Underwood, 303.3

Amoco Production Co. v. Alexander, 302.9, 303.1, 303.7, 303.10, 303.11

Amoco Production Co. v. Braslau, 303.22

Amoco Production Co. v. First Baptist Church of Pyote, 303.7

Amoco Production Co. v. Smith, 305.25

Anadarko E&P Co., L.P. v. Clear Lake Pines, Inc., 303.5

Anadarko Petroleum Corp. v. Thompson, 303.24

Anderson Development Corp. v. Coastal States Crude Gathering Co., 313.18

Andretta v. West, 304.1

Anglo-Dutch Petroleum International, Inc. v. Greenberg Peden, P.C., 305.4

Antwine v. Reed, 305.13

Archer County v. Webb, 303.24

Argyle Independent School District v. Wolf, 305.26

Arthur Andersen & Co. v. Perry Equipment Corp., 313.18

Atlantic Richfield Co. v. Hilton, 312.16

Austin Lake Estates, Inc. v. Meyer, 312.2

B

Bachler v. Rosenthal, 303.16, 303.19

BACM 2001-1 San Felipe Road Ltd. Partnership v. Trafalgar Holdings I, Ltd., 312.12

B.A.L. v. Edna Gladney Home, 312.7

Ball v. Dillard, 302.2

Banker v. Breaux, 305.22

Barfield v. Holland, 301.1–301.6

Barfield v. Howard M. Smith Co. of Amarillo, 312.5

Bargsley v. Pryor Petroleum Corp., 303.15–303.18, 303.20

Barrow-Shaver Resources Co. v. Carrizo Oil & Gas, Inc., 305.4, 305.10, 305.19

Bartush-Schnitzius Foods Co. v. Cimco Refrigeration, Inc., 312.2

Bashara v. Baptist Memorial Hospital System, 305.24

Basic Capital Management, Inc. v. Dynex Commercial, Inc., 305.22, 313.19

Bass [In re], 304.1, 304.2

Baxter v. Palmigiano, 300.11

Beeman v. Worrell, 305.24

Bell v. Lyon, 301.2–301.6

Bendalin v. Delgado, 305.19

Bender v. Brooks, 313.4

Benge v. Williams, 314.2

Best Buy Co. v. Barrera, 305.25

Black Lake Pipe Line Co. v. Union Construction Co., 305.24, 312.6

Blackmon v. XTO Energy, Inc., 303.13, 303.23

Blount v. Bordens, Inc., 300.8

Kraft v. Langford, 313.7

L

LaChance v. Hollenbeck, 313.18
Lambert v. H. Molsen & Co., 305.10
Land Title Co. v. F.M. Stigler, Inc., 305.6
Larson v. Ellison, 300.8
Lemos v. Montez, Introduction 4(c)
Lennar Corp. v. Markel American Insurance Co., 312.2
Lesley v. Veterans Land Board, 304.1, 304.2, 313.16
Lightning Oil Co. v. Anadarko E&P Onshore, LLC, 302.2, 302.4
Lindsey Construction, Inc. v. AutoNation Financial Services, LLC, 305.4
Liu v. Yang, 305.20
Lone Star Gas Co. v. Hutton, 313.8
Longoria v. Lasater, 301.2
Ludt v. McCullum, 313.5, 313.7
Luecke v. Wallace, 304.1, 313.16

M

Madison v. Gordon, 312.18
Mandell v. Hamman Oil & Refining Co., 313.14
Mandell & Wright v. Thomas, 312.13
Mandril v. Kasishke, 312.11
Manges v. Guerra, 304.1, 313.16
Martin v. Amerman, 301.1
Martin v. Glass, 303.4, 303.9
Mary E. Bivins Foundation v. Highland Capital Management L.P., 305.25
Massachusetts Bonding & Insurance Co. v. Orkin Exterminating Co., 312.4
Matthews v. Matthews, 312.6
Matthews v. Sun Oil Co., 303.19
Mayers v. Sanchez-O'Brien Minerals Corp., 303.23
Mayfield v. Benavides, 302.5, 313.3, 313.4
McAllen Hospitals, L.P. v. Lopez, 305.4
McCuen v. Huey, 301.2

McCullough v. Scarbrough, Medlin & Associates, Inc., 305.25
McDonnold v. Weinacht, 301.4–301.6
McGill v. Johnson, 302.8
MCI Telecommunications Corp. v. Texas Utilities Electric Co., 305.2, 305.22
Meaders v. Moore, 301.2
Mengden v. Peninsula Production Co., 305.1
Merriman v. XTO Energy, Inc., 302.2, 302.3
Merryfield v. Willson, 305.25
Metromarketing Services, Inc. v. HTT Headwear, Ltd., 312.14
Mid-Continent Casualty Co. v. Global Enercom Management, Inc., 305.12, 305.13
Middle States Petroleum Corp. v. Messenger, 312.4
Midwest Oil Corp. v. Winsauer, 303.22
Mieth v. Ranchquest, Inc., 313.7, 313.8
Miller v. Gray, 305.10
Milner v. Milner, 305.3
Mims v. Beall, 313.16
Mistletoe Express Service v. Locke, 313.18
Mitchell v. C.C. Sanitation Co., 312.6
Monarch Marking System Co. v. Reed's Photo Mart, Inc., 312.8
Montgomery County Hospital District v. Brown, 305.19
Moore v. Jet Stream Investments, Ltd., 303.25
Moore v. Vines, 302.8
"Moore" Burger, Inc. v. Phillips Petroleum Co., 305.23
Morgan v. Bronze Queen Management Co., 305.13
Morris v. Reaves, 312.18
Morrow v. Shotwell, 312.14
Moser v. Tucker, 301.2
Moser v. U.S. Steel Corp., 302.1, 302.2
Motsenbocker v. Wyatt, 300.13
Mowbray v. Avery, 305.26
Murray v. Crest Construction, Inc., 305.24
Mustang Pipeline Co. v. Driver Pipeline Co., 305.3, 312.2
Myrtle Springs Reverted Independent School District v. Hogan, 313.19

S

SUBJECT INDEX

[Decimal references are to PJC numbers.]

A

Acceptance (contract)
general question on, 305.12
revocation of offer, 305.13

Accommodation doctrine, 302.3

Accord and satisfaction (contract), 312.12
distinguished from novation, 312.10

Actual notice of third-party claim, 312.18

Admonitory instructions to jury, ch. 300
adverse inference, 300.10, 300.11
bifurcated trial, 300.4
burden of proof, Introduction 4(e), 300.3
charge of the court, 300.3, 300.4
circumstantial evidence, 300.8
to deadlocked jury, 300.9
discharge of jury, 300.5
on discussing trial, 300.1–300.3, 300.5,
    300.6
electronic technology, jurors' use of,
    300.1–300.3
Fifth Amendment privilege, 300.11
if jurors separate, 300.6
if jury disagrees about testimony, 300.7
after jury selection, 300.2
note-taking by jurors, 300.2, 300.3
oral instructions, 300.1, 300.2, 300.5
parallel theories on damages, 300.12
preponderance of the evidence,
    Introduction 4(e), 300.3
privilege
    Fifth Amendment, 300.11
    generally no inference, 300.10
proximate cause, 300.13
on spoliation, 300.14
after verdict, 300.5
before voir dire, 300.1

Adverse inference
Fifth Amendment privilege, 300.11

generally no inference, 300.10

Adverse possession, ch. 301
generally, 301.1
accrual of action, 301.2–301.6
acknowledgment of title, 301.2–301.6
attorney's fees, 301.2–301.6
burden of proof, 301.2–301.6
claim of right, 301.2–301.6
color of title, 301.2
continuity of possession, 301.2–301.6
cotenants, 301.2
defined, 301.2–301.6
elements generally, 301.1
enclosed land, 301.4–301.6
fence, 301.4–301.6
five-year, 301.3
forged deeds, 301.3
hostile possession, 301.2–301.6
identification of property, 301.2–301.6
lease holdover, effect, 301.1, 301.2
limitation on acreage, 301.4
muniments of title, 301.2
peaceable possession, 301.2–301.6
purpose, 301.1
quitclaim deeds, 301.3
recorded instrument held by claimant,
    301.6
repudiation of title, 301.2–301.6
severance of mineral estate, 301.2–301.6
tacking, 301.2–301.6
ten-year, 301.4
three-year, 301.2
title, 301.2
title instrument lacking, 301.4
twenty-five-year, 301.5, 301.6

Affirmative defenses. *See* Defenses

Agent, authority of (contract), 305.5

Agreement. *See* Acceptance (contract);
    Contracts

309

DIGITAL DOWNLOAD DOCUMENTATION

Texas Pattern Jury Charges—Oil & Gas
Digital Download 2020

The complimentary downloadable version of *Texas Pattern Jury Charges—Oil & Gas* contains the entire text of the printed book. If you have questions or problems with this product not covered in the documentation available via the URLs below, please contact Texas Bar Books at 800-204-2222, ext. 1499 for technical support or ext. 1411 for orders and accounts, or at **books@texasbar.com**.

Additional and Entity Licenses

The current owner of this book may purchase additional and entity licenses for the digital download. Each additional license is for one additional lawyer and that lawyer's support team only. Additional and entity licenses are subject to the terms of the original license concerning permitted users of the printed book and digital download. Please visit **www.texasbarpractice.com/knowledgebase/article/how-to-get-access-for-other-lawyers** for details.

Usage Tips and Other Information

For information on digital download licensing, installation, and usage, visit the Texas Bar Practice Knowledge Base at **www.texasbarpractice.com/knowledgebase**.

Downloading and Installing

Use of the digital download is subject to the terms of the license and limited warranty included in this documentation and on the digital download web pages. By accessing the digital download, you waive all refund privileges for this publication.

To install this book's complete digital download, follow the instructions below.*

1.   Go to **https://manage.texasbarpractice.com**:

   If the site prompts you to log you in, do so using the email address associated with this purchase.

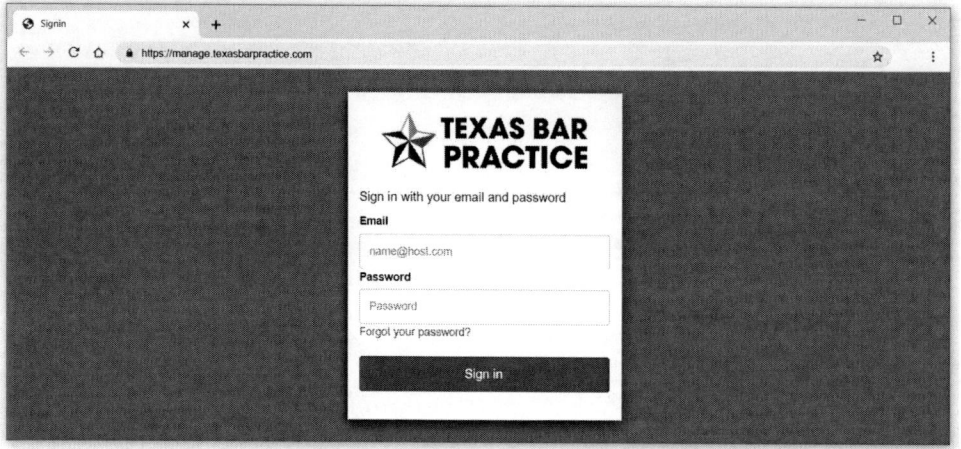

Once logged in, you should see the user icon in the upper right-hand corner of the page.

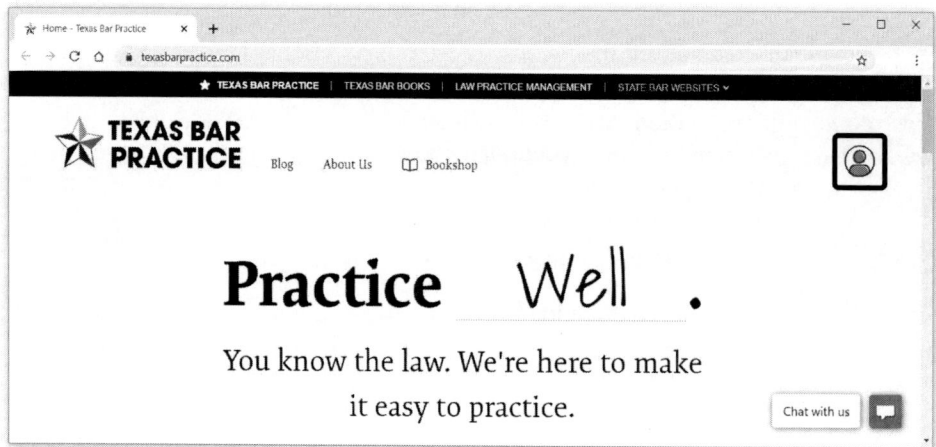

2. Go to your account:

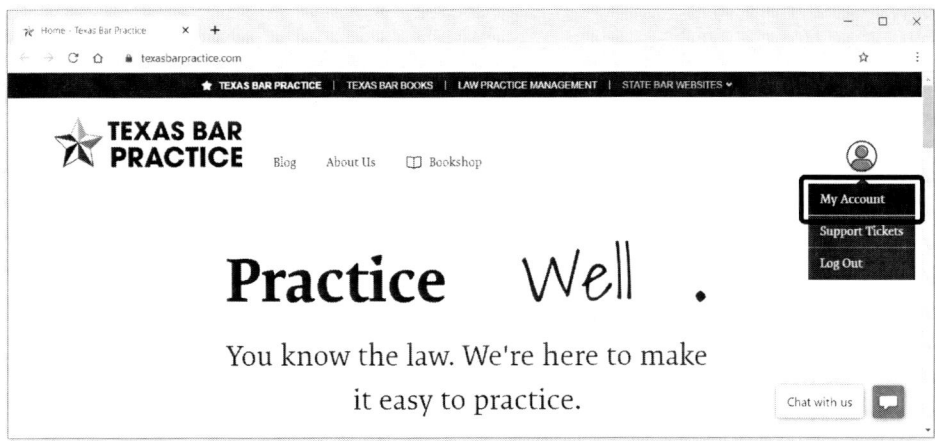

3. Select the library of the individual or organization associated with this download, and click the download button next to the book's title.

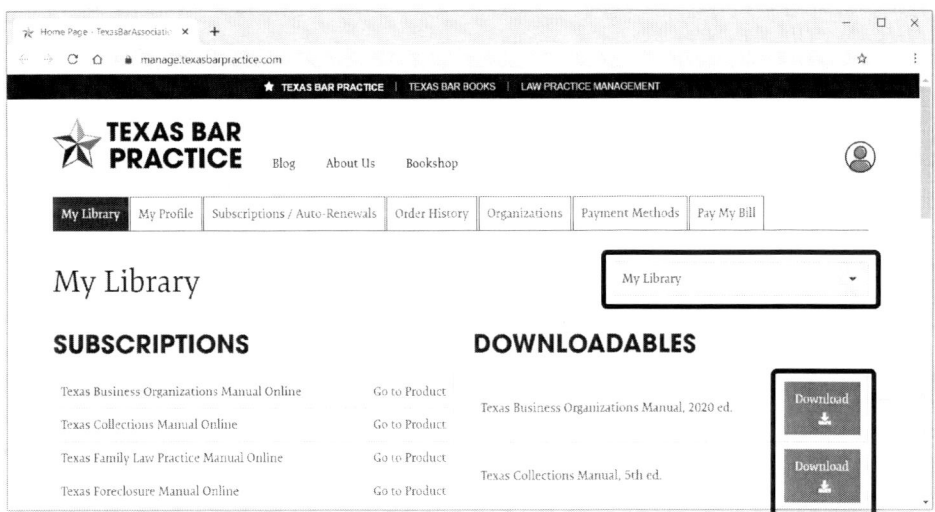

*Notes:

*   If you have never logged in to our site, the purchaser of this book should follow the instructions at **www.texasbarpractice.com/knowledgebase/article/already-a-customer**.

*   If you purchased the book as an organization, see **www.texasbarpractice.com/knowledgebase/texas-bar-practice-accounts**.

If you need any assistance, you may chat with us online or email us at **books@texasbar.com**.

USE OF THE MATERIAL IN THE DIGITAL DOWNLOAD IS SUBJECT TO THE FOLLOWING LICENSE AGREEMENT.

License and Limited Warranty

Grant of license: The material in the digital product and in the documentation is copyrighted by the State Bar of Texas ("State Bar"). The State Bar grants you a nonexclusive license to use this material as long as you abide by the terms of this agreement.

Ownership: The State Bar retains title and ownership of the material in the files and in the documentation and all subsequent copies of the material regardless of the form or media in which or on which the original and other copies may exist. This license is not a sale of the material or any copy. The terms of this agreement apply to derivative works.

Permitted users: The material in these files is licensed to you for use by one lawyer and that lawyer's support team only. At any given time, the material in these files may be installed only on the computers used by that lawyer and that lawyer's support team. That lawyer may be the individual purchaser or the lawyer designated by the firm that purchased this product. You may not permit other lawyers to use this material unless you purchase additional licenses. **Lawyers, law firms, and law firm librarians are specifically prohibited from distributing these materials to more than one lawyer. A separate license must be purchased for each lawyer who uses these materials.** For information about special bulk discount pricing for law firms, please call 1-800-204-2222, ext. 1402, or 512-427-1402. Libraries not affiliated with firms may permit reading of this material by patrons of the library through installation on one or more computers owned by the library and on the library's network but may not lend or sell the files themselves. The library may not allow patrons to print or copy any of this material in such a way as would infringe the State Bar's copyright.

Copies: You may make a copy of the files for backup purposes. Otherwise, you may copy the material in the files only as necessary to allow use by the users permitted under the license you purchased. Copyright notices should be included on copies. You may copy the documentation, including any copyright notices, as needed for reference by authorized users, but not otherwise.

Transfer: You may not transfer any copy of the material in the files or in the documentation to any other person or entity unless the transferee first accepts this agreement in writing and you transfer all copies, wherever located or installed, of the material and documentation, including the original provided with this agreement. You may not rent, loan, lease, sublicense, or otherwise make the material available for use by any person other than the permitted users except as provided in this paragraph.

Limited warranty and limited liability: THE STATE BAR MAKES NO WARRANTIES, EXPRESS OR IMPLIED, CONCERNING THE MATERIAL IN THESE FILES, THE DOCUMENTATION, OR THIS AGREEMENT. THE STATE BAR EXPRESSLY DISCLAIMS ALL

IMPLIED WARRANTIES, INCLUDING THE IMPLIED WARRANTIES OF MERCHANTABIL-ITY AND OF FITNESS FOR A PARTICULAR PURPOSE. THE MATERIAL IN THE FILES AND IN THE DOCUMENTATION IS PROVIDED "AS IS."

THE STATE BAR SHALL NOT BE LIABLE FOR THE LEGAL SUFFICIENCY OR LEGAL ACCURACY OF ANY OF THE MATERIAL CONTAINED IN THESE FILES. NEITHER THE STATE BAR NOR ANY OF THE CONTRIBUTORS TO THE MATERIAL MAKES EITHER EXPRESS OR IMPLIED WARRANTIES WITH REGARD TO THE USE OR FREEDOM FROM ERROR OF THE MATERIAL. EACH USER IS SOLELY RESPONSIBLE FOR THE LEGAL EFFECT OF ANY USE OR MODIFICATION OF THE MATERIAL.

IN NO EVENT SHALL THE STATE BAR BE LIABLE FOR LOSS OF PROFITS OR FOR INDIRECT, SPECIAL, CONSEQUENTIAL, OR PUNITIVE DAMAGES, EVEN IF THE STATE BAR HAS BEEN ADVISED OF THE POSSIBILITY OF THOSE DAMAGES. THE STATE BAR'S AGGREGATE LIABILITY ARISING FROM OR RELATING TO THIS AGREEMENT OR THE MATERIAL IN THE FILES OR IN THE DOCUMENTATION IS LIMITED TO THE PURCHASE PRICE YOU PAID FOR THE LICENSED COPYRIGHTED PRODUCT. THIS AGREEMENT DEFINES YOUR SOLE REMEDY.

General provisions: This agreement contains the entire agreement between you and the State Bar concerning the license to use the material in the files. The waiver of any breach of any provision of this agreement does not waive any other breach of that or any other provision. If any provision is for any reason found to be unenforceable, all other provisions nonetheless remain enforceable.